D0984218

日本民俗学研究

STUDIES IN JAPANESE FOLKLORE

Chief Translator: Y A S U Y O I S H I W A R A

Assistant Translators: Kayoko Kodama, Masako Suzuki, Matsuya Yamamoto

Assistant Editors: Pamela Casagrande, Maurice D. Schmaier

Studies in Japanese Folklore

GENERAL EDITOR

RICHARD M. DORSON

ADVISORY EDITORS

Toichi Mabuchi   *Tokihiko Oto*

KENNIKAT PRESS
Port Washington, N. Y./London

STUDIES IN JAPANESE FOLKLORE

Copyright © 1963 by Indiana University Press
Published in 1973 by Kennikat Press by arrangement
with Indiana University Press
Library of Congress Catalog Card No.: 72-85289
ISBN 0-8046-1725-2

Manufactured by Taylor Publishing Company   Dallas, Texas

ACKNOWLEDGMENTS

The idea for this volume was conceived when the editor held a Fulbright appointment as visiting professor in the department of American Studies at Tokyo University in 1956–57. An initial grant from the Asia Foundation of Japan to the Minzokugaku Kenkyusho, the Japanese Folklore Research Institute, to cover translation costs launched the enterprise. The encouragement of the late Kunio Yanagita and the good will, friendship, and exemplary patience of the contributors during the long period of the book's gestation have made its completion possible. Professor Toichi Mabuchi spent three weeks in Bloomington in July, 1961, exhaustively reviewing the manuscript and comparing the translations against the originals. Miss Yasuyo Ishiwara, the chief translator, has continued to supply needed information across the Pacific with unfailing promptness. In 1957 Professor Ichiro Hori, the son-in-law of Professor Yanagita and one of the contributors, visited us in Bloomington and conferred with me on the manuscript, as did Kayoko Saito (now Kodama), an assistant translator, in 1958. Hiroyuki Araki and Tokuichiro Matsuda, while graduate students in folklore and linguistics at Indiana University in 1960 and 1961, also helped the editor deal with translation problems.

Indiana University has made possible the publication of this volume by supporting a Folklore Monographs Series and an editorial assistantship for the series. Guthrie T. Meade, Jr., Mary Felder, Maurice D. Schmaier, and Pamela Casagrande have held this assistantship and worked with the manuscript at various stages. Supplementary funds for international volumes that will enlarge the scope of the Indiana University Folklore Series were received under a general grant from the Ford Foundation to Indiana University in 1961.

The Japanese characters in this book were all drawn by Mrs. Tomoko Kodama. Those appearing on the first page of any given paper represent the name of the author.

TABLE OF CONTENTS

序説

PART ONE | INTRODUCTION

Bridges between Japanese and American Folklorists

BY RICHARD M. DORSON

Our age has witnessed valiant efforts on both sides of the shrinking Pacific to achieve understanding between East and West. Yet one active generation can only begin to redress the balance tilted so heavily toward the transatlantic community. In the field of folklore, as in other branches of learning, ties formed by cultural origins and intellectual models have bound the United States to Europe. Colonists and immigrants brought with them Old World folk traditions, and in recent times American folklorists have followed the methods and theories of their European colleagues. Meanwhile Asia and Africa have remained largely outside the international community of folklorists. Although the tradi-

3

tions of folklore on those continents are extraordinarily fertile and flourishing, the number of professional folklorists in Asia is tiny and in Africa, virtually nonexistent. Among the Asian countries, only Japan has developed a mature science of folklore. Unfortunately, the copious reports and investigations by the Japanese are almost completely unknown and unavailable to Western folklorists.

During her long period of isolation, enforced by the Tokugawa Shoguns from the early seventeenth century until the Meiji Restoration of 1868, Japan effectively walled herself in from the global expansion of Europe. From Victorian England went forth colonial administrators, Anglican missionaries and leisurely travelers who collected native traditions around the world, the better to understand the peoples they governed, proselytized, and curiously observed. Consequently the westerner can turn to English editions of tales and myths from India, China, Oceania, Australia, Africa, and many countries of Europe. But Japan has remained largely *terra incognita* for the student of folklore. No Englishmen, nor any Europeans save the handful of Dutchmen stationed at the lone trading post of Nagasaki, were permitted to talk to Japanese, until the naval forces of Commodore Matthew Perry in 1853 persuaded the Shoguns to accept the world. One polyglot American, Lafcadio Hearn, who in 1890 came to live in Japan, wrote about the legends of his adopted land for the English-speaking audience, as did in a casual way a number of his countrymen; and travelers from France and Germany also published accounts of Japanese manners, tales, and customs.[1]

Still the situation differed radically from that in the colonial countries which the Victorian folklore collectors had tapped. During the ferment of the Meiji Restoration, folklore theory found a place among the array of arts and sciences the Japanese imported overnight to transform the Land of the Rising Sun into a modern nation-state. No short-term traveler, or even long-term resident, could match the dedication and knowledge of the Japanese scholar patiently examining his own folk culture. Throughout the twentieth century the volume of publications on Japanese folklore has steadily mounted, under the direction of Kunio Yanagita, born in 1875, who founded and guided the destinies of his chosen field. Patriarchal Yanagita, member of the Japan Academy and recipient of many honors, himself published nearly 100 books and over 1,000 articles; and research is so active that for the postwar decade 1945–55 alone a bibliography of 138 pages was needed to register the published materials on Japanese folklore.[2] This prodigious scholarship is locked up in a language that few American folklorists will ever master.

A comparative folklorist needs access to all the resources he can command. He does not intend to become a Japanese or Chinese or Philippine specialist, but he ardently desires to examine Asian oral literatures, if these have been recorded, and to read the treatises of Asian folklore specialists, if such exist. The problem for the Western scholar is to unlock this national treasure-house of folk traditions and folklore commentary. Though vexing, his dilemma is less acute than that faced by anthropologists who sought to study "culture at a distance" in countries barred to them during wartime, and resorted to such expedients as interviewing prisoners of war, studying film strips, and combing documents. In the present instance, one can penetrate the language curtain, and secure a fair view of the content and study of Japanese folklore, by piecing together annotated bibliographies, abstracts of articles, scattered and buried translations, and occasional reviews in Western languages.

The one systematic and comprehensive descriptive bibliography was published by the French Japanologist, René Sieffert, as "Etudes d'ethnographie Japonaise" in the *Bulle-*

tin de la Maison Franco-Japonaise (Tokyo), Nouvelle Série, Tome II (1952), pp. 9–110. This work affords an overview of the publication outlets, topics of investigation, and general scope of the professional Japanese folklorists—that is, of Yanagita and his school. Sieffert lists eighty general and regional folklore periodicals, and 378 publications, arranged in six main divisions, with succinct synoptic notes for each entry. The divisions cover "General Works," "Occupations," "Recreations," "The Economy," "Social Structure," and "Religious Phenomena," the last including ritual, magic, and oral literature.

A supplement to Sieffert's bibliography for the decade since 1951 is available in a bibliographical guide of 101 pages which the Kokusai Bunka Shinkōkai (The Society for International Cultural Relations) issued in Tokyo in 1961. This is Volume VIII, "Manners and Customs, & Folklore" of the *K. B. S. Bibliography of Standard Reference Books for Japanese Studies with descriptive notes.* Tokihiko Ōtō, who chose the 243 entries, Yasuyo Ishiwara, who translated his annotations into English, and Fanny Hagin Mayer, who served as editor, had also worked together in the Japanese Folklore Institute. All of the fifteen divisions in this bibliography relate to folklore, with sections, as in Sieffert's listing, on "Dwellings, Clothes, and Food" and "Family and Local Organization," which reveal the depth of interest in rural folk life. In addition to headings on "Popular Beliefs and Superstition," "Festivals," and "Legend and Folktale," there is, curiously, one topic called "Folklore," by which the Japanese refer to complete ethnographic treatments of folk culture, chiefly field monographs of single villages. Unlike Sieffert's work, the K. B. S. bibliography excludes articles and deals only with books. As in Sieffert, full data on number of pages, size, and number of plates or photographs is included.

In his brief but pithy introduction, Sieffert reviews the career of Yanagita after his interest in village folk life was aroused during his rounds as a youthful official in the Ministry of Agriculture. In 1910 he organized a group, Kyōdo-kai (Association for Local Studies), to pursue field research in the countryside. That year he published the pioneer volume of collected Japanese oral folktales, *Tōno Monogatari*, told by the farmer Sasaki Kizen of Tono-machi in Iwate-ken.[3] Also in 1910 appeared *Ishi-gami Mondō*, an exchange of letters between Yanagita and several scholars on "Stone Carved Deities" and the folk beliefs concerning stones as symbols of deities.[4] These are his earliest listed works. In 1913 he founded the journal *Kyōdo Kenkyū (Local Studies)*, in 1925 *Minzoku (Ethnos)*, in 1928 *Tabi to Densetsu (Travels and Legends)*, and in 1935 *Minkan Denshō (Popular Traditions)*. A fundamental reorientation in the viewpoint of Yanagita is seen in the change in name in 1935 of the Japanese Folklore Society from Minkan Densho no Kai to Minzoku Gakkai, employing the more scientific term for folklore, and reflecting a shift from the literary and picturesque conception of folk materials in his early career to the more systematic and analytical character of his later researches. In 1948 he created the Minzokugaku Kenkyūsho, the Folklore Research Institute, endowing it with his own splendid library quarters and holdings.

Sieffert comments admiringly on the overwhelming dominance of Yanagita in the field he founded. From 1913 on, when Yanagita filled *Kyōdo Kenkyū* with so many articles he had to sign them with several pseudonymns, *"sa biographie devient une immense bibliographie."* In the three decades from 1920 to 1950, every Japanese folklore work of value had benefited from his counsels, and often as not bore his prefatory remarks.

In the list of publications cited and briefly summarized by

Sieffert, the name of Yanagita (spelled "Yanagida") appears in every one of the thirty subdivisions of the six main categories. In the first section, of fifty-seven items listed thirty-three are by Yanagita, and most of these are solid studies of 300 to 500 pages; they include a manual on methods of field research, a social history of the Meiji and Taishō eras (1868–1925), a treatise on historical method in folklore studies, and an ethnographic report on the village of Kitakoura.

Actually these figures are somewhat misleading, since many of the books are collections of articles or new editions, and some are cooperative works bearing the name of the master but executed by his disciples. Thus the first title in the bibliography, the *Minzokugaku Jiten,* or *Dictionary of Japanese Folklore* (1951), a work of 714 pages containing 897 articles, carries his name as the author but is the collaborative effort of his institute.

The three major cooperative works of the Minzokugaku Kenkyūsho directed by Kunio Yanagita have been translated into English and are available on microcards. Masanori Takatsuka undertook the translations and George K. Brady of the University of Kentucky edited them for English style.[5] The *Minzokugaku Jiten* opens the door to the folk themes and concepts of a whole new culture area, and is invaluable as an introduction to an unfamiliar nomenclature. Its model is the *Wörterbuch der deutschen Volkskunde* by Oswald A. Erich and Richard Beitl (Leipzig: Kröner, 1936). Entries deal with subjects of legends, household articles associated with taboos and charms, names of festivals, terms for kinship relations, and theories of Japanese folklore study. The extensive entry on *"Densetsu, Legends,"* for example, deals with the characteristics and carriers of legends, with their classification and study, and with "Legends and Japan." Other theoretical definitions are found under *"Mukashibanashi,* Folktales," *"Minkan Shinkō,* Folk Religion," "*Minzokugakushi,* History of Folklore," "*Minzoku Goi,* Folklore Vocabulary," "*Minzoku Shiryō,* Folklore Materials."

A series of entries taken at random can illustrate the comprehensiveness of the dictionary: Misaki, a subordinate tool deity; *misogi,* water purification; *miso shōyu,* bean paste; *michi uta,* road song; *michikiri,* quarantine magic; *mitsumine shinkō,* the Mitsumine cult; *minakuchi matsuri,* irrigation-water rite; *mibun,* social standing; *mimai,* expression of sympathy; *mimifusagi mochi,* "ear-stopping" rice cake; *miyage,* a present; *miyaza,* a parishioner's league. In such entries Japanese village life appears honeycombed with magic and ritual, to such an extent that the folklore dictionary takes on the character of an occult counterpart to a conventional dictionary. The *Minzokugaku Jiten* condenses and synopsizes many monographs and field reports of Yanagita and his school.

The *Studies in Mountain Village Life* (1937) and its companion the *Studies in Fishing Village Life* (1949) in particular supplied much of the information for the dictionary. These collaborative investigations used as their starting point a detailed questionnaire of 100 topics covering the full range of rural folk life, prepared by the Kyōdo Kenkyūsho (Institute for Local Studies) and printed as a handbook. Field collectors followed these questionnaires in obtaining their data, and they were also distributed to interested persons throughout the country. Usually one fieldworker visited a particular village. The final results were then written up by contributors assigned to different chapters. The earlier volume reduced these items to sixty-five chapters, and the sequel, the completion of which was interrupted by the war, contained twenty-five. Prefectural and village authorities, elementary-school teachers, and volunteers lent their assistance.

These task-force surveys reached into the very heart of Japanese folk tradition, the remote and isolated villages tightly bound by ancestral cults and kinship lineages and fenced off from the outside world by the *dōsojin,* the guardian deity of the village boundary line. The mountain-village study considered such topics as "The Origin of Villages and Ancient Families" (over a hundred ascribing their origins to fugitive warriors of the Heike-Genji civil wars), "Great Events of Villages," "Obsolete Occupations," "Village Visitors," "Cooperative Labor and Mutual Assistance," "Division of Hunting Spoils," "Tabooed Plants," "Community Rituals," and "Lucky Families and Persons." In Chapter 24, "Figures Prominent in Oral Tradition," Kiyoko Segawa conjectures that these figures have degenerated into laughing stocks from an original semidivine status. The types of persons remembered in the majority of villages include a man of great strength, a very heavy eater (two types also conspicuous in American town lore), and an expert singer and dancer. A good walker was reported in eight villages, a very funny person in four, with single instances emerging of such eccentrics as a expert tree-climber, a man with a mania for lawsuits, a famous calligrapher, and an old man who never took off his clothes.

Segawa also indicates the attitudes of villagers toward these figures of legend: a liar is regarded favorably for his interesting stories so long as they harm no one; formerly a heavy eater was praised but he is now despised as a glutton.

The *Studies in Fishing Village Life* seems more sharply focused than its predecessor, perhaps since the sea and fisheries make a more definite impact on folk institutions than does mountainous land. A number of the chapters concern social and economic aspects of the fisheries; the more strictly folkloristic reports treat "Weird Beings of the Sea,"

"Places Sacred to Sea People," "Taboos of Fishermen," and "Festivals Pertaining to Fishermen."

The Western reader will experience some disappointment on reading the three publications to come from these imaginatively conceived and earnestly prosecuted enterprises. As a consequence of their cooperative nature, they tend to be sketchy and lightweight. Authors use extracts of reports obtained by many fieldworkers, and quote examples from one or another *mura* to illustrate their topic, giving the effect of a digest or summary. What is sacrificed in depth, however, is compensated in breadth and generalization about the character of legend, rite, and taboo throughout Japan.

Other than these joint works, almost all of Yanagita's voluminous writings are untranslated. His social history, *Japanese Manners and Customs in the Meiji Era,* has, however, recently been rendered into English from the original Japanese edition of 1931.[6] The Meiji revolution in Japanese society (1868–1912) has particular implications for the folklorist, since this is the dawn of modern Japan, and the time of seeming overthrow of ancient tradition. Yet in the chapter on "Religious Life" (chap. 13, pp. 291–316) Yanagita points out the strong underlying conservatism which preserved old beliefs in a new environment, or renewed them after an interim of disuse. In fact the popular beliefs which the government was attempting to discredit by strengthening state Shinto were even expanded, since the shrine guilds were opened to all families in the community, and not just to the old families related to the deity. Near Lake Suwa villagers had held a divination ceremony, dating back to the Heian period (794–1185), for the deity whose path across the ice could be traced by cracks, which portended prospects for the fall harvest. An early Meiji decree halted the ceremony, but in 1892 it was revived. Industrialization did not necessarily interrupt the old ideas. Villagers reported that foxes and badgers were heard to knock at doors to deliver telegrams, and were seen to stand on railway tracks and halt trains; worshipers sent supplicating postcards through the mails addressed to shrine deities; and all bus- and streetcar-drivers carried protective amulets.

Some idea of the range and specialities of Yanagita's co-workers and disciples who are represented in the present volume can be gained from the analytic bibliographies of Sieffert and Ōtō.

Takayoshi Mogami contributed two chapters to the mountain-village survey, three to the fishing-village report, and one to a collection of essays edited by Yanagita, *Nihon Minzokugaku Kenkyū (Studies in Japanese Folklore,* 1935). These covered diverse subjects, such as the trade and exchange practices of nomadic groups, village attitudes toward farm laborers, magico-religious sanctions for distribution of the fishing catch, and communal ownership of land in farming hamlets. In 1951 he published an ethnographic study of the village of Kurokochi, and in 1956 brought a series of individual reports to fruition in *Mairi-baka,* a book about the traditional double-grave system of rural Japan. This is a typical pattern for the training of a Japanese folklorist, who might first participate in coordinated projects directed by Yanagita, engage in an individual field inquiry, and at length specialize in some aspect of folk religion.[7]

The leading folktale scholar of Japan, Keigo Seki, has specialized in one of the genres first explored by Yanagita. The two collaborated in 1942 on a substantial manual and handbook for collectors, *Nihon Minzokugaku Nyūmon (Introduction to Japanese Folklore).* The same year Seki published a folktale collection from the peninsula of Shimabara in Nagasaki-ken, *Shimabara Hanto Mukashi-banashi,* as Volume I in a general series of folktales from various districts and islands of Japan edited by Yanagita. In a 1941 treatise on the method of studying folktales, *Mukashi-bana-shi,* he acknowledged his debt to the Finnish folktale scholar Antti Aarne, and then applied the Finnish historical-geographical method to well known Japanese tale types, such as the battle between the monkey and the crab. Turning his attention to classification, Seki constructed a comprehensive index of Japanese folktales in six volumes, *Nihon Mu-kashi-banashi Shūsei.* This work arranges Japanese tale types in an orderly scheme, providing the most complete oral text to illustrate each type, giving bibliographical references to and summaries of the variants, and indicating their regional distribution. Part I (1950) dealt with "Animal Tales," Part II (3 volumes, 1953–55) with "Proper Folktales," and Part III (2 volumes, 1957–58), with "Jokes." As a companion work, Seki prepared an edition of 240 representative tales from all regions of Japan, *Nihon no Mukashi-banashi* (3 volumes, 1956–58). At the end of the third volume, the author provides commentaries and a bibliography of source collections and research studies.[8]

In 1943 the former director of the Minzokugaku Ken-kyūsho, Tokihiko Ōtō, wrote a volume jointly with Professor Yanagita on Japanese customs, in an historical series on contemporary Japanese civilization. This work, *Sesō Shi,* reveals the broad "folk-life" orientation of the Japanese folklorists with chapters on clothing, food, and houses; social organization; economic activities; education and recreation; religious practices; and instruments of cultural diffusion.[9] Ōtō contributed to *Studies in Mountain Village Life* four chapters on the subjects of tabooed plants and animals among village clans, and purification rites preceding festivals. In an article in English about votive tablets, which appeared in *Contemporary Japan,* Ōtō describes the func-

tion and forms of these roughly painted, small wooden
boards offered to deities in shrines and temples. Thus the
deity of the Ōte Shrine in Ashikaga, reputed to cure arth-
ritic fingers, receives ex-voto tablets portraying the right or
left hand; a deity of the Mizushi Shrine miraculously heal-
ing women's diseases is offered tablets showing the lower
half of the female body. Wealthy persons have even commis-
sioned famous artists to paint framed votive tablets.[10]

A counselor of the Minzokugaku Kenkyūsho, Tokuzo
Ōmachi, collaborated with Yanagita in 1937 on a systematic
study of folk terms connected with marriage customs. The
influence of Arnold van Gennep is seen in Ōmachi's essay
on rites of passage, from birth through puberty to marriage
and death, in an article "Kankon sōsai no hanashi," translated in Cultural Nippon in 1941 as "Ceremonial Practices
in Japan—Birth, Majority, Marriage, Death and Festival."
His stated purpose is to reconstruct the attitudes and ceremonial practices of the early Japanese concerning these
stages of life, through the illustrative examples of folklore.
One such example is the sacrifice of babies in impoverished
families, which restores them ritually to their guardian
deities. Ōmachi's general interest in rites of passage led to a
special inquiry on the ashiire-kon form of marriage, treated
in a sixty-four page monograph issued in 1950 by the Minzokugaku Kenkyūsho, and discussed in the present volume.[11]

Taro Wakamori, a professor of history who began editing
the new monthly journal Minkan Denshō in 1935, has like
Ōmachi interested himself in social relationships within the
folk society. A collection of his articles issued under the
title Nihon Minzoku Ron (Treatise on Japanese Folklore)
in 1947 contains a major paper dealing with social structure
in ancient Japanese society. A substantial work published
in 1951, Rekishi to Minzokugaku (History and Folklore),
applied the historical method to ethnological materials, and

considered the evolution both of social structure and of certain popular beliefs, such as the cults of Jizō (a guardian deity of children) and of the hearth deity. In a 1949 paper Wakamori dealt with the subject of social relations among neighbors, employers and workers, and within age groups and religious organizations. In a sixty-six-page treatise, *Nihon-jin no Kōsai* (*Social Intercourse of Japanese People*), written in 1953, he discussed such matters as the etiquette of visiting and of exchanging gifts.[12]

One prolific female folklorist combines her interests in the traditional role of women and in the life of fishing villages. Kiyoko Segawa has written research papers on the activities of women in the folk culture of inland and coastal villages, concentrating on such subjects as women dancers in the Bon and other festivals, child-rearing practices, and the occupation of *ama* (women divers). These essays were brought together in 1942 in *Kaijo Ki* (Account of Women Divers), and the same year in *Kimono* she described changes taking place in ritual costume and the daily clothing of women in rural districts. A full-length study (1943) on fish-vendors, *Hanjo,* dealt with the wives of fishermen who sell the catch to inland markets, and discussed their apparel, portage, and modes of exchanging marine for agricultural products. Naturally Segawa contributed major chapters to *Studies in Fishing Village Life,* on the traditions of *ama,* on pregnancy and menstrual taboos, and on childbirth customs such as the accouchement hut. A field report on the island of Himaga in Aichi-ken, *Himagashima Minzoku-Shi,* appeared in 1951, and her investigations into the techniques and traditions of women divers culminated in a book on *Ama* in 1956.[13]

The head of the Fishery Research Institute in the Ministry of Agriculture and Forestry, Katsunori Sakurada, has appropriately concentrated on the folk culture of fishermen,

studying masculine roles in the fishing village as Segawa
studied the feminine. In 1934 he published an intensive
field report on the folklore of fishing villages (*Gyoson Minzoku-shi*), with discussions of boat types, methods of naviga-
tion and fishing, the specters of the sea and spirits of the
boats, and proverbs of the waves and weather. A collection
of articles entitled *Gyojin (Fishermen)*, appearing in 1942,
concerned the social organization of adults and youths in
the fishing village, the festivals and rituals connected with
the catch, and traditions defining the boundaries of fishing
sites. To *Studies in Fishing Village Life* he contributed a
chapter on relations between coastal and interior villages,
and for *Studies in Mountain Village Life* he wrote sections
on tabooed farming and wooded areas, and consequences of
taboo violation.[14]

The foremost student of Japanese festivals is Narimitsu
Matsudaira, whose doctoral dissertation at the University of
Paris was published in French in 1936 as *Les Fêtes Saison-
nieres au Japon (Province de Mikawa)*.[15] Matsudaira begins,
"*Le Japon reste un pays de folklore*"; and in the seasonal
festivals of country villages he finds deep wells of folk custom and belief undisturbed by the official edicts of the Meiji
government. Part I describes particular festivals: Hana-
matsuri, Mikagura, Kagura, and Déngaku; Part II treats
folk-religious beliefs in spirits, gods and demigods associated with the festivals; Part III deals with the village organization, divisible into corporate and personal relationships, arising from the festivals. From 1941 to 1944 Matsudaira edited twenty-four numbers of a journal devoted to
festival research, *O-matsuri*. His book *Matsuri* in 1943 focused on the communal aspects of village life at festival
time, and analyzed twenty important festivals which he had
observed. A sequel study published in 1946, *Matsuri: Honshitsu to Shosō (Festivals: Characteristics and Morphology)*,

considered the elements structuring festivals, such as the supernatural figures of cult worship. In a 1957 paper, "Le Rituel des Prémices au Japon," Matsudaira dealt specifically with the harvest ritual, *niiname,* observed from ancient times by emperor and peasant alike.[16]

Another Japanese folklorist who studied in France is Nobuhiro Matsumoto, whose dissertation was published in Paris in 1928, under the title *Essai sur la Mythologie Japonaise.*[17] This study distinguished three local sources of cult tradition for the Japanese classic myths recorded in the *Kojiki* and *Nihongi:* worship of the god of water and thunder centered at Izumo, worship of the sun god at Yamato, and the cult of maritime tribes in Kyushū. A subsequent historical and comparative treatment of these mythological themes appeared in 1946 as *Nihon Shinwa no Kenkyū (A Study of Japanese Myths).*[18] Matsumoto offered a useful survey of the Japanese folklore scene in 1924, "L'etat actuel des études de folklore au Japon," in *Japon et Extrême-Orient,* commenting on the work of Yanagita, of Shinobu Origuchi and his *"études remarquables"* on Japanese antiquity, of the botanist Kumakusu Minakata who examined popular beliefs in the twelve signs of the zodiac, and of the folk narrator Kizen Sasaki who published his own tales.[19]

The son-in-law of Yanagita-*sensei,* Ichiro Hori, has specialized in *minkan shinkō,* or religious folk beliefs. An early investigation, written jointly with his father-in-law in 1948, concerned 223 *jūsan-zuka* (graves called thirteen mounds) and analyzed origin legends of these mounds or *tumuli* for foreign influence which might have affected the Japanese ceremony of mound-building. His first major work on *Minkan Shinkō* appeared under that title in 1951; it initially considered interrelations between folk narrative and folk belief, and then examined the relation between the belief system, with its concepts of ancestor and spirit worship, and the social organization of village families and clans. This was followed by a two-volume *Study in the History of Japanese Folk Religion* (*Waga-kuni Minkan-shinkō-shi no Kenkyū*) (1953–55), reconstructing the archetypal forms and genetic development of Japanese supernatural beliefs, and classifying them typologically.[20] Hori has also written articles in English (and is the one contributor to do so in this volume). A two-part paper in *Numen*, 1958–59, "On the Concept of *Hijiri* (Holy-Man)" provides a closely documented historical account of the shamanistic religious leaders contributing to rural folk Buddhism from the Heian period to the present.[21]

While studying and lecturing at Harvard University and the University of Chicago from 1956 to 1958, Hori prepared another important paper in English, "Japanese Folk-Beliefs," which was published in the *American Anthropologist*.[22] This article deals with the social structure and historical factors determining the multiple religious organizations found in a typical Japanese village, rather than with the actual content of magico-religious folk belief. Hori traces a complicated pattern: "I believe that the essence of Japanese folk-beliefs lies in the interaction of two belief systems: a little tradition, which is based on blood or close community ties; and a great tradition, introduced from without, which is adopted by individual or group choice. Multilayered, coexistent and syncretistic beliefs are found everywhere in Japanese rural society" (p. 405).

The little tradition refers to the indigenous folk system: a symbolic rather than an animistic or nature religion, culminating in advanced Shinto. The great traditions include the philosophical importations of Buddhism, Confucianism, and Taoism. From the little tradition with its concept of ancestor worship developed the primary kinship unit of the village, the *dōzoku*, consisting of a main family and branch families linked by patrilineal kinship. The dōzoku forms a core group for social and economic activities and for annual ritual observances, such as the New Year and the Bon festivals.

These dōzoku groups, deifying ancestors thirty-three years after death, in time produced tutelary deities for the whole village. Cults of other religious organizations center around various deities imported by missionaries. One phenomenon particularly important for the proliferation of local deities is *goryo-shin,* the idea that spirits of the hostile dead can wreak vengeance on the living. The goryo-shin age flourished from the eighth to the twelfth centuries, and eventually induced three main systems of counter-magic, Nembutsu, Shugendō, and Onmyō-dō, each with its own religious organizations. The complexity and abundance of the deities and their cult groups cannot easily be summarized, and in a village of 682 families in Nagano-ken Hori counted 114 shrines and stone symbols.

During the past decade the Minzokugaku Kenkyūsho and its leading members have sponsored several enterprises, in addition to those already mentioned. The institute edited a seven-volume Series of Regional Folklore Accounts under the supervision of Yanagita, from 1949 to 1951, bringing together field reports on folk life in remote villages of Japan. Yanagita wrote about Kitakoura on Sado Island, Ōmachi on Takaoka in Ibaraki-ken, Segawa on Himaka Island in Aichi-ken, Sakurada on Tokuyama in Gifu-ken, and Mogami on Kurokōchi in Nagano-ken.[23]

Two pictorial publications of the Folklore Institute presented scenes of folk life. An "Illustrated Book of Annual Rites" (1953) arranged the seasonal folk festivals in calendrical order under 128 headings, illustrating them with three color prints and fifteen plates, and appending a bibliography of annual festivals. The "Graphic Record of Japa-

nese Folk Customs" (1955) offered 744 gravure pictures
with accompanying text to depict regional customs.[24]

A number of important publications have been written
by other folklorists besides the present contributors, and a
few additional K. B. S. entries may be cited to suggest their
variety. A three-volume report on "Folk Beliefs in Japan,"
including both collected materials and interpretive essays,
was issued in 1949 by the Research Committee on Superstitions established under the Ministry of Education. The
Attic Museum published in its Memoir No. 28, "Diary of
a Farmer's Diet on Kikai-ga-shima," a record of the daily
meals of a farmer in Kagoshima-ken for the year 1936. A
glossary and list of local sayings connected with food was
appended. A 972-page "Dictionary of Japanese Calendar
Customs" by Masanobu Nishitsunoi appeared in 1958,
covering annual festivals and observances of past and pres
ent, with some reference to analogous foreign customs. A
pictorial study, published in 1959, on "The Rice-Field Deity
—Rituals of Rice Production in Japan," with commentaries
in Japanese by Hideo Haga and in English by Iwao Ishino,
illustrated rice-cultivation rites in six districts.[25] A striking
folio-size volume on *Japanese Women's Folk Costumes,*
published in 1960, contains 121 full-page, half-page and
quarter-page paintings, a number of which are in color, by
Tadaichi Hayashi. Women from rural districts all over
Japan are seen attired in work trousers and heavy blouses of
many patterns, engaged in a host of occupations: carrying
bundles on their backs, picking fruit, digging in the fields,
and dressed for pearl-diving, coal-mining, and stone-cutting.
The introductory descriptions of the illustrations, and the
captions, are in English as well as Japanese.[26]

One scholarly journal published in English, German, and
French devotes its contents exclusively to folklore and ethnology of the Far East, and represents an especially rich re-

source for the westerner. Its title, *Folklore Studies,* has carried a subcaption "Journal of Far Eastern Folklore" on its cover since Volume XII, 1953, when its sponsorship shifted from the Catholic University of Peking to the Society of the Divine Word Research Institute of Oriental Studies in Tokyo.

Folklore Studies was founded and has continuously been edited by Matthias Eder, a clerical scholar equally at home in Chinese and Japanese and the Western languages. Born 15 November 1902 at Abtenau bei Salzburg in Austria, he pursued philosophical and theological studies in the mission seminary St. Gabriel in Mödling, near Vienna, from 1923 to 1930. From 1930 to 1934 he served as a missionary priest in Japan. He then studied successively with Wilhelm Schmidt at the University of Vienna, with Orientalists in Paris, and with Richard Thurnwald at the University of Berlin. His doctorate was taken in three fields, Japanology, anthropology, and Sinology. From 1938 to 1949 he held the post of professor of anthropology at Fujen University in Peking, where he founded the Ethnological Museum of Fujen University, and initiated *Folklore Studies.* In 1949 he barely escaped from Peking ahead of the Chinese Reds, leaving thousands of his slides behind. Since 1949 he has lived in Tokyo, and has served as professor of anthropology at Nanzan University in Nagoya.

Dr. Eder works closely with the Japanese folklorists, translating, abstracting, and reviewing their writings in the pages of *Folklore Studies.* A valuable translation that he has rendered for Western folklorists is the history of Japanese folklore studies (*Nihon Minzokugaku*) by Kunio Yanagita, printed in Volume III (1944) as "Die Japanische Volkskunde: Ihre Vorgeschichte, Entwicklung und Gegenwärtige Lage." The table of contents, translated into English, is given here.

A "Foreword by the Translator" (pp. 1–2) pays tribute to Yanagita on his seventieth birthday, as the pioneer of Japanese folklore science and the major contributor to the rich scholarship unfolded in the history of the field now offered in German translation.

This historical survey of the development of folklore studies in Japan could well be emulated for the United States, England, and other countries. While the account is descriptive rather than analytical, such a treatment is needed for the Western reader, who must first familiarize himself with the unfamiliar names of authors and collectors and the unfamiliar titles of monographs and journals. This end the history serves well, offering in effect a running bibliographic commentary, from the classical literary works and the pre-Meiji chronicles, travels, and topographies containing traditional materials, up to the systematic field inquiries and theoretical and classificatory works of the twentieth century. The history also covers the organizational side of folklore's struggle for recognition—the societies, conferences, lecture series, and academic footholds—a story much the same around the world, wherever folklore has endeavored to rise from dilettantism to university status.

A few turning points are here singled out. In the writing and teaching of a late-nineteenth-century scholar like Bin Ueda the terminology for the field was not yet standardized. Through his knowledge of English literature, Ueda came to know the work of the Victorian folklorists in England. In 1911 he taught an introductory course on *minzoku densetsu* (folklore traditions) in the upper girls' school of the Kyoto district, relying on Gomme's *Handbook of Folklore* (1890) with its strong ethnological emphasis. Eventually *minkan denshō* came to stand for the content and *minzokugaku* for the method of folklore. Before these terms came into general use, the interest in folk traditions centered around *Kyōdo Kenkyū,* the title of a lively journal founded in 1913 by Yanagita and Toshio Takagi, a student of Japanese mythology and traditional narrative. *Kyōdo Kenkyū* can be translated in German as *Heimatforschung* and in English as *Local Life Studies.* This journal continued until 1917, and was revived from 1931 to 1934. *Kyōdo Kenkyū* included reports on local history and population, customs and crafts, agricultural methods, clothing, food and dwellings, community organizations, religion, and oral traditions. Another periodical influencing the development of the field was *Tabi to Densetsu* (*Travels and Legends*) which printed articles and reports on customs of marriage, birth and death, folk medicine, children's games, and folktales, frequently in the midst of tourist rambles. The more centralized and professional direction of folklore studies can be dated by the journal *Minzokugaku,* which in 1929 for the first time used this scientific term to denote the study of oral literature. In 1935 the first general folklore conference was held, for a week in March in the outer park of Meiji Shrine, attended by delegates from most of the districts of the country. From this meeting resulted the handbook, published that year, *Nihon Minzokugaku Kenkyū* (*Studies in Japanese Folklore*), and the formation of a national folklore society, Minkan Denshō no Kai, which began to issue a monthly periodical (still published), titled *Minkan Denshō.*

These annals of the Japanese folklore movement ended in 1944, four years before the establishment of the Minzokugaku Kenkyūsho (Folklore Research Institute), but this and other developments are described in a later article by Hiroji Naoe, also translated by Eder, on "Post-War Folklore Research Work in Japan."[27] Yanagita donated his private library, which had escaped the ravages of World War II, to the new institute which he founded to succeed the Kyōdo Kenkyūsho (Local Studies Research Institute), a group he had directed since 1935. The primary purpose of the Folklore Research Institute was to train younger specialists in Japanese folklore, since no universities were performing this function. The already existing Japanese Folklore Society, numbering some two thousand members around the country, provided a natural audience for publications of the institute.

Although Naoe's survey covered only the years 1945 through 1948, and pointed out the serious postwar difficulties of travel and financial support impeding folklore research, his report revealed considerable activity. Such fields as sociology, jurisprudence, and the history of religion were now drawing increasingly on folkloristic investigations of traditional family systems, labor organizations, and religious ceremonies in agricultural villages. Communist scholars had also found an interest in the folklore field, but the school of Yanagita thoroughly rejected the Marxist materialistic concept of history which saw inviting prospects in the historical reconstruction of peasant traditions.

The institute issued a semiannual bulletin, compiled a bibliography of Japanese folklore classifying post-Meiji publications, and sponsored field surveys of single villages and glossaries of folk vocabularies. The chief accomplishment of Japanese folklore after the war was a *Glossary of Names of Japanese Fairy-Tales* (March, 1948), issued through the Japanese Broadcasting Company under the supervision of Yanagita. This work classified 240 groups of tales under fifteen headings, giving a plot summary, the geographical distribution, and literary references for each tale, thus summarizing the past thirty years of research on *mukashi-banashi.* Yanagita himself had concentrated on indigenous folk religion in the postwar years, and his books on ancestor worship, clan deities, and Buddhist mountain temples were brought together in 1947 under the title *The New Nipponology.*

Supplementing Naoe's report is a 1959 appraisal by Eder himself of "Japanese Folklore Science Today."[28] Remarking on the flood of Japanese folklore publications, Eder surmised that folklorists were now completing research digested and perfected during the postwar years, rather than producing books at the invitation of publishers to meet a popular demand. In the new monographs, source books, and encyclopedias he perceived greater objectivity toward the national folkways, more rigorous methods, and even sharp self-criticism of Japanese folklore science as overly insular. Because of his own comparativist, ethnological, and culture-historical position, Eder singled out for highest praise a group of papers published under the title *The History of Japanese Folklore Science and its Fields of Activity* (*Nihon Minzokugaku no Rekishi to Kadai*), issued as Volume II in the thirteen-volume "Encyclopedia of Japanese Folklore Science," published from 1958 to 1960. Eder provides detailed summaries of the introduction by Masao Oka, and of "The Historical Development of the Japanese Culture," by Minoru Shibata; "Sociological Character of the Japanese Folklore Studies," by Keigo Seki; and "The Regional Character of Japanese Folk Customs," by Katsunori Sakurada and Tsuneichi Miyamoto. Sakurada and Miyamoto speak for concern with causality rather than mere description in the discussion of regional customs; Seki asks that folk customs be studied in relation to social groups and classes; Oka insists that the assumed homogeneity of Japanese folk culture be analyzed into its historical components introduced from east and southeast Asia.

Two other volumes in the series synopsized by Eder are *Dramatic Performances and Amusements* (Vol. 9, *Geinō to Goraku*), and *Regional Investigations and Studies of Folk Customs* (Vol. 11, *Chihōbetsu Chōsa Kenkyū*). Each is an unusual stock-taking of the abundant materials in Japanese folk culture. In *Geinō to Goraku*, the variety of magico-religious dances, such as Kagura and *dengaku*, of Buddhist dances dramatizing Chinese and Indian tales, of ritual puppet shows, of Nō and Kyōgen plays drawing upon folk sources, all vitally connected with folk religion, can well bewilder a westerner. The ambitious survey of studies on folk customs inventories the research work done in Okinawa, Hokkaido, and all forty-two prefectures in between: histories of local folklore societies, bibliographies of local publications, photographs of local folklore materials. Eder points out that the prefectural units do not necessarily coincide with cultural unities (a point that applies of course to our own state boundaries). Thus Nagano—formerly Shinano—prefecture falls culturally and geographically between the northern and southern areas. Yet from early Meiji times the Shinano Education Society took a lead in local cultural and historical matters, encouraging *kyōdo-shi,* or descriptions of district folkways, and these monographs led to the journal *Kyōdo Kenkyū* founded by Yanagita in 1913, which in turn ushered in the period of systematic folklore studies.

In this multiple review, Eder also summarizes the contents of two recent works on the Japanese farmhouse. *Minka-chō (Notebook on the Farmhouse)* by Shūchū Kurada was published in the monograph series of the Folklore Research Institute in 1955, and deals with farmhouse types from northern to southern Japan. Also in 1955 appeared a regional monograph, *Tōhoku no Minka (The Farmhouse of Northeast Japan)* by Tsuyoshi Ogura. Only recently has the history of architecture in Japan looked beyond Shinto shrines, Buddhist temples, and mansions of the nobility to farmers' dwellings, and, as is true in European folk-life research, the folklorists have claimed this line of investigation.

The subject of *geinō,* alluded to above, is further discussed by Eder in a review of two books by Yasaburō Ikeda.[29] Geinō may be described as the interweaving of religious dance and dramatic performance in the traditional cult observances of Japanese villagers. The word *geinō* does not apply to purely artistic dance, song or drama *(geijutsu),* although such forms as Nō and Kabuki have sprung from

geinō. Geinō's distinguishing features are its specific connections with annual festivals and places of worship, its
enactment by and for members of the cult group, and its
oral transmission. As Japanese folk belief centers around the
seasonal greeting and leave-taking of the agricultural deity,
so geinō provides the ritual-theatrical procedures for worshiping the deity. "The essence of the geinō exists in the
expecting, welcoming, and sending off the gods, spirits, and
ancestor-souls," Eder writes. The mimic dance appears to
have been the original form of such devotions, but the
matsuri (festival) has evolved into a folk pageant. In many
geinō the prominence of decorated floats, trees, bridges, and
natural boundaries suggests places where the traveling deity
was believed to rest, and where he should be reverenced.

Yasaburō Ikeda has written two thorough and copiously
illustratd treatments, Geinō (1955) and Nihonjin no Geinō
(1957). The earlier work deals with the subject historically,
and the sequel classifies the forms of geinō, illustrating the
examples with monochrome photographs. Ikeda, a disciple
of Shinobu Origuchi, the authority on the history of Japanese folk customs, taught history of dramatic art and
Japanese literature at Keio University in Tokyo, and was
active for the Japanese Broadcasting Company.

Besides carrying the three historical surveys of Yanagita,
Naoe, and Eder, Folklore Studies contributes to a knowledge
of Japanese folklore through translated and original publications, and by an invaluable "Review of Reviews" section
which abstracts articles appearing in Japanese folklore
journals.

A study of exceptional interest is "The Kappa Legend"
by Eiichirō Ishida, professor of anthropology at Tokyo University, who employs the comparative method eschewed by
Japan-centered folklorists.[30] Beginning with texts of kappa
traditions assembled by Yanagita from all over Japan, Ishida

examines analogous examples throughout Asia and Europe of gods, goblins, and dragons who seek, like kappa, to cover mares and to pull horses into a nearby body of water. In his historical reconstruction, Ishida regards oxen as predecessors of horses in the fertility rites of prehistoric agricultural societies throughout the Eurasian continent. In Japan a special form of the mare-coveting water god appeared in a degenerate divinity resembling a monkey, the kappa. What seemed like a local folklore tradition thus appears to have world-wide associations.

Another similar study, "Das Pferd in Sage and Brauchtum Japans" by Nelly Naumann, complements Ishida's investigation of kappa in concentrating on the mare which the kappa covets. Bringing together much data on folk-religious ideas and observances connected with the horse, Naumann finds in the horse complex lunar-myth and phallic elements, and likely influences from the silkworm myths and cults of China.[31]

The first translation of field-collected tales to appear in English was printed in 1952 as the major portion of the journal. Fanny Hagin Mayer translated the "Japanese Folk Tales" of Kunio Yanagita from the revised edition of his *Nippon no Mukashi-banashi* (1942, first edition 1930). Mrs. Mayer is the one American who had made contact with the Minzokugaku Kenkyūsho. Born in Iowa in 1899, she was brought to Japan at the age of one by her father, a missionary in Tokyo. Mrs. Mayer left Japan in 1914, but in 1947 she returned with the occupation forces as a member of the Civil Affairs Team at Niigata Prefecture, holding the position of assistant education officer until 1949. In the years following she taught at Japanese women's colleges and studied at Sophia and Tokyo Universities, becoming increasingly interested in Japanese folk literature. The collection which Professor Yanagita suggested she translate contains 108 tales written in simple form for children, but they were based on field texts and represented many of the best-known traditional animal, demonic, and humorous village tales of the country. An illustrated book edition of the translation appeared in 1954.[32]

Eder himself contributed two original treatises, and directed the translation of a third, all in the sphere of folk religion. In his notes Eder acknowledges the debt in his own work to the Japanese studies. An extensive description of "Jahresbrauchtum im japanischen Dorf" by Hisayoshi Takeda, in 1949, with 195 accompanying photographs, concentrated on seasonal rites and fetes in the farming districts of Kantō and Chūbu and part of Tōhoku.[33] A foreword by Eder explains his desire to see this work translated in order to provide Western ethnologists with information on the wealth of festival, custom, and usage in the rural life of the Japanese, as a prelude to comparative studies. In his own study two years later on "Figürliche Darstellungen in der japanischen Volksreligion," Eder discussed the images and representations of deities made from stone and straw which play a central role in the calendrical observances. His first section follows Takeda's work with its heading "Im Jahresbrauchtum gebrauchte Figuren." In the next four sections, Eder considers such well known deities as Oshira-sama, who is believed to reside in puppets manipulated by female shamans; Funadama-sama, the guardian deity of boats; two deities of fortune, Ebisu and Daikoku; and stone deities like Jizō.[34] In a subsequent article Eder dealt with beliefs and rituals connected with the deity of the rice fields, the most revered supernatural being in agricultural folk Shintoism and folk Buddhism.[35]

Still other monographic papers deserve mention. U. A. Casal brought together many scattered references from literary works and field reports on two ubiquitous themes in

Japanese legend, the transformation antics of foxes and badgers, and the miraculous feats ascribed to Kōbō Daishi.[36] Casal, a retired Swiss businessman, married to a Japanese wife, and a resident of Japan for more than forty years, has accumulated massive materials on Japanese folklore, in the tradition of Basil Hall Chamberlain, M. W. De Visser, and other foreign residents who made themselves familiar with "things Japanese." However, in the papers by European scholars like Eder and Casal, and even by the Japanese ethnologist Ishida, we still do not directly perceive the work of the Japanese folklorists.

In the department "Review of Reviews" initiated by Eder in 1951 in *Folklore Studies* to "enable students of Oriental Folklore and Ethnology to follow up the activity and achievements of Japanese scholars in those fields" (p. 117), a bountiful feast is spread before the Western folklorist. Beginning with Volume X, Number I, the department has synopsized the contents of articles appearing in *Minkan Denshō*, the monthly organ of the Japanese Folklore Society, and in the quarterly of the Folklore Research Institute, *Nippon Minzokugaku,* a more detailed and scholarly publication, begun in May, 1953, whose topics and authors, however, remained pretty much the same as in *Minkan Denshō*.

These careful summaries covering eight productive years (1949–57) of Japanese folklore research provide us with a close view of the basic field studies from which the book-length monographs, encyclopedias, and general series develop. Almost all these abstracts are longer or shorter reports of customs and traditions in outlying villages and districts. Japan emerges from these digests as a folklorist's paradise. The perfect laboratory situation is here: the high civilization in which the folk culture is still vital and functional. Unlike Victorian England, post-Meiji Japan does not need to talk about "antiquities" and "survivals," and seek to reconstruct full-fleshed forms out of fragments and oddments; the entire complex of folk festival-dance-song-costume-legend-belief is visible and vigorous. For whereas cultural anthropology deals holistically with the traditional culture of a non-literate society, folklore has defined for its special province the submerged culture of the "lower orders"—to use the Victorian phrase—of the literate and imperious culture. One fortunate consequence of this opportunity to see closely and fully a full-bodied folk culture is the chance to determine its focus and function.

As one field report after another presents its data, the centrality of ritual in the category of folklore forms becomes apparent. In the United States we are accustomed to think of indexes of tales and ballads, superstitions and proverbs and riddles, but not of customs and observances, which do not lend themselves to the neat classification systems for texts. Yet the same patterns of textual variations familiar to students of English ballads and European folktales appear in the shifting blends and re-formations of ritualistic elements recurring from Aomori in the north to the Amami Islands in the south. A typology of regional rituals of worship almost constructs itself. Nor is there any danger here of Frazerian over-pressing of analogies; these are all rites from the same culture, with components as clearly identifiable as motifs in a folktale.

The seasonal rituals to welcome the field deity in the spring and see him off to the mountains in the winter in turn generate varied forms of tradition. Songs and dances are part of the rituals. Masks and portable shrines, dolls, ex-voto offerings and gala costumes are physical accessories to ritual worship. Legends coexist with festivals, as Ogura discovered (and writes about in this book) in his field work in the Noto Peninsula, collecting texts of legends at the annual festivals. The demonic creatures like *kappa* and *tengu* and the shape-shifting fox, so conspicuous in legend, all bear some relationship to the deities of mountain, stream and field.

The economic life and social organization of the Japanese peasant continually touch on *minkan shinkō*. The major food-procuring activities, namely rice cultivation and deep-sea fishing, require propitiation of the deities at every point, and a host of lesser observances as well, all involving charms and taboos. The social structure and interpersonal relationships are shaped by family and clan-group ancestral spirits, or *kami,* who too must receive ritual respect. In a challenging article in this volume, Matsumoto hypothesizes a genetic connection between the ancestral spirits and the field deities.

Some of the abstracts in the "Review of Reviews" may be cited to support these general comments. A number of articles describe the regional similarities and variations in deity beliefs. In "A Study on the Field-God" the folktale collector from Niigata-ken, Kenichi Mizusawa, documents the syncretism between the New Year deity, field deity, mountain deity, and ancestral spirit, whose festival rites tend to overlap and merge.[37] As a result of inquiries among 250 towns and villages in Kumamoto-ken, Manabu Maruyama uncovered a distribution area of belief in a supernatural being called "Yamawaro," hirsute and childlike, which lived on mountains in the winter and in rivers and ponds in the summer, and so was identified both with kappa and tengu.[38] Again "A Study on the God of the Kitchen-Hearth" demonstrates that Kamado-gami is a deity both of the hearth fire and of the crops. The same writer, Hirobumi Gōda, further investigates these interrelationships in an essay on "Multiplicity and Overlapping of Household Deities." Commenting on such well-known gods of good fortune as Ebisu and Daikoku—along with Kamado-gami, the hearth deity, Okama-sama, the furnace deity, and Kōjin, the ill-mannered deity—he observes: "Their individual functions are not always and everywhere clearly defined, and we find them shifting from one to another. The development seems to have started with a fire god who had, or still has, connection with agricultural fertility and ancestor souls."[39] In one of his studies on Jigami, the earth deity whose cult is reported throughout Japan, Hiroji Naoe speaks of Jigami's identification with *yashiki-gami,* the deity of house and grounds, with ancestral spirits, and with the rice-field deity.[40]

The varying elements of Shintoism and Buddhism in a given cult complex contribute both to the stability and fluidity of minkan shinkō. In a report on the Kōshin cult, Tatehiko Ōshima offers the opinion that the deity Kōshin was derived from the Hindu god Shiva, and then incorporated into the mountain- and field-deity complex. Eder adds a parenthetical note that his own field investigations on this question revealed no Taoist residue in Kōshin.[41] Manabu Ogura reached the same conclusion, namely that "The belief in the god Kōshin has many ramifications with other beliefs though it belongs neither to the Shintoistic nor to the Buddhist creed."[42] Yoshiyuki Kōjima points out the submergence of Buddhist features in kin-group rituals in villages of Iwate-ken, where a Buddhist picture scroll or statue, which is the object of worship, is kept by the head family for worship by the branch families; "the festival is essentially an affair of the sib." The Buddhist picture or image exercises a magico-religious function, compelling each worshiper to remain faithful to its cult all his life.[43] A report by Katsuaki Ogoshi on cult groups in Izumi-gun emphasizes the Shinto-Buddhist syncretism still apparent in folk rituals originating during the pre-Meiji period, before the

official separation of the two faiths. Ogoshi's description of
a ceremony performed on New Year's Day and again on the
first day of the ninth month, by the Myōjin Association
whose function is to pray for a good crop, typifies a folk-
Shinto fertility ritual.

At 10 o'clock in the morning the old members gather in the
shrine office. They bring two logs of cryptomeria, each about
24 feet long. The association members take their seats on both
sides of the logs and first a plate of pickled radish is passed
around. Then follows the dinner. When all are seated for it,
they take a foot long stick of oak or cherry into their hands and
worship the god in the alcove (*tokonoma*), while the door is
closed and the room is completely dark. Next a taper is lighted,
a big drum is beaten, and a flute is played. With music the god
is called down. Rice-wine is offered to him and a Shinto prayer
(*norito*) is recited. While they beat the matted floor (*tatami*)
with their sticks, they move around in the room on their knees
wresting the sticks from others. The ensuing tumult ends when
the Shinto minister beats a gong. The assembly is then dis-
banded. The rite aims at producing a good crop of the early
rice (*wase*). For producing a good crop of the middle and late
rice, the rite is repeated twice. If in the brawl with the sticks
none of the participants has suffered bodily harm, good crops
can be expected.[44]

Credence in and supplication to cult figures are not confined to the rural villagers. Writing on Inari, the agricultural deity associated with the fox and occasionally with
fisheries, Keiichi Kameyama observes, "In modern times
Inari is worshipped more by businessmen and inmates of gay
quarters as the god bestowing prosperity on them, less by
farmers."[45]

In one particularly striking case of syncretism, the villagers of Iojima on the island of Oki-no-shima outside Nagasaki Bay mingle Catholic with folk-Shinto ritual. They

observe the mass, baptism, and the cross, while they also maintain the Tanabata festival, worship Kōjin-sama, the kitchen deity, and keep the custom of *kadomatsu,* or planting pine trees at the entrance of the house on New Year's Day.[46]

Phallic and sexual elements in the fertility rites are plainly indicated in some reports. In Yamanashi-ken and Nagano-ken stone figures of the boundary deity Dōsojin are seen in male and female form or simply as stones in the shape of male and female genitalia. At the Dōsojin festival in Kitakoma-cho, onlookers rub their bodies with paper strips attached to a huge human figure made of wheat straw, and indulge in phallic worship.[47] Again from Kitakoma in Yamanashi-ken we hear of a special festival to *iwai-gami* (celebrated deity) at which members of the *maki* (a kinship association) make replicas of the male and female sexual organs and offer them to the deity. Childless married couples request members to make figures in their behalf. In feudal times the villagers danced nude in the hall before the deity.[48]

One recurrent theme emerging from the journal articles is the intimate connection between minkan shinkō and oral folk narrative. Without getting into the controversial myth-ritual theory of folklore origins, we can observe a common fount of magico-religous traditional belief nourishing both rite and legend.

Traditions about foxes, the commonest theme of supernatural encounters in Japan, differ vastly from European animal tales, for the fox possesses, or once possessed, the character of a deity. As Keiichi Kameyama points out, the fox-belief is enmeshed with the cult of Inari, a messenger deity. Inari frequently changes to a fox, and fishermen who believe in Inari listen to the cries of the fox to hear Inari's portent for a good or poor day's catch.[49] In a report from

Shimane-ken on "The Fox," Takatoshi Ishizuka finds that families still worship *kitsunegami,* the fox deity, and practice sorcery with his help, a practice which leads other villagers to fear and avoid intermarriage with fox-possessed families. More than half the families in Izumo and Oki were believed to be possessed by an evil fox spirit, who would follow a bride coming from a possessed family, and remain with her descendants.[50] The seriousness with which fox possession is regarded still today is seen in the following abstract:

A report from Akita Prefecture, Katsuno District, Akebono village, Kurozawa. To cure a mad woman a sorcerer was called. He found that the woman was possessed by a malignant fox. To drive the fox out he denied all food to the woman. He applied pepper on her nose, eyes and mouth, rubbed her body with red-hot sticks which were otherwise used to handle charcoal in the brazier. Then he bored holes into her breast and abdomen, all with the result, that the woman died after three days. Such cases of barbarous treatment of lunatics are still heard of from far-away mountain villages where a good number of sorcerers are still held in high esteem.[51]

A legend found all over Japan tells of a water creature who borrows rice bowls from a village family and returns them intact. In a common variant, a kappa appears in the guise of a beggar to request the bowls, and rewards the family with riches. Analyzing 150 texts, Toshio Kitami finds these legends closely connected with worship of the water deity, a cult originating in simplest form from wet rice culture. Chopsticks and wooden bowls drifting downstream led stranded and isolated groups, seemingly through the agency of the water spirit, to friendly and prosperous settlements.[52] Discussing "Water Women in Folktales," Midori Tade-numa sees for the central motif the remuneration given by a water spirit to a human being who has thrown a useful object into the water. In many of these stories a happy event occurs on New Year's Eve, and this day is characterized in fact by ritual offerings to the water deity. In a companion article on "The Pond-snail in Tales," Tomiko Yokoyama considers legendary traditions in which a pond snail, who is a demigod, marries a village girl and changes into a handsome hero. The evidence shows that villagers regard snails living in ponds and swamps as messengers of the water deity, or the water deity himself, and pray to them for protection against fire and to bring rain. Since the snails leave the ponds to spend the winter in the mud, creep into the rice fields when the spring rains soften the mud, there to multiply, and disappear in autumn, farmers linked their cycle with the arrival and departure of the field deity.[53]

So-called fairy tales, or "mukashi-banashi," often are seen to be fictional versions of legends, with their roots in minkan shinkō. Eiichirō Ishida finds a sea divinity behind the tale type of which the best-known example is Momotaro the Peach Boy, the story always included in English editions of Japanese fairy tales for children. Ishida discusses Momotaro in terms of "The Mother-Son Complex in Japanese Religion and Folklore." A divine boy from the water world born miraculously from a dragon, water spirit, thunder god, or a known father, benefits mankind in various ways; he and his mother are worshiped together. Using the method of comparative ethnology, as in his treatise on the kappa, Ishida finds the genesis of these folktales in a telluric mother-goddess from the ancient Near East and India.[54]

A picture of the activities of a field collector in the remote countryside can be obtained from reviews of five books by Kenichi Mizusawa, all published in 1957 and 1958, and an article on his field methods, by Fanny Hagin Mayer. Principal of an elementary school in Nagaoka-shi, Niigata-ken, in the "snow country" of west-central Honshū, Mizusawa belongs to the Niigata Folklore Society and the Folklore Society of Japan, and depended "largely upon Mr. Kunio Yanagita for reference and guidance in technique."[55] Following up leads from his students to their parents and grandparents, Mizusawa has located a number of narrators in mountain and lowland communities, which, during winter, he visits on skis. Often he will ski ten miles into the hills beyond the bus lines to reach a hamlet. He writes the stories down in the local dialect, and depends on subsequent visits to solve puzzling points, wishing to keep the storytellers comfortable and at ease without interrupting their delivery. In publishing the tales he retains all the original earthy and humorous idioms, and appends dialect glossaries explaining in standard Japanese the meaning of local terms and phrases. In one volume, instead of appending a glossary, he rendered the dialect into conventional Japanese in parallel columns. Each tale is identified by narrator, locality, and year of recording.

The arrangements of the collections show imagination and logic. In *Echigo no Minwa (Folktales of Echigo)*, the bulk of the tales, fifty-five out of seventy-seven, follow three old divisions of the prefecture, with one storyteller representing each region. In the two volumes of *Tonto Mukashi Atta Gedo* (an opening formula), the tales all come from the area of Nijimura, and one narrator fills the entire first volume with 122 texts. The introduction furnishes details of the narrator, a ninety-year-old woman, Nagashima Tsuru, and is supplemented by eight photographs and a hand-sketched map. The sequel volume emphasizes folk crafts and customs in the region, directly relating twenty-seven tales to local beliefs and practices. The full total is 134 tales recited by fifty-one narrators, ranging widely in age, from nineteen small communities; many stories are of the short, humorous variety, as they are nowadays in the United States and Europe. Thirteen photographs show scenes of folk life. In *Tonto Hitotsu Attaten Gana* (another opening formula), Mizusowa printed the repertoires of two storytellers, (who, this time, lived in more accessible towns on the plains) one aged ninety-four and the other forty, who each told him over a hundred tales. Finally in *Iki Ga Pon To Saketa* (a closing formula), Mizusawa grouped 135 tales, including many variants of previously published texts, from thirty-six narrators according to the eastern, western, northern, and southern regions of his home town of Nagaoka. These substantial collections, averaging from three to four hundred pages and affording opportunities to compare variants and individual and regional repertoires, testify to the industry and rewards of a zealous regional collector.[56]

Folksong is also closely linked with ritual, but as a part of ceremonial observance rather than of magico-religious belief. A whole set of regulations and taboos governs the appropriate time, place, sequence, and style of singing traditional folksongs. If field-planting songs were sung at an inappropriate time, they would bring the mountain deity down from the mountain top in a wrathful mood. When a smallpox epidemic broke out in Kagoshima-ken, the villagers sang and danced in their best clothes to the deity of epidemics; during its height they dressed as beggars and toured the villages collecting money for medicines and incantations, singing and dancing in another manner. These songs and dances had to be faultless, in order to placate the deity.[57] In a paper on "Traditions Regarding Boatmen's Songs," Sōichirō Fukushima categorizes boat songs according to their use by fishermen: while worshiping at festivals, rowing, setting nets, waiting for the tide, launching boats, celebrating the New Year. A tendency exists to make the long phrase ending such songs, which expresses a wish for bright moonlight, favorable tides, and success on the voyage, the main burden of the song.[58]

These illustrations could be expanded almost indefinitely to suggest the pervasive character of minkan shinkō in Japanese peasant life. Other abstracts from *Minkan Denshō* and *Nippon Minzokugaku* deal with such topics as Chichibu dolls in religious ceremonies, divining with gruel, charms against thieves, the connection of a place name with a summer ritual, worship of the dog spirit by pregnant women to ensure easy delivery, the magical properties of sedge hats. All these beliefs and practices interlock and interlace in a universe governed by spirit-powers.

One exception to the internal preoccupation of the Japanese folklorists is found in the work of Toichi Mabuchi, an anthropologist with extensive field experience in southeast Asia, who became a member of the Folklore Research Institute. Mabuchi has considered analogies and genetic relationships of traditional beliefs in the Ryukyus and in Formosa with the body of Japanese custom and ritual.[59]

A special mention should go to Hiroko Ikeda, first trained by Yanagita, who crossed the Pacific to take a doctorate in folklore at Indiana University with Stith Thompson. Her unique control of both the Japanese sources and the method of motif analysis has enabled her to construct an important index of international tales in Japan and to write articles identifying Japanese folktales in Korea and among the North American Indians.[60]

In view of the breadth of Japanese folk culture, one school of research can scarcely deal with all its facets, not even so comprehensive a school as that of Yanagita. A separate group with quite a different emphasis has addressed itself to Japanese folk art, under the leadership of Sōetsu Yanagi, who founded the Japanese Folk Art Society (Nihon Mingei Kyōkai), with the artists Kanjirō Kawai and Shōji

Hamada, in 1931, as well as the Japanese Folk Art Museum (Nihon Mingei Kan) and the journal *Mingei* (*Folk Art*) in 1936. In an informative article, "Notes on Japanese Folk Art," Matthias Eder discusses this movement and reviews the beautifully designed book on *The Folk Arts of Japan* by Hugo Munsterberg (Tokyo: Charles E. Tuttle Company, 1958) which draws much of its material from Yanagi and his museum.[61] Eder makes the point that this folk-art movement is primarily interested in aesthetic recognition for, rather than historical research of, its subject. The conscious awareness of folk-art and craft traditions has even led four sophisticated artists to become in effect folk artists: Hamada and Kawai as folk potters, Keisuke Serizawa as a folk dyer, and Shikō Munakata as a print-maker following folk models. Yet the folk arts belong to the province of Japanese folklore science, since figures and pictures and costumes and decorations are intimately bound to native religion, magic and myths. In the field of folk toys especially are the Shinto and Buddhist popular beliefs in spirits, demons and ghosts fully reflected. *Ema* or ex-voto pictures hung in shrines and temples, and even in horse stables, and stone sculptures and carvings of such deities as the children's guardian Jizō and the boundary guardian Dōsojin also relate the popular arts to the popular religion.

This introduction has dwelt on the work of the Japanese folklorists whose essays will appear in the following pages. If one were to seek access to those materials of Japanese folklore gathered and translated by other hands than those of the disciples of Yanagita, he could compile a considerable bibliography. Collections exist of folktales, folksongs, proverbs, customs, and folk comedies or *kyogen*.[62] Illustrated accounts discuss legendary themes in art in general,[63] and in special modes such as the carved and decorated *netsuke* worn on the obi.[64] American cultural anthropologists prob-

ing into Japanese village life have written ethnographies—
notably the field studies of Suye Mura by John Embree, of
Takashima by Edward Norbeck, and of Niike by Richard
K. Beardsley, John W. Hall, and Robert E. Ward—[65]
which incidentally consider minkan shinko. From his Suye
Mura experience came Embree's sheaf of earthy *Japanese
Peasant Songs* published as Memoir 38 (1944) of the American Folklore Society. The treatise on Japanese mythology
(1928) by Masaharu Anesaki in the Mythology of All Races
series (Vol. VIII), composed by a specialist in art history, offers useful comments on oral folklore, particularly in the
chapter on "Local Legends." Scattered through such journals as *Monumenta Nipponica, Transactions and Proceedings of the Japan Society of London, Japon et Extrême
Orient, Contemporary Japan, Transactions of the Asiatic
Society of Japan, Deutsche Gesellschaft für Natur- und
Völkerkunde Ostasiens,* and the folklore quarterlies can be
found many papers bearing on Japanese folk traditions.[66]
Yet in their totality these collections and interpretations
yield external and fragmented views of Japanese folk culture. Only the industrious group of Japanese folklorists are
working systematically and in concert to explore the folk
institutions and traditions of their civilization. Their inde-
fatigable labors and substantial achievements well merit the
envy and admiration of their colleagues overseas.

Notes

1. As early as 1895 Fr. von Wenckstern's *A Bibliography of the
Japanese Empire* (Leiden, 1895) could list eighty-two publications in
Western languages on "Fairy Tales, Folklore, Proverbs and Supersti-
tions" published from 1859 to 1893 (XVII, 223–27).

2. *Nihon Minzokugaku Bunken Mokuroku (Japanese Folklore Bibliographical Index)* (Tokyo, 1955). Compiled by the staff of the Minzokugaku Kenkyūsho, Taro Wakamori editor-in-chief.

3. An enlarged edition with 299 additional tales was issued in 1935 (K.B.S., entry 37).

4. A second edition appeared in 1941 (K.B.S., entry 147).

5. See Sieffert, entries 1, 10, 11, for the original Japanese editions. *Studies in Fishing Village Life (Kaison Seikatsu no Kenkyū)* and *Studies in Mountain Village Life (Sanson Seikatsu no Kenkyū)*, as translated by M. Takatsuka and edited by G. Brady, are in the University of Kentucky Press Microcards Series A, Modern Language Series Nos. 1 and 2 (1954). *The Japanese Folklore Dictionary (Minzokugaku Jiten)* is in Series A, Modern Language Series No. 18 (1958).

6. Charles S. Terry (trans.), *Japanese Culture in the Meiji Era* (Centenary Culture Council Series, Vol. IV [Tokyo: Obunsha, 1957], 335 pp.). Cf. Sieffert, entry 12.

7. Sieffert, entries 18, 73–75, 175, 189–90; K.B.S., entry 125.

8. Sieffert, entries 2, 327, 329, 344; K.B.S., entries 207, 208. A selection from the *Nihon no Mukashi-banashi*, translated by Robert J. Adams, has been published in the "Folktales of the World" series (Chicago: University of Chicago Press, 1963).

9. Sieffert, entries 13, 308–11.

10. Tokihiko Ohtow [*sic*], "Yéma, or Votive Tablets," *Contemporary Japan*, XI (April, 1942), 585–98, with 3 plates.

11. Sieffert, entries 17, 227; K.B.S., entry 120. "Kankon sōsai no hanashi" appeared in *Nihon Minzokugaku Kenkyū*, 1935, pp. 197–232, as one of a collection of essays on Japanese folklore by the disciples of Yanagita. A translation appeared in *Cultural Nippon*, IX (December, 1941), 14–58.

12. Sieffert, entries 6, 43, 208; K.B.S., entry 111.

13. Sieffert, entries 20, 41, 77, 78, 174, 238, 315; K.B.S., entry 92.

14. Sieffert, entries 69, 70, 173, 312–14; K.B.S., entry 79.

15. Subtitled *Étude descriptive et sociologue* (Paris: Librairie orientale et américaine, G. P. Maissonneuve, 1936), 172 pp.

16. Sieffert, entries 250, 251. A general article by Matsudaira in English translation, "Festivals in Japan," appeared in *New Japan*, VI (1953), 315–20. Although the festivals have been influenced by major organized religions, "what interests us most is the fact that the people's faith in the primitive age forms the basis of all the festivals" (p. 318). The *Bulletin de la Maison Franco-Japonaise* (N. S. IV, No. 2,

1955 [Tokyo, 1957]) carried three papers by Matsudaira: "Le Rituel des Prémices au Japon" (pp. 1–48); "Les fêtes du Japon" (pp. 49–58); and "La cosmologie japonaise telle que la suggère l'observation des fêtes" (pp. 59–70).

17. (Paris: Librairie Orientaliste, Paul Geuthner, 1928), 144 pp. Cornelius Ouwehand has written that Matsumoto and Kazuo Kigo "belong to the earliest advocates of the introduction of folklore studies into the field of mythology" ("Some Notes on the God Susa-no-o," *Monumenta Nipponica*, XIV [1958–59], 387).

18. Sieffert, entry 319.

19. No. 10, October, 1924, pp. 228–39. The same number contains "Une collection de folklore japonais," pp. 279–92, a bibliographical review article by Serge Elisséev, giving detailed summaries of a number of field collections.

20. Sieffert, entries 149, 292; K.B.S., entries 128, 129. Volume I of the last work is titled "Tradition and Folktales," and Volume II "Religious History in Japan."

21. *Numen, International Review for the History of Religions*, Vol. V, fascs. 2–3, pp. 128–60, 199–232.

22. LXI (June, 1959), 405–24.

23. *Zenkoku Minzoku-shi Sōsho*, K.B.S., entry 36.

24. *Nenchu-gyoji Zusetsu*, K.B.S., entry 163; and *Nihon Minzoku Zuroku*, K.B.S., entry 80. In both text and notes, translated book titles which appear alone are given in quotation marks.

25. K.B.S. entries 103, 135, 162, 133.

26. Edited, with an "Explanation of Illustrations" (pp. 1–16) and a "Glossary of Japanese Folk Costume Terminology" (pp. 17–19), by Keitaro Miyamoto; published by the Ie-no-Hikari Association.

27. *Folklore Studies* (hereafter *FS*), VIII (1949), 277–84. Reprinted in *Midwest Folklore*, III (1953), 213–22.

28. FS, XVIII (1959), 289–318. For the full listing of the *Encyclopedia of Japanese Folklore Science (Nihon Minzokugaku Taikei)* see K.B.S., entry 33. Four of the present contributors served with Masao Oka on the board of editors; Mogami, Omachi, Sakurada and Seki. A review of Vols. 3 and 4, jointly titled "Society and Folk Customs," and a listing of the contents of Vol. 8, "Religious Beliefs and Folk Customs," by M. Eder are in *FS*, XX (1961), 329–39.

29. Ibid., XVII (1958), 239-41.

30. Kenichi Yoshida (trans.), "The *Kappa* Legend: a Comparative Ethnological Study on the Japanese Water-Spirit *Kappa* and Its

Habit of Trying to Lure Horses into the Water," ibid., IX (1950), i–vi, 1–152, with a two-page color print and twenty figures; from a revised version of *Kappa Komahiki Kō (Kappa Luring Horses into Water)* (1948), specially prepared by the author.

31. *FS*, XVIII (1959), 145–287. English summary on pp. 271–72, with twenty-four plates following p. 287.

32. Ibid., Vol. XI, No. 1, 1952, pp. 1–97. Book edition (Tokyo: Hokuseido Press, 1954), 299 pp.

33. *FS*, VIII (1949), 1–269., K.B.S., entry 166, *Nōson no Nenchū-qyōji (Annual Observances in Rural Districts)* (Tokyo, 1943), 590 pp.

34. *FS*, Vol. X, No. 2, 1951, pp. 197–280, with twenty-five photographs and drawings.

35. "Die Reisseele in Japan und Korea," ibid., XIV (1955), 215–44.

36. "The Goblin Fox and Badger and Other Witch Animals of Japan," ibid., XVIII (1959), 1–94; "The Saintly Kobo Daishi in Popular Lore (A.D. 774–835)," ibid., pp. 95–144.

37. Ibid., XIV (1955), 266–67.

38. Ibid., pp. 273–74, "The Distribution Area of Traditions of the Strange Being Yamawaro.",

39. Ibid., XVI (1957), 300, 316.

40. "The Earth God (Jigami) and the God Kōjin (Rough God)," ibid., pp. 315–16.

41. "The Kōshin Cult and the Ritual Called Nijūsanya in Reference with the Mountain God and the God of Paddy-fields," ibid., pp. 316–17.

42. "Kō in Kaga and Noto Provinces," ibid., pp. 310–11.

43. "The Mairi-no-hotoke: 'Buddhist Deities' Worshippe⁀ by Individual Kinship Groups," ibid., XVII (1958), 263–64.

44. "Cult-groups *(miyaza)* and Agrarian Rites in Izumi Provinces," ibid., XVIII (1959), 330–32; quoted from p. 331.

45. "The Belief on Inari as Fishery-god," ibid., Vol. X, No. 2, 1951, pp. 297–98. R. P. Dore gives data on urban folk-religious beliefs in "The Individual and the *Kami*," *City Life in Japan* (Berkeley and Los Angeles: University of California Press, 1958), pp. 329-38.

46. Doi Takuji, "Customs of the Underground Christians," *FS*, XIV (1955), 264–65.

47. Yoshinori Ōmori, "Dōsojin and Graveyards in Kōshū," ibid., p. 268.

48. Mison Yoneyama, "On *maki* in *Kitakoma*," ibid., Vol. XI, No. 1, 1952, p. 102.

49. Loc. cit.

50. *FS*, XIV (1955), 259.

51. Sasaki Kinishiro, "A Case of Superstitious Killing of a Mad Woman," ibid., p. 277.

52. "A Cross Section through the Japanese Conception of Other Countries," ibid., pp. 258–59.

53. Ibid., XVII (1958), 259–60, 260–61.

54. Ibid., XVI (1957), 297–99. Abstracted from the *K.B.S. Bulletin*, No. 15 (November–December), 1955.

55. Fanny Hagin Mayer, review of "Four Japanese Folk Tales Published by Kenichi Mizusowa," in *FS*, XVII (1958), 243.

56. Ibid., pp. 243–45; ibid., XVIII (1959), 319; F. H. Mayer, "Collecting Folk Tales in Niigata, Japan," *Midwest Folklore*, IX (summer, 1959), 103–9. Mizusowa also published an earlier collection from Miyauchi in 1956, *Mukashi Attantengana (Once-upon-a-Time Stories)*.

57. Tomiko Baba, "Avoidances in Folksongs," *FS*, XVII (1958), 258.

58. Ibid., XIV (1955), 257.

59. See his "Folklore Science and Ethnography in the Investigation of Okinawa," ibid., Vol. XI, No. 1, 1952, p. 106; "Okinawa and Formosa," ibid., pp. 125–26; "Spiritual Predominance of the Sister over the Brother in the Southern Ryukyus," ibid., XVI (1957), 301.

60. See "A Type and Motif Index of Japanese Folk Literature" (Diss., Indiana University, 1955), recorded on microfilm by Microfilm Service, Ann Arbor, Michigan, 1955; " 'Kachi-Kachi Mountain'— A Japanese Animal Tale Cycle," in W. D. Hand and G. O. Arlt (eds.), *Humaniora, Essays in Literature, Folklore, Bibliography, Honoring Archer Taylor on his Seventieth Birthday* (Locust Valley, New York: J. J. Augustin, 1960), pp. 229–38; "Relationship between Japanese and Korean Folktales," *Internationaler Kongress der Volkserzählungsforscher in Kiel und Kopenhagen* (Berlin, 1961), pp. 118–23.

61. Ibid., XVII (1958), 228–35. Yanagi has published *Folk-Crafts in Japan* (Postal Administration Ministry [Tokyo, 1936]) (rev. ed.; Tokyo: Hōbun-Kan, 1960), 57 pp., 19 plates. Munsterberg writes: "The underlying spirit of Japanese folk art is best described by the term *shibui*, which is difficult to translate, but implies a subdued, subtle, and austere quality in contrast to the gaudy brilliance found in the shrines at Nikko and in so much of the decorative art of the Edo period. . . . The whole effect is one of a plain, functional beauty which avoids ostentation, and in that way it is quite different from much of the folk art of Europe, which tends to be gay and colorful

and to show a far greater variety of design" (*The Folk Arts of Japan* [Tokyo: Charles E. Tuttle Company, 1958], p. 30). Cf. Yanagi, Foreword, p. 16.

62. The following are representative titles. FOLK NARRATIVE: David Brauns, *Japanische Märchen und Sagen* (Leipzig, 1885); Richard M. Dorson, *Folk Legends of Japan* (Rutland, Vermont, and Tokyo: Charles E. Tuttle Company, 1961), with bibliography, pp. 245–48; Fritz Rumpf, *Japanische Volksmärchen* (Jena, 1938). FOLKSONGS: *Japanese Peasant Songs*, compiled and annotated by John F. Embree, with the assistance of Ella Embree and Yukuo Uyehara (Memoirs of the American Folklore Society, XXXV [1944]); Georges Bonneau, *L'Expression Poetique dans le Folk-lore Japonais* (Paris: P. Geuthner, 1933); Iwao Matsubara, *Min-Yo, Folk-Songs of Japan* (2nd rev. ed., Tokyo: Cosmo Publishing Co., 1946). FOLK DRAMA: Shio Sakanishi (trans.) *Japanese Folk-Plays: The Ink-Smeared Lady and Other Kyogen* (Rutland, Vermont, and Tokyo: Charles E. Tuttle Co., 1960). PROVERBS: Aisaburo Akiyama, *Japanese Proverbs and Proverbial Phrases* (3rd ed., Yokohama: Yoshikawa Book Store, 1940); Hitoshi Midzukami, *A Collection of Japanese Proverbs and Sayings (With Their English Parallels)* (Tokyo: The Kairyudo Press, 1940); Rokuo Okada, *Japanese Proverbs and Proverbial Phrases* (Tourist Library Series No. 20 [Tokyo: Japan Travel Bureau, 1955]). CUSTOMS: William H. Erskine, *Japanese Customs, Their Origin and Value* (Tokyo: Kyo Bun Kwan, 1925), and *Japanese Festival and Calendar Lore* (Tokyo: Kyo Bun Kwan, 1933); Frederic de Garis, *We Japanese, being descriptions of many of the customs, manners, ceremonies, festivals, arts and crafts of the Japanese* (Miyanoshita, Hakone: Fujiya Hotel, Ltd., 1950); Mock Joya, *Quaint Customs and Manners of Japan,* 4 vols. (Tokyo: Tokyo News Service, 1951–55).

63. Henri L. Joly, *Legend in Japanese Art: A Description of Historical Episodes, Legendary Characters, Folk-Lore, Myths, Religious Symbolism, Illustrated in the Arts of Old Japan* (London and New York: John Lane, 1908).

64. Adrienne Barbanson, *Fables in Ivory: Japanese Netsuke and Their Legends* (Rutland, Vermont, and Tokyo: Charles E. Tuttle Company, 1961); Egerton Ryerson, *The Netsuke of Japan illustrating Legends, History, Folklore & Customs* (London: G. Bell & Sons, 1948); Madeline R. Tollner, *Netsuke, the Life and Legend of Japan in Miniature* (San Francisco: Abbey Press, 1954).

65. Takao Sofue, "Japanese Studies by American Anthropologists:

Review and Evaluation" (*American Anthropologist,* LXII [April, 1960], 306–17), contains a convenient bibliography.

66. Some representative articles from the periodical literature are Ensho Ashikaga, "The Festivals for the Spirit of the Dead in Japan," *Western Folklore,* IX (1950), 217–28; Felicia G. Bock, "Elements in the Development of Japanese Folk Song," *Western Folklore,* VII (1948), 356–69; U. A. Casal, "Far Eastern Monkey Lore," *Monumenta Nipponica,* XII (April–July, 1956), 13–49; idem, "Inari-sama, the Japanese Rice-deity and other Crop-divinities," *Ethnos,* XIV (1949), 1–64; F. J. Daniels, "Snake and Dragon Lore of Japan," *Folklore,* LXXI (1960), 145–64; W. L. Hildburgh, "Japanese Popular Magic connected with Agriculture and Trade," *Transactions and Proceedings of the Japan Society,* London, XII (23rd Session, 1913–14), 22–83; idem, "Some Parallels between Minor Superstitions of Japan and of Great Britain," ibid., XVII (28th and 29th Sessions, 1918–20), 2–29; Henri L. Joly, "Bakemono," ibid., IX (19th and 20th Sessions, 1909–11), 16–48; W. D. Preston, "Japanese Riddle Materials," *Journal of American Folklore,* LXI (1948), 175–81.

Opportunities for Folklore Research in Japan

BY KUNIO YANAGITA[1]

Mid-twentieth-century Japan offers the folklorist a rich harvest of ancient legends, tales, crafts, and folk observances. In hundreds of little offshore islands and in mountain or rural communities remote from large cities, millions of elderly Japanese still feel it their duty to preserve and hand down their ancient traditions. These traditions are especially worth collecting because they reveal that the Japanese have for centuries remained fundamentally one people. Today, ninety million Japanese live on some three hundred islands extending from Hokkaido in the northeast to the Ryukyu Islands in the southwest. These people experience great differences in climate; their planting and harvesting seasons vary by as much as three or four months; and they speak distinct dialects which vary from region to region. Yet in spite of these differences, communities far removed from each other have been found to possess remarkably similar folkways and culture.

Japanese folk traditions have for centuries remained largely uninfluenced by foreign ideas even though Japan has experienced several immigrations of people from abroad. It is true that contact with Korean and Chinese craftsmen and teachers as early as the fifth century, and with Europeans and Americans in modern times, has brought outside influences to Japan; but it is no less true that outside of the big cities, sixty to seventy per cent of the population still follow the beliefs and way of life traditional to Japan.

Visitors to small, remote Japanese communities will find many an open-hearted old man or woman ready to describe the ancient traditions to them. The collector is especially welcomed, for the old folk, seeing young people in increasing numbers leaving their communities to obtain work in larger towns, are filled with worry that the precious lore of the past will not survive. Through the help of a young local teacher, a little circle of such old people was assembled by this collector in Nagano-ken. When I began to ask questions about local customs and traditions, one old woman burst into tears of joy and exclaimed: "Is the time come when we may tell these things to strangers who come to inquire?" Throughout Japan old villagers like this woman wait to share the lore they have preserved with folklorists rugged enough to undertake first-hand research in these isolated areas.

The foreign folklorist will find long-enduring and relatively undisturbed folk traditions in Japan. In Western nations, traces of old patterns have been well recorded through folklore research for so long that at present there is little left to find. By contrast, everything in Japan that is traditional can still be found and still awaits careful attention by scholars. This is not to say, however, that no start has been made toward recording Japanese traditions. Faced with the enormous possibilities for folklore study when I first learned of this point of view,[2] I urged my countrymen to observe and to record each and every old custom, tradition, or activity in their local regions, with the result that published materials soon accumulated; but they were burdened down with unrelated details. At present, the studies are proceeding more systematically. I myself have particularly turned my attention to old religious beliefs and practices of the common people in Japan.

Although the uncompromising march of Christianity has all but obliterated traces of ancient faiths in the West, Japan offers scholars an opportunity to observe and study still-vigorous traits of old religious ideologies. Beneath the Buddhism of modern Japan, the folklorist will find vestiges of ancient mountain and ancestor worship. Even though the priest in the rural areas shaves his head as a Buddhist priest must, he is still identified more with older faiths and observances. Buddhist temples can be found everywhere today for the convenience of believers; but when the temples were first introduced, they were erected at the base of mountains, whose names they took. There seems to have been an attempt by the early teachers of Buddhism in Japan to identify their faith with the pre-existing one, which attached religious significance to mountains. Traces of the belief that the souls of the dead gather in the mountains still are found in place names and in dialectal words and phrases. Today the funeral and anniversary rites for the dead are usually Buddhist, and worshipers offer fitting compensation to the Buddhist monks for their services; but the people continue to associate the souls of their remote ancestors with kami, a pre-Buddhist concept surviving from ancient times.

There are several dangers to be considered by foreign

scholars in Japan. They may be misinformed by friendly Japanese who are too intent upon establishing a common ground with them. Or they may be misled by untrustworthy written sources: for instance, in thinking that they study genuine Japanese culture through the works of women writers of the Heian Period (794-1185) who wrote about life in palace circles where Chinese modes prevailed. A degree in Buddhistic theology will not help the student of Japanese faiths. To avoid these dangers, I have been urging my countrymen to distinguish between elements traditional in Japanese culture and elements derived from foreign countries, and to study more intensively before trying to interpret Japan to foreign inquirers. On the other hand, I would like to welcome folklorists in greater numbers to come to Japan to examine and to enjoy the rich, ancient lore of traditional narratives and beliefs and folk arts and manners, which retain their strength in spite of the modern ways evident in the metropolitan centers.

Notes

1. This article is a summary of Mr. Yanagita's remarks during an interview in Japanese with Mrs. Fanny Hagin Mayer, at his home in Tokyo on April 19, 1957. Mrs. Mayer rendered the translation.

2. Mr. Yanagita refers to his readings in the anthropological school of English folklorists of the late nineteenth century.

百姓

PART TWO | RICE FARMERS

Seasonal Rituals Connected with Rice Culture

BY TOSHIJIRO HIRAYAMA

Almost all the main agricultural rituals performed in Japan are connected with rice culture. In these narrow and mountainous islands which are always faced with threats of typhoons, the cultivation of wet rice has ever been attended by toil and stress. Owing to such conditions, the Japanese have, on the one hand, exerted tremendous efforts to develop techniques of intensive farming of the existing rice fields, and on the other, they have since ancient times strictly observed a number of rituals to ensure the safety and abundance of their crops. These rituals are performed in conjunction with the actual processes of production. By means of comparative studies of the many rituals and functions which are still transmitted and practiced in various parts of Japan, we may be able to reconstruct phases of historical change which Japanese beliefs have undergone during the past 2,000 years.

What we call annual festivals have passed through a great many public changes since the court of Yamato (the first imperial court in the history of Japan) adopted the Chinese calendar at the beginning of the seventh century A.D. Moreover, after the adoption of the Gregorian calendar in 1872, knowledge of the occidental calendar has generally prevailed among the people. Yet the primeval annual fes-. tivals, no doubt formed from a complex ritual connected with rice culture, and based on the naïve conception that a year begins with the annual sowing and ends in the harvest, have long been transmitted from generation to generation in the rural areas; and clear traces of them still remain in many parts of Japan today, even though they do not accord with the calendar cycle propagated by the government.

i

Rituals connected with rice culture are, in brief, rituals held for the deity or deities of the rice field. The ancient myths indicate the various names which are applied to the rice deity and other agricultural divinities who came to be worshiped in shrines throughout Japan. However, the rice-field deity in question here has neither been protected by any official or nobleman nor been honored in the national shrines during any historical period; he has received homage only from the farmers. Consequently, it is the deity which has existed in a popular faith that has developed naturally, without the interference of specific religious policies. This deity is widely known as *ta-no-kami* (the deity of rice fields), but it has other names, too. It is called *nō-gami* in the Tohoku area (Aomori, Iwate, Akita, Miyagi, Yamagata, and Fukushima prefectures), *saku-gami* in both Yamanashi and Nagano prefectures, and *tsukuri-gami* in the Kinki area (Shiga, Mie, Wakayama, Nara, Kyoto, Osaka, and Hyogo prefectures). All of these names signify "deity of agriculture." In the San'in region (a part of Yamaguchi, Shimane, and Tottori prefectures), the deity is called *i-no-kami*. *I* means "wild boar," the twelfth of the twelve horary symbols, which is assigned to October. Along the Inland Sea there are villages which refer to this deity as *ji-gami*, meaning "deity of the earth." Ebisu-gami in the eastern part of Japan, as well as Daikoku-gami in the western part, are syncretized with ta-no-kami. These figures were formerly worshiped as the beneficent deities of commerce and manufacturing in towns and cities in the medieval period from the thirteenth to the sixteenth centuries, and were later welcomed as agricultural deities in rural areas.

The rituals for the deity of the rice field are performed on many occasions according to the growing stages of rice plants. In the past the entire village participated collectively in such rituals, whereas at present they are held simultaneously in each home in a given village. The main rituals are held several times a year, as follows: the inviting and the welcoming of the deity, before cultivation is begun in the spring; the *minakuchi matsuri,* at the time of the sowing of the seed in the rice nursery; the *sa-ori,* when the seedlings of rice are transplanted to the rice field; *sanobori,* when the transplanting is completed; and the farewell to the deity, at the end of the harvest in autumn. There is, in addition, a ritual prayer for a good crop, which is performed at the beginning of the year. In traditional Japanese belief, the deities are invited to appear at appropriate occasions and are sent off again afterwards, since they do not live continuously with men but emerge from the land of the gods to receive offerings. The deities in the shrines have undergone metamorphoses through the influence of Buddhism, but the rituals used in serving the deity of the rice field remain relatively unchanged from olden times.

A traditional belief almost constant throughout Japan is that the deity of the mountain comes down to the village in the spring and becomes the deity of the rice field; then after protecting the rice during its cultivation, he returns to the mountain again in the autumn. The time of arrival and departure of the deity differs between the northern and southern parts of Japan, due to the difference in climate and its relationship to agricultural production. In most cases, the rituals are held in February and in October of the old lunar calendar, but there are some places where they are held in March and November. The days on which the rituals are held also vary from place to place. For example, in the Hokuriku region (Niigata, Toyama, Ishikawa and Fukui prefectures), villagers serve the rice-field deity on the fifth day of the month in both spring and autumn and serve the mountain deity on the ninth day. The months of the rituals have become confused through the simultaneous use of the lunar and solar calendars. The i-no-kami ritual in western Japan is held on the day of *I* (the Wild Boar) in October, and the Shimo-tsuki matsuri in Kyushu is held on the day of Ushi in November. Shimo-tsuki is an old name for November, and Ushi (the Ox) ranks as the second of the twelve horary signs. The ji-gami ritual is held on the day of *shanichi*[1] both in spring and in autumn. Shanichi was the day for serving the deity of the earth in China also, and hence some relationship may exist between the ceremonies observed on this day in the two countries. Presumably, these rituals were originally held around the night of the full moon. Since ancient times there have been held at the court of Japan the *toshigoi-no-matsuri* (a ritual prayer for a good crop) in February and *niiname-no-matsuri* (ritual of thanks for the crop by tasting the first fruit of the rice) in November, at both of which the emperor himself formerly presided. Such court festivals are based on the same beliefs as are the rural observances.

Many changes have occurred in the rituals for the rice-field deity—even within one village the ceremonies may vary from season to season—and the place of worship has changed as well. In former days the people might stand in the rice field to welcome the deity in spring, whereas at present they generally hold this ritual inside the house. On this occasion they start a fire in the kitchen early in the morning and pound steamed rice in the mortar, making heavy sounds with the pounder, as the traditional saying bids them, for it is said that the deity will descend from heaven on hearing these sounds. The prevalence of the custom prohibiting anyone from entering the rice field before this day suggests an older usage, in which the people went to the rice field, there to welcome the deity descending from the heavens. In the autumn the peasants used to serve the rice-field deity around the pile of reaped rice plants after the harvest, whereas today they usually bring the sheaves to their houses and hold the rituals there. At this time, with loud sounds from the pounder, they again crush the steamed rice to make the *mochi* (rice cake).

ii

The specific rituals connected with rice cultivation will be considered next. First of all, the people soak the rice seeds in water early in the spring. They often call this water *waka-mizu* (young water). At about the same time that the deity of the wet rice field is welcomed at the homes of the people, the rice seeds are sown in the fields. In the Tōhoku area, the blossoms of the *kobushi* (a kind of magnolia) are given the name *tanemaki-zakura*, which means "the cherry blossoms that bloom at the time of sowing," and farmers actually begin sowing when the flowers come into bloom. In Kyūshū sowing commences when the lark starts to sing. People in the eastern part of Japan recognize the time for sowing when the remaining snow in the high mountains is shaped like the seeds of rice. Usually the rice farmers initiate their work by watching the changes in nature and in the activities of the animals—perhaps as they did in pre-calendrical times.

Immediately after sowing the rice seeds in the bed, the farmers heap mud at the inlet of the rice field, place flowers or erect branches there, offer parched rice in front of them, and worship the deity of the rice field. This is the rite called *minakuchi matsuri* (irrigation-inlet rituals) and is observed most commonly in eastern Japan. In some places the rice farmers erect a branch in the midst of the rice field. This branch is neither a mere decoration nor a sign, but serves as a *yorishiro* (an object upon which the deity rests). In Nagano-ken they call it *tananbo,* or the "bench for the deity of the wet rice field." In Fukushima-ken they call this consecrated tree *nae-mi-dake.* Today it is merely a bamboo measuring stick used to measure the growth of the seedling (*nae*), but it was once the symbol by which farmers consecrated the seedlings. (The wood signs called *nae-jirushi,* used in the Tohoku area to mark the boundary of one's land tenure, originally had a similar purpose.) These trees, like the pine trees erected at the entrances of houses on New Year's Day and the flowers that decorate altars during the Bon festival, are gathered from the forests and from the mountains, the home of the deities. In some villages the people put up the sticks which have been used to make rice gruel, the food eaten on the fifteenth of January. In certain districts, sacred tablets given by the priests of the shrines and temples to the villagers at their spring festivals are inserted in the fork of a willow or chestnut tree. The parched rice offered up at this ritual is made out of the unhulled rice left over from planting. In many places this practice is explained on the grounds that the farmers seek to divert the birds from eating the sown rice by offering them the parched rice. Usually the food which has been offered in a ritual is shared by the performers; however, the parched rice offered in this ceremony must not be eaten by the members of the family who hold the ritual but should be left for the village children. In some places children walk from door to door asking for the parched rice and reciting a spell to drive away the birds. From this practice we can see that the offering of parched rice at minakuchi matsuri has the ritualistic implication of invoking a rich crop.

After the rice has been sown, the people must not touch the growing seedlings for about thirty-three days. This is a tabooed period in which they pray for the growth of the rice seedlings, and those who violate this prohibition are warned that they will lose their eyesight. Also it has been told that the seedlings should not be touched because they are about to bud. When the period of *nae-imi* (the taboo against handling the rice seedlings) passes, the villagers take up *ta-ue,* the transplantation of the rice seedlings. In preparation of ta-ue, they begin digging the main rice field into which the seedlings will be transplanted as soon as the minakuchi matsuri is over. The soil is tilled and fertilized, the levees are hardened, and water is drawn into the rice fields. Then the day of ta-ue comes.

iii

The ta-ue is the most important process in the work of rice cultivation. The greatest ritual of the year accompanies this labor of transplantation.[2] Some scholars believe that the farmers did not transplant in ancient times but sowed the rice seeds directly in the fields; but even if we admit the existence of a primitive way of direct sowing, the technique of rice transplanting can be traced back to a period earlier than the fifth or sixth century A.D. Ta-ue, therefore, has been observed as an agricultural method for at least fifteen hundred years.

In the past, the transplantation of rice plants was cooperative work involving all the people of a village. It was directed by the head of a labor group presumably based on an extended kinship relation. This headman rallied the villagers to cooperate, and at the same time presided at the rituals held for the deity of the rice field. The productive as well as the religious activities of the villagers have long been carried out by this communal organization. This is presumed to be the prototype of a large-scale organization for ta-ue, which has existed till recently in the Tōhoku and Hokuriku areas, and was managed by a great landlord; he was the head of both the kinship group and the farmers, and controlled the subordinate peasants known as *nago* and *hikan*.[3] In the Noto Peninsula, on the day of ta-ue the head of an old family stood beside the rice field with a bamboo stick in his hand and directed many *taudo* (the villagers who join the ta-ue) by leading the songs. In many instances all the villagers have helped with the ta-ue of a great landlord, and the small farmers were not permitted to work at their own transplanting until the ta-ue of the landlord was finished. In the mountainous part of the Chūgoku area, even though the labor groups have been dissolved and changed, the old form of the rice transplantation has been handed down as a joyous function. Sometimes all the villagers, and sometimes a united body of over ten families, cooperate in transplanting the rice plants.

The leader of these labor groups is called *sage*. This position is assumed by a man who is skilled in the work and who is well versed in the ritual. He holds a *sage* stick in hand

and takes the lead in the ta-ue songs, which consist of several hundred stanzas. The labor is divided between the male and female taudo who gather there. Men take part in tilling the soil, leveling the ground, and carrying and distributing the seedlings. Women transplant the seedlings, since the sacred labor of ta-ue has traditionally been the work of the female. These females, who are called *sa-otome,* wear new clothes, white towels on their heads, and red cords around their waists. In addition, there are some who play flutes and beat gongs and drums. All of these people together form a group and transplant the rice plants all day long as a divine service. The smooth procedure of the work depends entirely on the skill of the *sage* in securing the cooperation of many taudo. With his songs he leads the hard work rhythmically.

The ta-ue ritual begins when the people welcome Sanbai-sama, the deity of the rice field, after taking the seedlings out of the rice bed early in the morning. They make a shelf in the field or heap mud at the inlet and erect there a branch from a chestnut tree. Before this altar they offer three bundles of rice seedlings. At this time songs of praise are sung to welcome Sanbai-sama. These songs depict the deeds of the deity and laud his virtues. The work advances with the songs. At noon, beautifully dressed *onari* (virgins in the service of the ta-ue ritual) bring the consecrated diet, and the people share it with the deity. Fish is always included in the food served on this day, a custom which suggests that fish was the original ritual diet, since an early type of offering, possibly Shintoistic but definitely not Buddhist, served the deity with a whole fish, including head, fins, and tail. The verses and melody of the song change as the time passes, and when the evening draws near, the tempo of both songs and labor accelerates. When the transplanting is finished, all sing together the song to send off Sanbai-sama. The verse that still widely persists is, "Come again next year, *o-ta-no-kami.*" Thus the deity is served and songs are sung to the accompaniment of musical instruments, while the women work cooperatively from morning until night to finish the transplanting of the rice plants in one day. The tradition of finishing the ta-ue of a household in a day's time is handed down in many villages. The fact that this function is often called ō-ta-ue (ō means "big") suggests the scale of transplanting in former times.

When the power of the stem family (that is, the family of the chief of the farmers) declined, and the branch families and the small farmers became independent, both the productive and the religious activities of the villagers shifted from a communal basis to one of cooperative labor between individual families. This change clearly appeared as the power of the medieval feudal lords became established. Moreover, the small-scale farmers who had newly attained independent status, such as they now have, needed temporary help only in times of heavy labor, as during ta-ue. A few people, grouped around members of a family unit, need more than one day within the short period suitable for transplanting, and must make haste in finishing the job. No more songs, no more festivities; only the hard work remains.

Thus the ta-ue ritual has taken two forms: the ritual that is performed in each family, and the ritual held by the whole village. The traditional practice and belief in completing ta-ue in a day have declined, and two stages of the ritual have emerged, one at the beginning and the other at the end of the transplantation. The form of the ta-ue ritual most prevalent today follows this pattern.

iv

The ritual held at the beginning of the transplantation is called by an old word, *sa-ori*. *Sa* seems to mean the deity of the rice field, *ori* being "to descend." Consequently, the word means the day on which the people invite the rice-field deity down from the mountain. This connection is also seen in the words Sa-tsuki and *sa-otome;* Sa-tsuki is the name of the month (tsuki) in which the rice transplantation is done and *sa-otome* refers to the maiden (*otome*) who transplants the rice seedlings. The sa-ori ritual is also called *sa-biraki* and *wasa-ue,* both signifying the onset of transplanting. These words suggest the idea that the deity descends and the people initiate the transplanting. In the eastern part of Japan, sa-ori takes place on the thirty-third day after minakuchi matsuri (when the taboo against touching the seedlings ends), and farmers once transplanted all their rice on this day, simply for the sake of formality. The prevalent practice for the ritual of sa-ori, however, is to transplant three plants or bundles of rice seedlings on a certain day in April of the lunar calendar. The remainder of the rice seedlings is transplanted whenever the season is suitable. As on the minakuchi matsuri, people sometimes erect a chestnut-tree branch in the rice field and decorate it with the flowers of the season. Nowadays, in many parts of Japan, these seedlings are regarded as offerings to the deity, but the erected tree branch would originally have been a symbol of the divine presence.

There are many local names for the ritual which is held at the end of the transplantation. *Sanobori* and *sanaburi* are representative names among many for this ritual signifying that *sa,* the deity, goes back to the mountain. In this ritual, the villagers also decorate or consecrate the seedlings of rice as they do in sa-ori. The ritual is usually held before the standing altar within a house, and the people who have joined in the transplanting are invited to a congratulatory feast. The sa-otome are given seats of honor at this banquet, because these women have played an important role in ta-ue. According to one explanation, this practice is based on an old idea which makes the fecundity of a woman parallel with the richness of the soil—as is indicated by the former custom of a priestess' presiding over the rice-planting ritual.[4] Following the ritual of sanobori, several days of self-confinement were formerly observed by the workers, but at the present time this period is used for rest and recreation.

The twofold character of this custom is of particular interest. One ritual is held by each household at the close of transplantation; the other is held by the whole village on an appointed day. In some districts, both rituals are held on the same day, while in other districts only one or the other is observed. And in still other places the ritual is not to be found at all. If we look at their geographical distribution, we find that the areas in which the sanobori ritual is held only once by a whole village encircle the places where it is held twice. From this fact we may be able to reconstruct historically the bifurcation of the ritual. The reason why these two forms of sanobori split off from the original single form honoring the departure of the rice-field deity becomes clear from the history of the village labor organizations. Up to recent times, the small farmers in certain villages took part only in the sanobori held by their stem family. When the small families subordinate to or branching out from the stem family became independent, the custom of holding sanobori at each home was instigated, and so brought a change in the nature of the village sanobori. Although in some villages the home and the village sanobori have been celebrated on the same day, their functions differ; the main purpose of the ritual at home is to send off the deity suitably by providing a congratulatory feast, whereas in the village shrine festivals the people pray to their tutelary deity for a rich crop and for protection against harmful insects, and they enjoy the holiday together. Thus the two forms of sanobori have become quite distinct.

v

After the transplantation of the rice seedlings is completed, the farmers turn their energies to eradicating the weeds that spring up in the rice field during the summertime. This is very toilsome labor and needs to be repeated two or three times. Along with this work they attempt with great effort to keep the water in the rice field standing at the appropriate level, and they conduct rituals and utter spells to protect the rice plants from injurious insects and from the strong wind.

When the water supply becomes insufficient, the farmers pray for rainfall in a widely observed ritual known as *ama-goi* (praying for rain). In ama-goi the villagers may gather at the shrine and pray for rain all night through, or they may kindle a large fire on the mountain or take some water believed to be endowed with a spiritual power and wait in their own houses for rain. Again, they may dedicate dances to please the deity of water, or even commit deeds to offend him and so precipitate a rainfall. If the rain continues to fall day after day and the people fear damage to the rice plants, a ritual is staged to pray for fair weather.

In former days, the curse of an evil spirit was believed to be responsible for the appearance of insects harmful to the rice plants. The belief that the spirits of people who die bearing grudges can cause epidemics is seen in documents of the seventeenth century, which liken the malignancy of noxious insects to the dreadful power of evil spirits. In the nocturnal ritual to drive away the insects, the villagers make a straw doll which they carry about and cast away at the border of the village, while a row of people with glowing torches in their hands parade through the streets loudly reciting a spell.

The first of September (two hundred and one days from the beginning of spring) the people believe to be an evil day. Since plants suffer much damage from strong winds, the people ask the priests of the shrines and the monks of the temple to pray and to hold a ritual to placate the deity of the wind. In some districts at this season the farmers go out into the rice field and speak words of praise to the rice plants to precipitate their sound growth and utter a spell to hasten the budding of the ears.

vi

The last stage in the series of rituals connected with rice cultivation comes with the autumn harvest rites. There are two rituals on this occasion, one at the beginning and the other at the end of the harvest. The autumn festivals were once the joint activity of all the members of the village, but now an autumn festival is held at the shrine, and the original rites are usually conducted in each house.

The ritual held at the beginning of the harvest is called *ho-kake*. The farmers reap a small portion of the rice ears (*ho*) before the real harvest to hang (*kake-ru*) in front of the deity, and offer parched rice taken from the new crop. The date of the ritual differs from place to place. In some districts it is held on August first, or at the time of the wind-placating ritual, while in others it occurs on shanichi in autumn. In some places the farmers hold the ritual on the very first day on which they actually reap the rice plants. The deity to be served should have originally been the deity of the rice field, since this is a day of thanksgiving for the rice crop. According to present-day customs, however, the first crop is offered not only to this deity but also at the shrine of the mountain deity, at the shrine of the village tutelary deity, at the family altar, and at the tomb of the ancestors. There is a fairly general trend for the deity of the rice field to be syncretized with such tutelary deities and also with the ancestral deities, all of whom are worshiped in a similar manner.

Kariage matsuri (finishing-of-the-harvest festival) is held when the harvest is over. Since Japan consists of islands which range a considerable distance from the south to the north, the climate varies, and consequently this ritual has come to be held roughly at three different times according to latitude. People in the Tohoku area call the days to which the number nine is attached *san-ku-nichi*,[5] and they choose one of these three days as the day of the ritual. Usually they choose the twenty-ninth. In the Kanto area, they hold the ritual on the tenth of October and call it *tōkan-ya* or *jū-ya* (the night of the tenth). In the Kansai area and in the western parts of Japan, they call the day of the wild boar, in October, I-no-ko (Child of the Wild Boar). The ritual is held on that day, and rice cakes shaped like piglets are eaten. Kariage matsuri in Kyushu is held still later, on the day of the ox in November, and is called *Shimo-tsuki matsuri* (November festival).

The ritual that comes at the end of the harvest seems to have been initially held in front of the *nio,* a heap made of the reaped rice plants. The vestige of this old custom can be recognized even today. In some districts the farmers make shelves on which to hang and dry the sheaves of rice plants. However, in many instances they hold this ritual inside the house rather than outside by the rice field. They take away the *kagashi* (scarecrow), which has threatened the birds all summer long in the rice field and erect it at a corner of the house to worship it there. This practice can be seen in the

ritual of tōkan-ya in Nagano prefecture, where the kagashi
is regarded as the symbol of the deity of the rice field. The
ritual of consecrating or offering up the sickle used in reap-
ing the rice plants is also widespread. O-ushi-sama in Kyūshū is now associated with Daikoku, an agricultural deity,
and is worshiped on the day of *ushi,* the ox. To serve this
deity, they reap the rice plants that have been left unreaped
for this day, take them home, and offer them at an altar
made of a mortar. Never do the people forget to include the
rice cakes (*mochi*) made from newly harvested rice, along
with some vegetable, in the offerings of this ritual. In most
cases, these rice cakes are covered with red beans. In an old
form of celebrating I-no-ko matsuri, they put *bota-mochi*
(rice-cake dumplings covered with sweet bean paste) in a
one-*sho* measuring cup and offer it up before a mortar. This
custom is also observed at Ushi matsuri. These rice cakes
might once have been eaten by the people who had joined
the ritual. Now that the ritual has come to be held at each
house, families present these rice cakes to each other.

The Shimo-tsuki matsuri and the Ushi matsuri in Kyūshū
are held long after the end of the actual harvest. The twenty-
third of November in the lunar calendar is the proper day
for these festivals, which are linked with many differing
traditions; among these festivals there are some which resemble the ritual connected with rice culture and others in
which the villagers worship their ancestor spirits. This is
now the date of our national holiday, Kinrō Kansha no Hi
(Labor Thanksgiving Day), the direct antecedent of which
is the harvest ritual held at the imperial court.

Originally the people stored the reaped rice plants for a
long time just as they were harvested; but from the Middle
Ages on they hastened to thresh them and to put the un-
husked or unpolished rice in bags made of rice straw, since
these bags of rice were the required form of tax payment.

Consequently, the *niwa shigoto* (the work done in the yard) such as threshing and husking rice, came to be included in the labor of the harvest season. At the end of each of these processes the farmers individually celebrate with a feast.

vii

Some agricultural rituals are also observed on one of the New Year holidays. The people's need to feel hopeful about the new year has brought forth many festivals during the first month. In the *ae-no-koto* ritual in the Noto Peninsula, the rice-field deity is worshiped on the ninth of January. The practice varies with individual villages and houses, but in general the families consecrate as a symbol of the deity a portion of the rice that has been harvested the previous year and that is to be used as seed rice in the coming year. It is believed that the deity will move from the house into the rice field when this ritual is over. On the eleventh day of January, the head of the family goes into the field and symbolically tills the land and transplants the rice plants, removing the snow if any has fallen. When he returns home a feast is given for him celebrating the occasion. This is the rite of *ta-uchi shōgatsu* (rice-field-cultivating for the new year) and is widely observed east of the Chugoku area. Along the Inland Sea, it is customary on the same day for all the members of the family to honor the deity of agriculture and to worship the rice field itself. This custom is not often found in Kyūshū. In the Tōhoku area, they celebrate the fifteenth as the first day of labor by simulating the trans-plantation of rice plants, enjoying the ta-ue dance, and decorating a wooden stick with small pieces of rice cakes, after the manner of the harvest in autumn.

On the nights of the full moon in January many rituals connected with agriculture take place. All of them strongly suggest magico-religous performances that are intended to ensure a rich crop for the coming year. In some districts they are held prior to the invitation to the rice-field deity; and presumably in their original forms these rituals were supposed to welcome and serve this deity, as we can see in an ae-no-koto ceremony in the Noto Peninsula. The reason for the change from the early form to the present one may be found in the adoption of the new (Gregorian) calendar, which no longer conforms to actual agricultural practices.

In summary, I have tried to reconstruct in brief the hypothetical prototypes of rituals in Japan concerned with rice culture, and to trace their changes up to the present in accordance with historical developments in agricultural society. My study has greatly profited from the work already accomplished by Kunio Yanagita and other senior students of folklore in analyzing and systematizing diverse folklore materials. Two other approaches remain open for further investigation in this field: historical studies based upon surviving documentary records, and comparative studies utilizing the data on agrarian rites observed among other rice-cultivating peoples.

Bibliography of Reference Books and Articles

Hayakawa, Kōtarō. *Nō to Matsuri (Farming and Ritual)*. Tokyo: Guroria Society, 1942.

Kurata, Ichirō. *Nō to Minzokugaku (Farming Rites in the Science of Folklore)*. Tokyo: Rokunin Sha, 1944.

Yanagita, Kunio. *Bunrui Nōson Goi (Classified Glossary of Farming Village Life)*, 2 vols. Tokyo: Tōyō-Dō, 1948.

――――. "Ta-no-kami no Matsuri-Kata" ("Rituals for the Rice-Field Deity"). *Minkan Denshō (Folklore)*, Vol. XIII, Nos. 3, 4, 5 (March–May, 1949).

Notes

1. Shanichi occurs twice a year, at the vernal and autumnal equinoxes, and always falls on a day designated as *tsuchi-no-e* (earth, in the older aspect). Because shanichi was understood to be the day of the earth, it was customary on this day to hold a festival for the earth deity. Moreover, shanichi came at important seasons for the farmers, at rice-seed-planting time in the spring and the harvest time in autumn.

2. Ta-ue was also called Sa-tsuki in earlier times, since it took place in May of the lunar calendar, Sa-tsuki being the old name for May. Ta-ue (literally "transplanting rice seedlings in the wet rice field") originally signified both the labor of transplanting and the associated ritual. With the increasing emphasis on the labor aspect of rice cultivation which became a principal industry of farmers under the control of samurai since the medieval period, the ritual aspect was weakened. Then in some districts the ta-ue festival has become separated from the actual rice planting.

3. Subordinate families like nago and hikan, whether or not related to the head family, lived under the latter's control and offered their labor in return for permission to cultivate some land for their own use. The nago system endured in a few villages until the end of World War II.

4. Ichirō Kurata, *Nō to Minzokugaku (Farming Rites in the Science of Folklore)* (Tokyo: Rokunin Sha, 1944), pp. 184–87.

5. San-ku-nichi (three ninth days) are the ninth, nineteenth, and twenty-ninth days of the ninth month of the lunar calendar. In China the ninth day of the ninth month was and is an important ceremonial day.

Mysterious Visitors from the Harvest to the New Year

BY ICHIRŌ HORI

One of the most significant phenomena in Japanese folk culture is the emphasis placed upon mysterious visitors and upon members of outcast groups who travel from place to place as magico-religious beggars and reciters.[1] Various beliefs, legends, and customs pertaining to these individuals have been collected from rural communities throughout Japan and from historical documents as well. Scholars who have gathered these folklore items view almost all of them as an integral part of traditional agricultural rites, festivals, or ceremonies which have taken place annually between harvest time and the New Year. Through careful comparison and analysis, these scholars have drawn the conclusion that much of the present-day lore about mysterious visitors derives from the original belief that strangers who appeared at harvest time or at the turn of the year were life-givers from the other world in heaven or from the eternal land overseas. The ancient Japanese believed these visitors came to instill new life power in rice seeds and in human beings in order to ensure vigorous germination in the approaching spring.

The concept of parallelism between the life cycles of rice and human beings arose from the primitive but seriously held feelings of ancient Japanese peasant philosophers who sought to explain the interrelationship between the four seasons of the year and the process of growth and decay of the rice plant. Seeing that nothing grew during the winter months, these peasants believed that the period from the harvest to seeding time was the most critical one, not only for rice plants but also for human beings, because the people waited in anticipation during this period to see if the rice seeds would sprout in the spring and ripen in the autumn. If not, no one would survive through the coming year. To help ensure survival, the peasants began to practice a considerable number of magical rites and ceremonies designed to promote the renewal and rebirth both of seeds and of human vitality. In time they may have developed a vague conception of a magical life-giver which, in turn, became particularized into a belief that an ancestral deity was the originator and sustainer of each individual life. Over the years the rice mother, or the corn mother, came to be regarded in the same light. Hence ancestor worship and its attendant customs, festivals, and rites, which may have developed from particularizations of the life-giver and rice mother, became one of the most pervasive characteristics of Japanese farming society.

i

Being so predominant throughout the whole range of Japanese folk beliefs, agricultural themes play a major role in almost all the annual festivals of Japanese peasantry.

The Bon festival in July of the lunar calendar, and the winter and New Year festivals as well, are among those the peasants consider most important. Agricultural rites and magic are contained in each of these festivals, in which mysterious visitors from the Other Land make their appearance to bless the people. The winter and New Year festivals will be particularly discussed in this paper for they occur within the period from harvest time to spring planting— the period in which most of the mysterious visitors appear.

The first of the winter festivals is the niiname-no-matsuri, the harvest festival of the imperial court. Traditionally observed by the emperor himself, it is one of the court's most important annual festivals. While its origin seems to date back to the early dynastic period when the emperor was regarded as the medium between the chief deity and the people, the festival has been carried on up to the present day. In fact agriculture has remained so essential to Japan that the coronation ceremony of the emperor continues to be simply the niiname festival on a larger scale.

According to the *Kojiki, Nihongi, Manyōshū,* and other Japanese classics, in ancient times each family had its own niiname festival. On the night of that festival a mysterious visitor or visitors came from the Other Land in order to be entertained at a sacred meal prepared from the new rice and other harvest crops. The *Manyōshū* contains several poems which celebrate this festival night, and which indicate that it was customary for a hostess or virgin member of the family to remain alone in attendance upon the visiting god or spirit, while the rest of the family gathered at the public festival place. One of these poems reads as follows:

> Who is secretly knocking on the front door of my house,
> On the night of the niiname festival,
> When I am observing abstinence alone,
> In order to serve the god of the rice field,
> After my husband has gone out?[2]

The niiname also is the focal point of a famous Japanese legend which concerns happenings on Mount Fuji and Mount Tsukuba on a night of the festival. This legend is contained in the *Hitachi Fudoki,* an ancient account of what is now Ibaraki-ken, compiled under imperial order at the beginning of the eighth century. The *Hitachi Fudoki* states that once upon a time Mioya-gami-no-mikoto (the Great Ancestor Deity) went from place to place in order to visit her descendants. Finally she arrived on Mount Fuji at sunset and asked for lodging for the night. However, the deity of the mountain replied: "Just tonight I am observing abstinence because this is the niiname night for the early-ripened variety of the rice plant. I am sorry, but I will not be able to give you shelter." Thereupon the ancestor deity cursed the mountain deity, saying: "So you won't give shelter to your ancestor! Henceforth the mountain you live on will be covered with eternal snow, and no one will be able to ascend your mountain to serve you. This is the fate your impiety and undutifulness to your ancestor have created."

Mioya-gami-no-mikoto received different treatment upon Mount Tsukuba. When she asked for lodging, the deity replied: "This is a festival night of niiname. Nevertheless, my Great Ancestor Deity, how can I refuse you?" And, having said these words, the deity of Mount Tsukuba served many kinds of fresh harvest food to his ancestor. In return, the ancestor deity invoked a blessing upon her pious offspring: "Oh my dearest offspring! Oh your highest shrine! You will be prosperous and enjoy life as long as heaven and earth exist, for many people will ascend your mountain to serve you!" According to the *Hitachi Fudoki*, Mioya-gami-no-mikoto's prophetic curses and blessings came true. Since then Mount Fuji has been covered with snow which never melts completely; hence the belief that no one could climb to the summit. On the other hand, even today many people gather on Mount Tsukuba, where they dance and sing, eat and drink, on the festival days in honor of its deity.³ This legend, and the poems of the *Manyōshū*, hint that the ancient Japanese people believed a deity from the Other Land visited them on the night of the harvest festival.

ii

Before the niiname-no-matsuri, many kinds of festivals and rituals take place on the night of the full moon in the first month of winter (October by the lunar calendar). On this night the *ta-no-kami-no-toshitori* (ceremony of a year's addition to the rice deity's age) is held in Tohoku province; in some villages in Kanto province this ceremony is also called the *daikon-no-toshiya* (New Year's Eve of the radish); on the same night the *i-no-ko-matsuri* (festival of the wild boar, one of the twelve horary symbols) is celebrated throughout the western and southwestern parts of Japan. These festivals are perhaps all related to each other; at least some form of connection is indicated by their common elements. Thus, in nearly all of them the village boys band together and visit every home. Together they carry a magic symbol, a rod made of straw or of two large stones bound together with rice-straw rope. The boys utilize this rod to beat on the ground or on each front door rhythmically, while they sing a magic formula.⁴ A typical song used for this purpose on the night of I-no-ko is as follows:

> I-no-ko is tonight;
> Tonight is I-no-ko,
> And those who do not solemnize the I-no-ko,
> Give birth to a demon!
> Give birth to a snake!
> Give birth to a child with a horn!
> There is a deity who is called Daikoku;
> First, he sits astride the rice bags;

Second, he smiles sweetly;
Third, he makes *sake*;
Fourth, he makes the world pleasant;
Fifth, he makes the world permanent;
Sixth, he gives the people good health;
Seventh, he makes the world peaceful;
Eighth, he enlarges the residence;
Ninth, he builds a storehouse here;
Tenth, having done all this he rests
    astride the rice bags.[5]

The ritual magic of this song and its accompaniment of rhythmic beats are supposed to subdue the noxious insects and demons or evil spirits that lurk behind each house or under the ground. Yet, if we compare this ritual with the original symbolic stamping on the stage or in the ring, an action still performed in the *kagura* (ancient sacred Shinto music and dances) and in the popular entertainments for the return of spring,[6] we discern that the stamping symbolizes the visits of the strange, powerful gods from the Other Land, who bless the people and banish evil spirits. These gods were so revered by the peasants that in some areas in former times sexual liberty was permitted with them on the night of the I-no-ko festival. This license appears to have been a survival of a ritual in which the hostess or virgin member of each family became the one-night wife of the guest deity during the niiname festival.[7]

Finally, from the tenth to the fifteenth of October according to the lunar calendar, the *jūya-nembutsu,* a rite of supplication to the Buddha or Buddhas for spirits of the dead, is held at Buddhist temples of the Shingon and Jōdo sects. Like the Bon festival in July, this rite probably represents a fusion of Buddhism with the ancient belief in seasonal visits by spirits of the departed.

iii

In November of the lunar calendar, many harvest festivals take place in Japanese rural society. On the ninth of the month, for example, the peasants of the Noto Peninsula, Ishikawa-ken, hold the ae-no-koto (rite of feasting) or ta-no-kami matsuri (festival for the deity of the rice field). The head of each farming family comes out separately to meet the deity and guides him to the fireplace for warmth. Then a bath is prepared for him, after which he is treated to the many foods made from new harvest crops and to the host's address of welcome and thanks. Even though the presence of the deity is symbolic rather than actual, each of these details is rigidly observed. For Japanese peasants believe such a deity does exist, even if he cannot be seen, and the peasants claim to know enough about him to maintain that he is blind, as a consequence of staying beneath the rice fields to guard the plants from harm. His presence in each household is symbolized by bags of rice seed. The most important food offerings to the blind deity are new harvest rice boiled with red beans and the two-forked *daikon* (giant radish), both of which are usually prepared for two guests. The food offerings which this deity has consumed only symbolically are offered to the household deities after the festival is over, and are then distributed to each member of the family.[8]

Around the twenty-third of November the *daishi-kō*, another kind of harvest festival, is held in the Tōhoku and Kantō areas, where the villagers imagine they are visited by mysterious spirits. Although these spirits are thought to be ghosts or goblins which have replaced the original deities, the widespread custom of serving the visitors gruel made from red beans and new harvest rice, and the observance of fasting and abstinence on this festival night, still survive.

As in the I-no-ko festival held in other parts of Japan, so in this harvest rite village boys take an active part; in the east-central part of Niigata-ken, they band together and march through their villages, repeating a meaningless set of verses in place of the original formula.[9]

iv

New rice with red beans, rice gruel with red beans, and the two-forked daikon all have important roles in Japanese harvest festivals. Each is an important offering to the deities as well as a sacred food for men. We have seen, for example, that rice gruel with red beans is used in the daishi-kō festival, and that both new rice with red beans and the daikon are primary offerings during the festival of ae-no-koto. So, too, the daikon plays an oblatory role in the tōkan-ya festival held on the tenth of October of the lunar calendar in several regions of central Japan,[10] in the Daikoku-age or Agari-ushi festival held on the day of the ox in November of the lunar calendar in northern Kyūshū, and in the Daikoku-no-toshitori (New Year of the Deity Daikoku) or Daikoku-no-yome-mukae (Marriage of the Deity Daikoku), which is usually held in the Tōhoku area on December ninth of the lunar year.[11]

Daikoku, referred to above, is a deity who originated as Ōkuni-nushi, a famous culture hero in Japanese mythology. Daikoku is also the Japanese name of a Buddhist guardian deity, whose Sanscrit name is Mahā-kāla. Purported to have come to Japan from China, Ōkuni-nushi became known as Daikoku, the Japanese pronunciation of the Chinese characters for Ōkuni (*nushi* is "lord). Then, after Mahā-kāla became the guardian deity of the kitchen in Buddhist temples, the Japanese peasantry identified him with Daikoku. Finally, as a combined culture hero and guardian deity,

Daikoku developed into the harvest deity responsible for good fortune in every rural community. Continuing to play this important role in mid-twentieth-century Japan, the deity Daikoku usually is enshrined in the special kitchen altar of each agricultural household.

The daikon also may have a symbolic signficance which many Japanese villagers comprehend. Villagers who transmit harvest rituals from generation to generation seem to be aware of the origins of the rituals. They sometimes disguise themselves as visiting spirits and chant prayers or magic formulas of their own making. These villagers may possibly regard the two-forked daikon as the most important offering to the deities because it symbolizes the bride of Daikoku; and when it is placed on the altar, a household member chants "Bride, Bride!" Referred to as the "Marriage Ceremony of Daikon" or the "Marriage Ceremony of the Deity Daikoku," this symbolic betrothal is deemed necessary to ensure an abundant harvest in the coming year. The fact that this and other harvest rituals in which the daikon is used as a sacred offering take place around the winter solstice and Christmas Day also suggests that the niiname festival of the imperial court once was held at these times. Before the Meiji Restoration, for example, it may have been held according to the lunar calandar on the middle "rabbit day" of November. In the pre-Meiji era it occurred close to the winter solstice.[12] But now it takes place according to the solar calendar on November 23.

The mi-kawari held in Chiba-ken near Tokyo is another harvest festival at the time of the winter solstice that is supposed to derive its significance from a famous Japanese culture hero. The people of Chiba-ken claim that the mi-kawari evolved from the legend of Prince Yamato-takeru, a semimythical and semihistorical hero who gave his life to unify the Japanese Empire. They say that he accomplished this unification by leading victorious expeditions to the east and west as ordered by his father the emperor, and that on one occasion he came from Yamato, the metropolitan district, and annihilated the powerful clans of the Ezo tribe. In commemoration of the Prince's battle with this tribe, which lasted from November 26 to December 5 of the lunar year, the villagers of this area (present-day Chiba-ken) even now must stay at home to observe abstinence during the ten-day period in which the fighting took place.[13] Needless to say, this legend is a far-fetched explanation of the long period of fasting and abstinence that is observed after the mi-kawari festival, and an equally strained rationale for the visit within this period of a strange, powerful god or spirit from the Other Land. Instead, the mi-kawari and the period of abstinence and fasting that succeeds it must be a survival of an ancient form of niiname festival, at which life-givers from the Other Land appeared to revitalize the rice seeds and human beings. The name mi-kawari might have originally signified the change or renewal (*kawari*) of the body or bodies (*mi*).

Other harvest festivals in Japan appear to have had the same origin as the mi-kawari. For example, the *ozakae matsuri* held at several Shinto shrines in Shimane-ken also makes use in the sanctuaries of divine clothes, seats, and carpets which are different from those used in the same sanctuaries during the New Year festivals. At each of these harvest celebrations, and also at the Otariya or Yugyō festival (for the visit of a divine spirit) held at the shrines of Futara and Kohata Jinsha in Tochigi-ken late in November and in the middle of December according to the lunar calendar, the *mikoshi* (portable shrine) is carried from one *buraku* (a hamlet or subunit of a village) to another. A final point of resemblance suggestive of a common origin for these festivals is that in all of them dengaku plays are performed in each hamlet at the resting place of the visiting mikoshi. Thus the mi-kawari, ozakae matsuri, and Otariya contain survivals from an ancient time when mysterious deities were believed to visit farming communities during the harvest festival.[14]

v

We have seen that, generally speaking, the winter festivals are characterized by spiritual visits of the deities to each family. This is also true of the Bon festival in July and of the many New Year celebrations as well. Many different types of visitors disguised as visiting spirits or deities, appear at the New Year as well as at the harvest. Among them are actors, minstrels, and magicians who usually belong to the outcast groups or to the special group of ritual performers attached to the large shrines and Buddhist temples. Before the Meiji Restoration these visitors even went from door to door giving blessings and purification for the coming year and harvest, accepting in return a small quantity of new rice or money.

In pre-Meiji times, and in some cases even in mid-twentieth-century Japan, mysterious visitors were said to have appeared at each home in their domain at the end of the year and once again in the early days of the new year. At the year's end, groups which included the *kama-harai, mono-yoshi,* and *sekizoro* went from house to house,[15] and shortly after the New Year's celebration their visits were repeated by other groups, such as the *Daikoku-mai, Ebisu-mawashi, haru-koma, haru-ta-uchi, kotobure, manzai, saru-mawashi,* and *tori-oi,* which even now are well known to the people and mentioned in local documents.[16] The names of these groups often originated in the songs, dances, or rituals the groups performed.

Among the groups which made their visitations at the year's end, kama-harai is one of the most interesting. Literally meaning "the purification of the fireplace," which is believed to be the residence of the fire deity, a household guardian, it is also the name of the lower class of female shamans who performed this purification ritual in the city of Yedo (present-day Tokyo). Although this group is no longer thought to exist, the purification of the fireplace at the end of the year continues to be an important annual function for Tokyo's lower-class and *petit-bourgeois* families.

Other groups of visitors at the year's end included the monoyoshi, the sekizoro, and a plethora of door-to-door magician-beggars. The monoyoshi derived their name, translatable as "All things are going to be good," from this fixed formula chanted in pre-Meiji times by the visiting magician-beggars in Kyoto. The sekizoro gained their name, which means "This is the end of the year," from a Japanese word used originally by the outcast beggars to open a blessing. But the magician-beggars, who still go from door to door in order to exorcise the evils and sins accumulated during the year, have no fixed group name of their own.[17]

The names of groups which made their magico-religious visits after the New Year owe their origin to the distinctive rite each group performed. In each case the group's title became that of the rite they had evolved. The Daikoku-mai and Ebisu-mawashi, for instance, derived their appellations from the performances of outcast magicians, some of whom still belong to the famous Ebisu Shrine of Nishinomiya, near Osaka. Originally magico-religious performers of rites in honor of Daikoku- and Ebisu-sama, these outcast magicians developed more specialized functions later on. Those who began to costume themselves as the deity Daikoku and to go from door to door dancing and singing, bestowing the grace of Daikoku and blessings for the New Year, became known as Daikoku-mai, after the rite they performed. And those who started to bring little dolls on a portable stage with them, and to sing, recite tales, and distribute the grace of Ebisu (a deity of good fortune and good harvest, worshiped by peasants, fishermen, and rural merchants, and ranked with Daikoku) became known as Ebisu-mawashi.[18]

Other outcast groups, including the haru-koma, haru-ta-uchi, saru-mawashi, and tori-oi, gained their names through the development of unique rites of their own. Literally meaning the "spring horse," the haru-koma rite was performed by outcast female minstrels who usually carried a colored wooden horse's head while they sang auspicious songs to the accompaniment of the *samisen* (a sort of three-stringed banjo) and drum or bell. The horse's head that they brought from door to door with them was believed to be the guardian of the silkworms and the vehicle of good fortune. Although the haru-koma group no longer exists as such today, its rite still is performed throughout Japan. In some areas, such as Tohoku, it is performed by the village youths, and in other areas by the wives or daughters of the outcasts.[19]

The haru-ta-uchi (literally "tilling the rice field in the spring") no longer exists as a rite or as the name of any group. Yet prior to the Meiji Restoration outcast actors performed the haru-ta-uchi annually on New Year's Day in Morioka-shi, Iwate-ken. To begin the rite the leading actor, wearing a mask representing the face of a beautiful girl, executed a dance which mimicked the processes of planting, digging the rice field, and transplanting and carrying the rice heads. Then, suddenly, he changed masks and completed the dance with one that was large and ghostly. This change of costume symbolized the transformation of the deity of the rice field into the deity of the mountain, for in

Japanese folk belief the rice-field deity descends from the mountain in early spring and returns as the mountain deity after the harvest.[20]

Unlike the haru-ta-uchi, the saru-mawashi (literally "the monkey show") still survives today, although in altered form. The outcast groups known as *saru-hiki* (literally, "one who leads a monkey") perform it every New Year in household after household. In the past they did so in order to purify the stables for the coming years, particularly those which belonged to households of the samurai class or to villagers who could afford stables of their own; for the monkey was considered to be the guardian of the stable and horses. At present, however, members of these groups function merely as storytellers who visit each house with their trained monkeys in order to give their plays. They have lost their magical function and have become itinerant entertainers instead.[21] Yet their fate is better than that of the outcast female magicians in western Japan, who performed the tori-oi (literally, "to drive away the injurious birds") to the music of the samisen, and better than that of the village boys or youths who performed it in the Tōhoku, Kantō, and Chūbu areas. In all of these areas the rite has died out, and with its passing tori-oi groups have vanished also.[22]

Gone from the Japanese scene, too, are the kotobure and manzai rites which, until the Meiji Restoration with its educational influence, were very popular in various parts of the country. Both rites were performed by members of special magico-technical minority groups rather than by outcast actors, minstrels, or magicians. The kotobure (meaning "to spread things abroad") was rendered by the lower-class priests of Kashima Shrine in Ibaraki-ken. Dressed in the robes of the lower priesthood and with symbolic fetishes on their neckbands, these priests, Kashima-no-Kotobure, went from house to house to perform this rite, which took the form of sung proclamations informing the people of auspicious times to plant grains and vegetables and to undertake other affairs in the coming year. It is taken for granted by scholars that the Kashima-odori (Kashima dance), which is very popular today in the Kanto area, was introduced by them during their annual New Year visits before the Meiji Restoration.[23]

The manzai was even more popular than the kotobure, and among its performers there were some families which had achieved special status from feudal lords and the emperor. Meaning "long live!" or "to live long," it was executed by two persons: a *tayū* (protagonist) and a *saizō* (buffoon). Usually the tayū sang joyful songs or recited auspicious formulas while the saizō pretended to pick a quarrel with him. In return he was beaten several times with the tayū's fan. The manzai rite originated as a magico-religious performance which manifested the superiority of the greater spirits from the eternal land over the spirit of the soil. Represented in the rite by the saizō, the spirit of the earth submitted finally to the greater spirit, which, according to the late Shinobu Origuchi, was represented by the tayū. In former times, several famous professional manzai villages, which also belonged to the minority groups, existed in Aichi-ken, Fukui-ken, Nara-ken and elsewhere in Japan.[24] During the feudal period some families from these villages even journeyed to the imperial palace or to the castles of their feudal lords where they paid their respects and gave manzai performances every New Year. After the Meiji Restoration the manzai's popularity dwindled, and some of its performers became stage vaudevillians.[25]

vi

The rites performed today or in the past by professional magico-religious outcast performers and beggars probably are connected with the traditional practices of village youths or boys at the harvest and New Year festivals. In general these practices fall into two categories: rites of purification and the expulsion of evil which usually take place between harvest time and the end of the year; and rites of blessing designed to assure a good harvest which usually are performed at the New Year. Among these rites of blessing, which take place on the night of *ko-shōgatsu,* or the "little New Year" (January 15 of the lunar calendar), attention should be called to two examples—one from the southwest islands of Okinawa and the other from the Tōhoku area.

In the Yaeyama archipelago, Okinawan islands, two young men are chosen on the night of the *puri* (a harvest festival) to go from house to house wearing two kinds of masks, their bodies clothed in grass or miscanthus leaves, to bless the coming year's good harvest.[26] Until recent times, the villagers imagined these visitors to be visiting demigods (named *nirai-kanai*) from the Other Land.

On the same night of the lunar calendar, January 15, two young men of Akita-ken in the Tōhoku area are chosen to go from door to door shouting and sometimes making prophecies about the new harvest. Wearing grotesque masks and straw coats, carrying wooden swords in their right hands and a box which holds a small fetish, these youths are welcomed and entertained by the host of each family despite their dreadful appearance. Yet the village boys and girls fear these curious visitors greatly because they are called Namahage, the name of the ogres which are said to punish idle children.[27]

vii

The rites of mysterious visitors are found throughout Japan in great variety and with many names. Their original meanings and forms have been lost. Still, it is possible to speculate on whether or not these rites have some connection with the seasonal festivals of members of tabooed classes in Polynesian and Melanesian societies described by Codrington, Rivers, and others. These islanders have believed in mysterious visitors for generations and still maintain that seasonal visitations are "the visits of dead ancestors" or "the appearance of ghosts." Furthermore, the names of the islanders' secret societies—such as the Duk-duk societies of the New Britain archipelago, the Ruk-ruk of Bougainville island, the Tamate of Banks Island, and the Areoi of the Marquesas—are supposed to be derived from words for "dead" or "death." Also, certain rituals of the Areoi society in the Marquesas Islands have been connected with the seasonal festival of the fire god Maui, whose name may have originated in the word *mauri* meaning "the dead."[28]

On the other hand, the rites of mysterious visitors may also have some connection with the many varieties of rice festivals, especially those associated with the harvest, found among the rice-culture peoples of Indonesia.[29] We find that the first crop offering at the harvest festivals is without exception related to a belief in the potent spirit of the dead. This may be inferential evidence that in ancient Japan the corn spirit was believed to die at the harvest and to be reborn at or after the winter solstice, or at the turning point of the winter monsoon. As in other primitive societies it may have appeared usually in the form of a young child, often accompanying a mother goddess or earth mother who represented the eternal reproduction of life.[30]

If the ancient Japanese did believe that the corn spirit died at the harvest and was reborn at the start of spring, then it follows that a prevalent Japanese folk belief already mentioned—that the rice deity comes down from the mountain in the early spring, and returns as the deity of the mountain after the harvest—possibly is a survival of this tradition. Other survivals too would seem to exist. For example, the rebirth of the corn spirit may be reflected in two subsequent rites which take place on and below Mount Horoha in Akita-ken. Following the *o-tojime-no-matsuri* (festival of closing the shrine's door) which takes place at Haushiwake Shrine on the summit, the *hōin-kagura* is held at the foot of the mountain on November 8 of the lunar calendar in the home of Ōtomo, the hereditary priest. There, Shinto priests who reside near the shrine and who are said to be the offspring of Ōtomo's old retainers, perform kagura music and dance many dances throughout the night.[31]

The rebirth of the corn spirit may be reflected also in the comparable ritual music and dance festivals held elsewhere in Japan. Some of them are known as *hana-matsuri* (literally "the flower festival"); others are called *hana-kagura*. The hana-kagura are a series of popular Shinto music and dance performances which take place from December to January of the lunar calendar in twenty or more villages in succession in the snowy, mountainous area of northeastern Aichi-ken. Begun in the evening, each performance starts with important Shinto services conducted by several main amateur actors under the leadership of a temporary head priest, who is called the *hana-negi* (flower priest).[32] Then follow various types of music and dance, including dances by boys, youths, and adult men. In one of them two adult performers masked as demons brandish a large broadaxe and stamp on the stage with all their might, for this effort is believed to generate sufficient magic power to conquer the evil spirits which might disturb the rice deity. Next, dramatic dances with such names as *negi* (priest), *miko* (female shaman), *okina* (old man), and *ouna* (old woman) are presented, several of which contain elements of fertility rites. In the morning the performance ends with a final set of dances, the last of which, called *hanagitō* (prayer to the flower) is said to request the "ascent of the deity."[33]

In other farming villages of the Tōhoku area magical rituals comparable to those described above are held during the New Year season. There the *hanami-shōgatsu,* the now extinct haru-ta-uchi, and many others have the same meaning and significance as the hōin-kagura and hana-matsuri, which possibly originated in ancient dengaku agricultural magic.[34] Thus, all of these rituals and ceremonies, as well as the magical dances and music, have important magico-religious connections with the growth of the rice or grain and with the lives of human beings. They are more than just advance purifications or blessings of a forthcoming good harvest.

viii

The winter festivals of the imperial court are far more than just ceremonies of purification or blessing. For, like the agricultural rites practiced in the Tōhoku area, they impart new life power to rice seeds and men. The day following the chin-kon (ritual for the renewal and repose of the emperor's soul), the members of the imperial court perform the niiname. Two days later come the kagura, the sacred dances and music in the holy palace of Seisho-dō. These are accompanied by offerings to the visiting deities from the Other Land, who are believed to accept them and give new life power to the emperor. If chin-kon, niiname, and the kagura are survivals of three different kinds of agricultural rites, it is interesting to note their uniformity today, and the no less striking uniformity of similar rites which still survive in popular tradition in both complex and degenerate forms.

Both niiname and the chin-kon focus upon the emperor's entertainment of mysterious visitors from the Other Land at a sacred meal of new rice and other harvest crops. In niiname, for example, the most important part of the rite is held by the emperor alone before a symbolic wooden bed with a wooden pillow and a bamboo stick as the holy of holies. There the emperor makes an offering of new harvest rice and crops to his ancestor goddess, and then sits down to dine with her. Scholars have suggested that the entire ceremony symbolizes the birth of the rice child from the great rice mother, the sun goddess, and that dining with his ancestral goddess symbolizes the renewal of the emperor's soul through the new, vital power she has brought from the Other Land.

It seems that chin-kon originated in a mythical rite which was performed for the first time under the direction of a shamanlike goddess named Ame-no-uzume in order to revive the sun goddess, Amaterasu. According to the *Kojiki* (Chapter 1), the sun goddess became so terrified when her impetuous younger brother, Susanowo the storm god, broke down the rice-field divisions she had made, filled up the irrigation ditches, strewed excrement in the palace where she partook of holy food, and continued such evil acts with more and more violence, that she closed the door of her heavenly rock dwelling, made it fast, and retired. Then, according to the myth, the entire country was obscured, and all of heaven was darkened. Hoping to remedy the situation, the gods convened the divine assembly, at which the following course of action was decided upon: The god of mirror made a mirror; the god of jewel fashioned a jewel; the god of divination and the god of prayer recited grand liturgies over these offerings; the god of strong hands stood hidden beside the door; and Ame-no-uzume put a sounding board before the door of the heavenly rock dwelling, and stamped on the board until she made it resound. Acting as if possessed by a deity, she pulled out the nipples of her breasts, and pushed down her skirt string almost to her private parts. All of these actions were meant to revive the sun goddess asleep in her cave, and thereby to restore light to the universe.[35]

Though the myth and the chin-kon ritual seem essentially far removed from each other, the rituals performed within them are similar in purpose. Both Ame-no-uzume in the myth, and the emperor in actual practice, seek the presence of an important goddess who can rejuvenate them. Among the eight symbolic and mysterious holy songs the *Kojiki* claims were used by Ame-no-uzume, there are some which illustrate still further the possibility that the chin-kon originated in her mythical rite. For example, each of the following songs tells of the descent of a mysterious visitor, the departed soul of the great ancestral goddess, Amaterasu or Toyohirume:

> We want to bring down the Great Soul,
> Of the Sun Goddess, Toyohirume,
> Who resides in the Sky;
> The Root [Substance] is a gold halberd,
> And the Branch [Shadow] is a wooden halberd!

> *   *   *   *   *   *   *

> Let's take a *tamachi*,[36]
> And plant the sacred clothes in the Soul-box,
> Flying her Soul, the departed soul of the Goddess,
> Just now coming down!

> *   *   *   *   *   *   *

> The Goddess whose Soul had flown away,
> And left for the Other Land,
> Is just now coming down!
> Bringing her Soul-box;
> Your soul has already left;
> Please return here!
>
> (From the *Nenjū-gyōji-hishō*)[37]

These songs possibly are connected with those of the
kagura, for many kagura songs likewise describe how the
deity's soul comes down secretly from the Other Land.[38]
If scholars verify this connection, then they will consider
the winter festivals of the imperial court as the background
for an all-important Japanese folk belief. This belief, of
course, is that the ancestral or great eternal mother goddess
who resides in the sky world or Other Land returns season-
ally to the families of her descendants in the land of the
living, that most of her visits take place during the period
from the harvest to the New Year, and that the purpose of
each of them is to instill new life power in the soul of the
rice plant as well as in the human soul which retains its life
by means of rice.

ix

In Japanese mythology, we find that the great creative
mother goddess, Izanami, died when she gave birth to Kagutsuchi the fire god, and that the goddess of plenty, Ōgetsu-
hime, was killed by the storm god Susanowo. We learn that
afterwards many kinds of seeds "were born in the body of
her [Ōgetsu-hime] who had been killed: in her head were
born silkworms; in her eyes were born rice-seeds; in her ears
was born millet; in her nose were born small beans; in her
private parts was born barley; and in her fundament were
born large beans."[39]
These myths reveal a consciousness of death behind the
ancient Japanese belief in the mother goddess and in the
goddess of food. They indicate that ancient Japanese peasant philosophers were concerned with the recognition and
experience of death and rebirth and with the ripeness and
sprouting of the different kinds of cereals upon which
human life depends. They suggest a belief in the individuality of spirit of each kind of grain—especially in the spirit of

rice, a most sacred food for the ancient Japanese—and a comparable belief in the individuality of the souls of human beings, who repeated the cycle of death and rebirth from generation to generation. Thought to be the source of a similar cycle in the rice plant, the rice mother also came to be regarded as the life-giver of human beings. But in the imperial court's mythology and rituals, it was necessary to transfer these functions to Amaterasu, the ancestral sun goddess of the royal family.

The winter season from harvest time until the New Year is a critical period for the spirit of the rice and for human beings too. For this is the time when the rice plant turns to seed and appears to have lost its power of growth. Many rituals consequently have been, and still are, practiced between the harvest and seeding time lest the rice spirit fall asleep forever or be disturbed by evil spirits. Since human life also is renewed through these functions, serious penitence, fasting, and abstinence are required of those who perform them. All of these performances once were based upon the idea that an original spirit created life, and made its continued existence possible from generation to generation. Because each family which entertained this spirit as a mysterious visitor believed it to be the spirit of their most distant ancestor, ancestor worship came to occupy a prominent place in Japanese agricultural society.[40]

Notes

1. Mysterious visitors of eminence, like deities or kami, are *marebito*; visitors belonging to an outcast group are *otozure-bito*. During the Tokugawa period (1600–1868) there were many outcast people in Japan. Some of them were untouchable, while others belonged to

magico-religious minority groups. These people, however, had many local names and functions. Among the untouchable class, the *eta* group was one of the largest and most typical; yet other outcast groups, such as the *tōnai* in the Hokuriku region, were considered higher in status. Among the magico-religious minorities, the *innai, jichū, maimai, manzai, onmyōji, shomonji, shuku,* and others gradually became degraded with the lapse of time from the *sacré pur* to the *sacré impur* classes, because they lost their particular magico-religious functions and became actors, reciters, and beggars. Their degeneration influenced other outcast groups so strongly that many of them assumed a multiplicity of particular names and functions. Members of the tōnai group, for example, soon were called *tōnai* only when engaged in the duties of prison guards and policemen. Otherwise, when they performed more lowly occupations, they were known by other names: *onbō* when engaged in obsequies as funeral directors; *sōji-no-mono* (cleaner or purifier) when employed in official services at a feudal lord's castle; and *kagoya* (palanquin bearer) when they visited from door to door to beg for rice or money. They were called by still other names when they took part in the production of lampwicks and straw sandals; indulged in small-scale fishing; or visited each house of their own class, as Daikoku-mai (Daikoku dance) in the spring, as *ayaori* (figured-cloth-weaving) in summer, and as sekizoro (end of the year) in winter. Later in Japanese history members of the eta group took part in further rites of visitation, including the manzai and harukoma, and became known by the special names of the magico-religious visitations in which they participated. (See *Minzokugaku Jiten* [*Dictionary of Japanese Folklore*] [Tokyo: Tōkyō-Do, 1951], pp. 408–9.)

2. Kenneth Yasuda (trans.), *Land of the Red Plains: Ancient Japanese Lyrics from the Manyōshū* (Rutland, Vermont, and Tokyo: Charles E. Tuttle Co., 1960), Chap. XIV, Vol. III, poem no. 3460, p. 433.

3. "Tsukuba-no-kori," in Yoshiro Akimoto (ed.), *Hitachi-Fudoki* (Tokyo: Iwanami Shoten, 1958), p. 39. In ancient documents it is difficult to discern whether the deities of Mount Fuji and Mount Tsukuba were gods or goddesses. Even though later documents of the medieval and subsequent periods indicate that Mount Fuji was occupied by a goddess named Konohanasakuya-hime, and that Mount Tsukuba was the dwelling place of a divine couple, I have deemed it best to refer to them only as anonymous deities.

4. Kunio Yanagita, *Saiji Shūzoku Goi (Folk Vocabulary of Annual*

Festivals in Japan (Tokyo: Minkan Denshō no Kai, 1939), pp. 577–91, 597–99.

5. From Edward Norbeck, *Takashima, A Japanese Fishing Community* (Salt Lake City: University of Utah Press, 1954), pp. 156–57.

6. These include the hana-matsuri, the hōin-kagura, the *sumō* wrestling game, the Nō and dengaku plays, and other forms of entertainment. Though *hana-matsuri* means literally "the festival of flowers," it is held in December of the lunar calendar in northeastern parts of Aichi-ken. The hōin-kagura festival, performed in former times by Shinto priests who were also *yama-bushi* or *hōin* (Buddhist ascetics), consists of Shinto music and plays which are given widely in the Northeast provinces. Sumō, a classic Japanese wrestling game, originated in the ancient agricultural magic and divination at one time performed officially at the imperial court each year. And finally, the Nō plays are the medieval lyric dramas of Japan, whereas the dengaku plays are ancient magico-agricultural music and dance presentations.

7. Shinobu Origuchi, *Kodai Kenkyū (Studies on Ancient Japan),* (Tokyo: Ōokayama Shoten, 1929), III, 1–82, 205–7. See also Ichirō Hori, *Wagakuni Minkan Shinkō-shi no Kenkyū (A Study of the History of Folk-Beliefs in Japan)* (Tokyo: Sōgen Sha, 1935), II, 686–88.

8. Idem, "Noto no Aenokoto ni tsuite" ("On the Harvest Festival in the Noto Peninsula"), *Niiname no Kenkyū (Studies of the Japanese Harvest Festival)* (Tokyo: Yoshikawa Kōbun-kan, 1955), II, 65–97.

9. Yanagita, pp. 609–24.

10. Tōkan-ya is "the night of October tenth," when the deity of the rice field returns to the mountain. To solemnize the deity's departure, the peasants prepare mochi (rice cakes) and offer them together with the daikon to a kagashi (scarecrow) brought from the rice field. On this night the village boys carry a magic symbol, a rod made from straw, and beat the ground with it. The tōkan-ya festival is also called *kagashi-age* (ascent of the scarecrow) or Daikon-no-toshitori (Daikon's New Year).

11. Yanagita, pp. 602–3, 670–71.

12. In the Japanese lunar calendar there are ten celestial stems and twelve horary signs which combine together to form the year, the month, and the day. The horary signs are rat, ox, tiger, rabbit, dragon, snake, horse, sheep, monkey, chicken, dog, and wild boar.

13. Hori, *Wagakuni Minkan Shinkō-shi no Kenkyū* (Tokyo: Sōgen Sha, 1955), IV, 454.

14. Ibid., p. 452.

15. Ibid., II, 554–65.

16. Ibid., pp. 566–96.

17. Ibid., pp. 554–65.

18. Ibid., pp. 567–73.

19. Ibid., pp. 578–79.

20. Kyōsuke Kindaichi, "Yama-no-kami-kō" ("On the Mountain-Deity"), *Minzoku (Folklore)* (Tokyo), Vol. II, No. 3, 1927, pp. 47–53; Ichirō Kurata, *Nō to Minzoku-gaku (Agriculture and the Science of Folklore)* (Tokyo: Rokunin Sha, 1944), pp. 111–28; and Yanagita, *Bunrui Nōson Goi (Classified Vocabulary of the Folklore in Farming Villages)* (Tokyo, 1948), pp. 142–50, 276–87.

21. Hori, *Wagakuni Minkan Shinkō-shi no Kenkyū*, II, 585, 593n.

22. Ibid., pp. 580–83.

23. Ibid., p. 569.

24. The manzai supposedly represents a transformation of the ancient diviners who specialized in the performance of Onmyō-dō, a Japanized branch-sect of Taoism. For further discussion, see Origuchi, III, 1–82.

25. Hori, *Wagakuni Minkan Shinkō-shi no Kenkyū*, II, 585–93.

26. Yanagita, *Kainan Shōki (Travel Records in Southwestern Japan)* (Tokyo: Ōokayama Shoten, 1925), pp. 161–66.

27. Yanagita: *Saiji Shūzoku Goi*, pp. 296–97.

28. Cf. R. H. Codrington, *The Melanesians: Studies in their Anthropology and Folk-Lore* (Oxford, 1891); J. G. Frazer, *The Golden Bough* (London: The Macmillan Co., 1913–15) (abridged ed., New York: The Macmillan Co., 1955); J. A. Moerenhout, *Voyages aux Îles du Grand Océan* (Paris, 1837), Vol. I; W. H. R. Rivers, *The History of Melanesian Society* (London: The Macmillan Co., 1941), Vols. I and II; and R. W. Williamson, *Religion and Social Organization in Central Polynesia* (Cambridge: Cambridge University Press, 1937).

29. These Indonesian rice festivals are described in Enkū Uno, *Maraishiya ni okeru Tōmai Girei (Rice Rituals in Indonesia)* (Tokyo: Nikkō Shoin, 1944).

30. See Frazer.

31. Yasuji Honda, *Shimo-tsuki Kagura no Kenkyū (A Study on the Kagura Celebration in November of the Lunar Calendar)* (Tokyo: Meizendō Shoten, 1954), pp. 3–82.

32. He is often called *tōya* (literally "duty house") instead of *hananegi*. The temporary priest, chosen by lot or according to the status

of his family in its home village, takes the part of a regular Shinto priest during each performance.

33. Kōtaro Hayakawa, *Hana-matsuri (Flower Festival)* (Tokyo: Oka Shoin,· 1939).

34. *Hanami-shōgatsu* means "flower-viewing on the New Year." During this ritual, ground-rice cakes in the shape of flowers are hung on willow trees or other trees with many small branches. The peasants use these branches to decorate their rooms. The haru-ta-uchi was a widespread New Year ritual of ceremonial digging in the rice field, which was performed in the garden of each house or in that of the main family. For a more extensive description of both rites see Yanagita, *Saiji Shūzoku Goi*, pp. 201, 402–3.

35. A complete version of this myth is in B. H. Chamberlain (ed.), *Kojiki (Records of Ancient Matters)* (Tokyo, 1906), pp. 61–65.

36. The meaning of *tamachi* now is obscure. However, many scholars suppose that it was miscopied in ancient times from a term, like *tamashii*, which may have signified a soul or a soul power.

37. *Nenjū-gyōji Hishō (Memorandum of Annual Rites)* was a manuscript of unknown authorship written in the latter years of the Heian period in the twelfth century. It was first published in *Gunsho Ruijū (Classified Collection of Books)* and reprinted in *Shinkō Gunsho Ruijū (New Edition of Gunsho Ruijū)* (Tokyo: Naigai Shoseki Kabushiki Kaisha, 1931), from which the above verses are quoted (LXXXVI, 518–19).

38. In kagura songs, though, the soul of the deity descends through the media of a symbolic branch of the sacred *sakaki* tree, a sacred stick, a holy bow, and the sacred *mitegura* (silk or paper cuttings), all of which are symbols of the deity.

39. Chamberlain, p. 71.

40. A complete study of the soul concept in Japanese folk culture should discuss the connection between the soul concept and the social structure upon which Japanese religious beliefs and practices are dependent. It should also describe the important relationship of the concept of the soul and spirit of the dead with the concept of the Other Land. In classic documents, such as the *Nihongi, Kojiki, Manyōshū, and Kogoshūi,* for example, the Other Land sometimes is imagined as a Tokoyo (Land of Eternal Life) beyond the sea. Yet this idea disappeared later in Japanese history, and today is retained only in Okinawan or Amamian folk belief. In its place, modern Japanese folklore almost always transmits the idea that the Other Land exists

on top of, or within, the sacred mountains. From these mountains the spirits of the dead are believed to return as visitors to their native homes several times a year, especially during the New Year season and at the Bon festival in July. These problems and the problem of how body and soul are connected in Japanese folk belief are treated in my paper, "Japanese Folk-Beliefs," in the *American Anthropologist*, LXI (June, 1959), 405–24.

漁

師

PART THREE | **FISHERMEN**

The Taboos of Fishermen

BY TOKIHIKO ŌTŌ

Taboos are a significant genre of traditional Japanese customs which affect the daily routine and ceremonies of the
life cycle. The features of these inherited prohibitions differ
from village to village in accordance with each community's
major occupation. Hunting, lumbering, and charcoal-making villages in the mountains, farming villages on the inland
plains, and fishing communities beside the sea each manifest
their own body of such customs. This article attempts to
survey the taboos peculiar to fishing villages and to compare
them with those of communities where other occupations
prevail.

Whatever the community's livelihood, two kinds of *imi*
(taboos) are found: those incorporated in rituals and the less
sacred taboos associated with the pollutions of childbirth

and death.[1] Both kinds have frequently been collected and studied by modern folklorists, in order to reveal to what extent each community has preserved old customs, or how much these customs have changed because of the village's modernization. The results of these studies indicate that taboos are fundamentally of communal concern, even though some of them in mid-twentieth-century Japan may belong only to particular individuals, occupations, or age groups. Thus, wherever a taboo seems to be the concern of just one segment of the community, this may well be an indication that modernization has been responsible for its declining importance.

i

Though fishery and agriculture each has its own set of taboos, these occupations also have some forms of imi in common. Farming villages often forbid sowing or any form of agricultural labor on certain tabooed days. Thus, in the eastern districts of Japan, on a day called *fujuku-nichi*[2] (the unripe day), no one sows seeds or transplants young seedlings, for fear that they would not ripen well.[3] And on *jika-no-hi* (the day of fire on earth)[4], as well, no planting is done; it is believed that straw made from wheat sown on this day will catch fire if it is used to thatch a roof.[5] Similarly, in the fishing villages of the Shima district in Mie-ken, fishermen are forbidden to go to sea on the twenty-fourth and twenty-fifth days of June.[6] Just as there are special fields which are never farmed in agricultural communities, so there are specific areas of the sea which may not be fished, and certain species that no one must catch. Usually the pond or portion of the sea belonging to a shrine or temple is forbidden to fishermen. For instance, sea bream in the pond of Tanjo-ji Temple in Kominato-machi, on the Pacific Coast of Chiba-

ken, are under taboo. A fisherman who catches a tabooed
fish brings sickness or injury to himself, and bad luck at sea
to the whole community.

Among the many forms of taboos common in every
type of Japanese village, those associated with childbirth
and death have survived most tenaciously. Death taboos
have undergone the least amount of change, for death is
still the event many communities abhor most. Childbirth
is also abhorred, but as a less severe pollution. Whereas
Japanese women once had to remain in secluded huts for
seventy-five days after the delivery of their children, today
the period of abstinence is usually reduced to twenty or
thirty days.[7] Men are still thought to be influenced by such
pollution, and consequently husbands, too, have various
restrictions placed upon their activities while their wives
are in parturient abstinence. They must refrain from participation in religious matters or in any affairs concerned
with deities. Nor can they work in the fields or forests for
seven days after the birth of their children. In particular,
charcoal-makers and hunters must strictly obey the taboos
at this time. If a man infected by his wife's pollution tries
to burn charcoal, the oven will be broken; if an infected
hunter enters the woods, he will find no game.

The situation is similar in fishing villages. There, husbands of parturient women are shunned, and other members of their households are considered infected enough to
contaminate a boat. Accordingly, during the women's seclusion none of the household sets foot in a fishing vessel, and
in some districts husbands are even forbidden to join in net
fishing along the shore. This taboo applies during the entire
period of pregnancy as well, although many husbands venture to go to sea then anyway, openly challenging the belief
that they will fail to catch anything. When they are daring
enough to break this taboo, it is usually because they have

prayed to their *uji-gami* (tutelary deity) for help.[8] Finally, at Sukari-mura, Kitamuro-gun, in Mie-ken a *watari-barami* (wandering pregnant woman) who arrives at the village is not made welcome, for the fishermen believe that this kind of woman will bring them a poor catch.[9]

Although fishermen invest the state of pregnancy with taboos, they also employ it in a contradictory manner to ensure themselves large catches at sea. Pregnant women are often key participants in rites designed to render the pregnancy taboos harmless. At Masaragawa, Sotokaifu-mura, on Sado Island, for example, a pregnant woman is placed aboard a new boat during its launching ceremony; and at Uchikaifu-mura on the same island, it is traditional for a woman with child to pick up the vessel's *jōnomi-ishi*[10] before it is offered to the *funadama-sama* (the guardian deity of the boat),[11] and equally customary for her to climb aboard on the starboard side while a prayer is chanted by the ship's carpenter. For these services she receives monetary payment from the fishermen, who believe that her presence during the launching ceremony will keep their catches from being poor.[12] It is also a general custom on Sado Island for fishermen to invite aboard men with pregnant women in their families whenever they want a large catch. However, this form of magic, called *ryō-zuke* (giving a catch), is very risky; the alternative result is a very large or a very small catch.

Similar rites are performed in agricultural villages to break the power of childbirth taboos. For instance, on Amakusa Island in Kumamoto-ken, pregnant women play an important role in ceremonies designed to ensure a good harvest. At the *sanobori*, a festival in late June following the rice-transplanting, in which both Ta-no-kami (the deity of the wet rice field) and Kōjin-sama (the deity of the earth) are celebrated, *sake* is offered to both deities. Two bundles of rice seedlings are tendered to Kōjin, and one shō of *sekihan* (rice boiled with red beans) is placed before Ta-no-kami. Then a pregnant woman takes the sekihan before it is consumed by the workers, who believe that her action will make their rice fields prosper.[13] Just as birth taboos are observed in fishery and agriculture, so too are prohibitions concerning death. In Senboku-gun, Osaka-fu, people who have just attended a funeral are forbidden to enter a rice field, because it is believed their presence would make the rice plants wither. In the village of Tsukui-gun, Kanagawa-ken, if someone dies, his family will not call on other households during the silkworm-raising period that year, for fear of infecting the worms with the death pollution.[14] Similarly, a fisherman does not go to sea for three to seven days after the death of a close relative, and sometimes the death of any villager—not necessarily a relative—is a serious enough pollution to cause everyone to take a three-day rest from fishing.

In spite of these apparent similarities, the death pollution is much less abhorrent to fishermen than it is to the residents of agricultural communities. Indeed, in a few cases fishermen even welcome it. In some parts of Kyūshū they consider it less ominous than the birth taboo, and even say that good luck will result if a person with *kuro-fujō* (the death pollution)[15] goes to sea. On Sado Island it is considered a good omen when a funeral procession happens to pass by a launching ceremony[16] and when someone related to the carpenter dies while the ship is being built. And at Unosumai-mura, Kamihei-gun, in Iwate-ken, fishermen believe they can increase their catch if they secretly take a *tatsu-gashira* (dragon head), which has been carried at the head of a funeral procession, and hide it in their boat.[17] All these beliefs may have their basis in the same kind of idea which has motivated fishermen to employ pregnant women in ritual magic in order to counteract childbirth taboos: if the childbirth pollution can cause fishermen poor luck, perhaps they can neutralize this pollution if pregnant women participate in launching rites. So too, if death pollution can contaminate their fishing boats, perhaps they can consciously employ it against the death taboos.

The attempts of fisherfolk to neutralize magically the death taboos are revealed most distinctly in their employment of corpses. Drowned men, often called *nagare-botoke* (floating Buddhas), are used in supplicatory rites aimed at increasing catches of fish, after their corpses are encountered floating at sea. Certain that these corpses will bring them good luck, fishermen are pleased to draw them into their boats and to transport them back to their villages. But if a corpse is sighted on the way to the fishing grounds, the fishermen ask it to stay put until their return; the corpse heeds the request and duly remains there. On the homeward voyage, it is lifted aboard according to one of various procedures, but usually on the starboard side. Then the boat sails for home, sometimes with a straw mat bound around its bow as a sign that a corpse is aboard. On their return to the village, the fishermen bury the body in the special graveyard set apart for drowned persons.

The primary reason why fishermen welcome such an unpleasant object as a floating corpse, and claim that it can be utilized in ritual magic, is that many corpses are believed to have the attributes of deities. Most bodies found at sea are those of the people who died in a distaster, and such disaster victims are deified throughout Japan. For example, on Eno-shima in Nagasaki-ken the spirits of the drowned are called *go-rō-ji*, a term which corresponds to the *go-ryō-jin* (*go-ryō-shin*) in standard Japanese, literally meaning "honorable spirit-deity" and also signifying "a deified revenge spirit."[18] In this connection it may be remarked that in inland regions, too, the villagers similarly deify the revengeful spirits of people who met violent deaths, in order to console the victims' hearts. *Misaki* is the name widely used for a spirit of this kind, a term which designates the spirit as the forerunner of a principal deity, or often as the deity's messenger or servant.

Dead persons are not necessarily deified unless they are victims of a disaster. The spirits of those who drowned themselves intentionally or of those whose bodies have floated ashore do not usually merit this honor in fishing communities. But it is felt that the spirits of those who have died bearing a grudge should be deified or honored, for the fishermen fear them as being violent and revengeful. In this category is a ghost which allegedly rises from the sea to call out to the boatmen, "Give me a ladle!" If its request is fulfilled, it uses the implement to pour water into the boat to make it sink. Hence the boatmen thwart its intentions by presenting it with a bottomless ladle. The spirits of shipwreck victims are also deified by the fishermen, and consequently these spirits of the dead can bring them good luck. As already mentioned, the corpses of these unfortunates are taken aboard in a specific manner, one which is sometimes very dramatic. One of the boatmen may speak to the corpse, asking if it will grant them a good catch in return for their kindness in picking it up. In the corpse's behalf, another fisherman may reply that it will surely make their fishing successful. The dialogue completed, the corpse will be lifted aboard. The logic of this dialogue may be reminiscent of the widespread Japanese custom of *narikizeme* (torturing the fruit tree), and of its analogues in countries other than Japan.[19] Observed in farming villages at New Year's time, nariki-zeme requires the master of the household to wound slightly with a hatchet a persimmon tree growing in his yard. As he does so, he asks, "Fruitful or not?" and a man hiding behind the tree replies, "I'll be fruitful." Japanese villagers believe this performance forces the tree to promise abundant fruit.

ii

Though agricultural labor is influenced much more than industrial labor by the natural conditions of climate and land, it is still more independent of nature's changes than the occupation of fishing. Whereas the period from sowing to harvest time is long enough to make the results of changes in natural conditions hard to perceive at once, the length of a fishing expedition is so much shorter that momentary changes in weather, wind, temperature, or tide can spell the difference between a good catch and a poor one. Fishing is so subject to the vagaries of nature and fortune that fishermen of equal skill, in identical boats, and at the same place at the same time, may haul in vastly unequal catches; consequently all of them try to bolster their luck through adherence to a vast number of taboos and through the practice of many forms of ritual magic. Only hunters can rival fishermen in this respect.

Both groups have many taboos involving childbirth and death. We have seen that fishermen are not supposed to go to sea while they are infected by either the birth or death pollution; similarly hunters are forbidden to set forth after game while they are in a comparable state of contamination. So, too, there is a parallel between other taboos in both occupations: The wives and children of fishermen and hunters must live in abstinence until the menfolk return from their work. Hunters' families must not eat any meat while the men are in the forest, and this is true for the households of fishermen. Formerly, in Higashitsugaru-gun in Aomori-ken, fishermen refrained from eating the meat of any four-legged animal before setting out to catch sea bream, and their families likewise were expected to abstain till their return. If, in addition, there happened to be a woman in childbed when they arrived home, the fishermen believed this might cause their catch to slip away. Thus they were obliged in such cases to spend the night elsewhere until the prescribed period after parturition had elapsed.[20]

Like their countrymen who subsist by hunting, Japanese fishermen pay special attention to their actions when they prepare to begin an expedition. As in most villages in Japan, residents of fishing communities are forbidden to use needles for mending or sewing buttons on their clothes at this time.[21] On the island of Himaka, taboos are enforced against the crying of children and the breaking of *geta* (clog thongs) before the fishermen set out. At Shimoukawa-mura, in Kyōto-fu, if fishermen should drop some rice before they leave, the conviction is that someone will be injured or the fishing will be poor.

Various deeds are tabooed once the fishermen are on board. To prevent bad luck, they must not recite any *utai* (verses from Nō drama); to keep the evil spirit away, they must not attempt to whistle;[22] and because the sea deity dislikes metal, earthenware, and the seeds of pickled plums, fishermen must not throw seeds or utensils overboard if they desire a catch of fish. When these objects are dropped in the water by mistake, someone must jump overboard to pick them up, or a Shinto priest must be asked to offer a prayer of apology to the deity when the boat returns. Fishermen also cannot bring beef, parched-bean paste, vinegar, rice boiled with red beans, or *kayu* (rice gruel) aboard their vessels.

Traditional stories are told in various localities to explain why kayu is tabooed at sea. The version common on the Harima-nada coast, along the Seto Inland Sea, is that Kannon (the deity who dispenses mercy) was originally carried by boat to the village of Ikeda in this area. When the deity's vessel, coming from the western region, entered the Harima Sea, the boatmen began to boil kayu and eat it. A storm was just then brewing, but the boatmen were sipping the porridge so noisily that they were unable to hear the thunder. Consequently the storm caught them unprepared, and they barely were able to float ashore at Ikeda. Since this near mishap, eating kayu aboard ship has become one of the fishermen's strongest taboos.[23] Another version, related by fishermen who sail the open sea of Munakata in Genkainada, Kyūshū, tells of a fine bell—rather than the deity of mercy—brought by boat to Japan from China. In olden times, they say, when the vessel bearing the bell reached the sea of Munakata, some of the boatmen began to wash rice for boiling. This action made the sea water cloudy, and the boat ran aground upon a hidden shoal; the precious bell fell overboard. According to the legend, the sea water has remained darkened around the spot where the bell sank, and to prevent further mishaps of this kind, fishermen have placed a taboo on eating kayu at sea.[24]

Japanese fishermen not only prohibit the consumption aboard ship of the meat of certain animals, such as snakes, cows, monkeys, and cats, but they also refer to them by substitute names. Using what is known as their *oki-kotoba* (open-sea language), fishermen refer to a *hebi* (snake) as a *naga-mono* (long thing); to an ushi (cow or ox) as an *okyaku* (guest); to a *saru*[25] (monkey) as an *ete-kō* (winner); to a *neko* (cat) as a *yokoza* (master's seat); to an *iwashi* (sardine) as a *komo-mono* (small thing); and to a *kujira* (whale) and an *iruka* (dolphin) as *ebisu* (from the name Ebisu-gami). Some of the animals so designated are more heavily tabooed than others, especially monkeys and snakes which the funadama-sama particularly abhors. Thus, if fishermen ashore see either of them, or hear the words *saru* or *hebi*, they will call off any plans to sail on that day. Too, they often use the phrase *saru o tore* (catch a monkey) as a rough oath when engaged in a quarrel on shore; and the fishermen of Ushijima in Nakatado-gun, Kagawa-ken, use *oka-no-anago* (sea eel on land)[26] in place of *naga-mono* for this term has become popular enough to be considered almost an ordinary expression.

Hunters also observe language taboos and use substitute terminology when they are at work in the forests. Their *yama-kotoba* (mountain speech), which must be used during the hunt in place of ordinary speech, has a vocabulary larger than that of open-sea language. Offenders against the taboos of yama-kotoba are dismissed from the expedition and sent back to their villages. Whereas a few words in the yama-kotoba vocabulary, such as *naga-mono* (for "snake") and *ete* (for "monkey"), bear close resemblances to those used in oki-kotoba, most of them are the hunters' unique expressions: *kusa-no-mi* (grass seed) for *kome* (rice); *oyaji* (father) for *saru* (monkey) or *kuma* (bear); *wakka* (an Ainu word for "water") for *mizu* (water); *hedari* (clotting of blood) for *chi* (blood); *magari* (curve) for *neko* (cat); *yase* (lean) for *ōkami* (wolf); *takase* (high back) for *uma* (horse); and *yama-no-negi* (priest of the mountain) for *usagi* (hare). These are just a few of the substitute expressions developed by hunters to protect themselves against the consequences of breaking language taboos.

iii

The taboos most peculiar to fishing villages are those which pertain to the fishing boat itself and to the manner in which it is operated and boarded. For example, no one aboard ship likes to be asked when the vessel will dock, for a question of this kind may result in the ship's never docking. No one must climb aboard at any place but the stern; boarding at the bow is forbidden to everyone except those who have come to offer sacred *sake* to the vessel's funadama-sama. Docking a boat bow-first is also tabooed; its stern must be closest to shore so that it will start on its next voyage with its bow facing the sea. Women must usually refrain from going aboard, especially if they are pregnant or menstruating, and fishermen particularly dislike to see a woman casting off the hawser of a floating vessel.[27]

The taboos of fishermen mentioned in this paper are not preserved today in every fishing village throughout Japan, but they can still be found wherever fishermen continue to seek their livelihood according to time-honored methods. Whether these taboos survive more tenaciously in fishing communities than in agricultural ones is a question not easily answered, even though it is generally recognized that fishermen are usually less progressive than farmers. Fishery remains dependent upon cooperative labor in common fishing grounds, and each fisherman's actions continue to influence everyone else working at the same place. For these reasons, individual conduct often can affect the lot of the entire community. In this kind of environment, fishermen remain very nervous about their actions. Even a woman's crossing their path can bring them a poor catch; dreams about ear shells, cuttlefish, or parents are bad omens, sometimes serious enough to keep them from going to sea,[28] and dreams about a woman may improve or worsen their luck.

We have seen that Japanese fishermen not only maintain abstinence and taboos to avoid bad luck, but also perform various kinds of ritual magic to draw good luck to themselves. The participation of pregnant women in launching ceremonies and the ritualistic employment of corpses are two of the most obvious examples. Since the rapid modernization of Japanese fishing villages in recent years has changed many conditions propitious to folklore, these rituals and taboos are now on their way toward total disappearance.

Notes

1. Japanese villagers remain filled with dread at the thought of breaking either kind of imi. Often they designate an imi of pollution by the term *hi* (fire), and use the words *hi o kuu* (to receive the influence of fire) or *hi-gakari* (infected by fire) to indicate to their friends that their actions at the time are controlled by a taboo. The connection between fire and taboo may derive from the belief that one must make his own separate fire whenever he is to abide by taboos of sanctity or pollution.

2. There are twelve fujuku-nichi in the Japanese calendar year, three of them in each quarter. Named after signs of the zodiac, these days are *ne* (rat) in the first month of each quarter, the day of *uma* (horse) in the second month, and the day of *tori* (chicken) in the quarter's final month. Farmers do not plant rice on these days because the plants would grow poorly if they did so.

3. Farmers say that anything planted on this day would be fit for consumption only on unhappy occasions or by people who are sick.

4. There are twelve jika-no-hi each year, one in each month. Named after the zodiacal signs, these days begin with *mi* (snake) in January, followed by the day of uma in February, and end with the day of *tatsu* (dragon) in December. It is said that on these days the earth is scorched, and thus planting is tabooed. Each month also has its *tenka-no-hi* (the day of fire in heaven) when thatching is forbidden. The first of these tenka-no-hi is the day of tori in January, and the last is the day of saru in December.

5. Kunio Yanagita, *Kinki Shūzoku Goi (Specific Glossary Concerning Taboos)* (Tokyo: Kokugakuin Daigaku Hōgen Kengyū-Kai, 1938), p. 73.

6. Jun'ichi Iwata, "Female Divers' Work in Shima District," *Shima (Islands)* (Tokyo), II (1934), 98. The annual festival of Isa-no-miya Shrine at Isobe-mura is held on June 24 and 25. It is said that the sacred shark comes from beyond the sea to attend the festival.

7. The taboo against allowing women to associate with other villagers for a prescribed period after childbirth is called *ara-mi* (rough abstinence), *aka-bi* (red fire), or simply *hi* (fire). See Yanagita, p. 3.

8. This is particularly the case at Kataku-ura, Izumo, in the district of Shimane-ken. See Tsuneichi Miyamoto, *Izumo Yatsuka-gun Kataku-ura Minzoku Kikigaki (Folklore Collected from Kataku-ura, Yatsuka-gun in Izumo Province)* (Tokyo: Attic Museum, 1942), p. 34.

9. Fishermen also believe that women, even those who are not pregnant, may spoil their luck if they happen to cross their path while they are on their way to the sea. See Shigeru Makita, "Mie-ken Kitamuro-gun Sukari-mura Goi" ("Folkloristic Glossary of Dialect in Sukari-mura, Kitamuro-gun, Mie-ken"), *Hōgen (Dialect)*, Vol. VIII, No. 1, 1938, p. 46.

10. A *jōnomi* is an outlet in a boat from which bilge water is poured out. An *ishi* is a stone, and in this context, one which is used to close this water outlet.

11. Fishermen and sailors worship the funadama-sama of their respective ships and usually place a representation of it (a small bag) in the wood at the bottom of a mast. The bag contains a woman's hair, a copper coin, dice, and a couple of male and female paper figures.

12. Kunio Yanagita (ed.), *Kaison Seikatsu no Kenkyū (Studies in Fishing Village Life)* (Tokyo: Minzokugaku Kenkyūsho, 1949), p. 282.

13. The sekihan is offered to the deity in an *isshō-masu*, a measuring utensil equal to one shō measure or 1.588 quarts.

14. Shigemitsu Suzuki, "Kanagawa-ken Tsukui-gun" ("Reports about the Tsukui District in Kanagawa-ken"), *Tabi to Densetsu (Travels and Legends)* (Tokyo), Vol. VI, No. 7, 1933, p. 86.

15. Kuro-fujō literally means "the black pollution." In contrast, the villagers of Kyūshū designate childbirth pollution by the term *shira-fujō* (white pollution) and menstrual contamination by *aka-fujō* (red pollution).

16. Yanagita, *Kaison Seikatsu no Kenkyū*, p. 282.

17. Ibid., p. 356. The tatsu-gashira is made of wood and paper and attached to the top of a bamboo stick. Sometimes the lower part is shaped like a bag, and is said to contain the soul of the dead person.

18. Kunio Yanagita and Ichirō Kurata (eds.), *Bunrui Gyoson Goi (Classified Glossary Concerning Fishing Villages)* (Tokyo: Minkan Denshō no Kai, 1938), p. 344.

19. Once again, taboos against contact with pregnant women do not imply that women have a completely negative effect upon the fishing

industry. Instead, even though they do not join the fishing expeditions at sea, they frequently engage in ritual magic designed to increase their husbands' haul of fish. When fishing is poor, the women of the village gather together to perform a *man-naoshi* (*man* means "luck"; *naoshi* means "improving") ceremony, in which they pray to the deity for a change of luck. Most commonly, they perform this ceremony in a temple or shrine, where they pass the time reciting chants and eating meals together.

20. James G. Frazer, *The Golden Bough* (London: The Macmillan Co., 1911), Vol. III, Part I, "Magic Art," pp. 20–22.

21. This taboo is also observed by hunters before they set forth from their villages, by farmers before they enter their fields, and by people in lesser occupations as well. Its strength among the fishermen of Himaka-jima, Aichi-ken, is discussed in Kiyoko Segawa, *Himaka-jima Minzoku-shi (Folklore of Himaka Island)* (Tokyo: Kōtō Shoin, 1951), p. 130.

22. Japanese miners share this taboo against whistling when they are beneath the ground.

23. Tsuneichi Miyamoto, *Suō-Ōshima o Chūshin to Shitaru Umi no Seikatsu (Sea Life Chiefly Around the Island of Suō-Ōshima)* (Tokyo: Attic Museum, 1936), p. 250.

24. Ibid.

25. The word *saru* also means "to go away" and is thought to be unlucky.

26. *Seto-Naikai Tōsho Junpō Nisshi (A Diary of a Journey Around the Islands in the Seto Inland Sea)*. [Project of the Attic Museum (Tokyo, 1940)], p. 137. The Attic Museum has been renamed Jōmin Bunka Kenkyūsho (Institute of Folk Culture).

27. Of course, women do go aboard fishing boats during launching ceremonies, and board other kinds of vessels as well, such as the boats they use for pearl-diving.

28. Yanagita, *Kaison Seikatsu no Kenkyū*, p. 353.

The Ebisu-gami in Fishing Villages

BY KATSUNORI SAKURADA

Ebisu-gami[1] is probably the most widely revered kami of the fishing industry and fishing villages in present-day Japan. However, the personification of Ebisu is not limited to that of Ebisu Saburo,[2] who is depicted as a fisherman with a red snapper under his arm. Sometimes he assumes the forms of a human corpse, a shark or a whale, or even a float (the Ebisu-aba)[3] tied to a fishing net. No one can explain what relationship exists between any of these particular objects and this kami of good fortune and wealth. Again we must admit that we are at a loss to explain what the name refers to when fishermen repeat "Ebisu! Ebisu!" while they kill fish by beating them on the head. The one conclusion that we can draw here is that Ebisu, as fishermen worshipfully call him, is the power who, they believe, grants them successful catches. Consequently, we may assume that a stone picked up from the sea bottom, a corpse, a shark, or any object believed to have power over the catch, has the potentiality of becoming Ebisu.

Fishermen still strongly believe in the force of luck which they call *man* or *gen*. Even when two boats are fishing alongside each other and employing the same method, one may strike and the other miss. When this happens, the custom is for the unlucky fishermen to ask for one or two fish from the other boat, in the belief that these will act as a charm to start a run for them. The practice, called *man-naoshi* (luck-mending), of drinking *sake* is widespread among fishermen whose spirits are depressed because of a continuous scarcity of fish. In agriculture, the combination of skillful tilling of the soil, adequate manure, and ordinary weather without extreme inclemency is sufficient to ensure good crops, and the efforts the farmers have made are usually rewarded. But the fisherman's labor does not always bring compensation. Fishing is still largely at the mercy of uncontrollable forces. It is no wonder, therefore, that fishermen recognize and worship whatever force seems to possess the power of granting a good catch.

This practice of calling by the name of Ebisu any power helpful to fishing provokes questions. We cannot determine historically whether this custom appeared after the image of Ebisu Saburo with a red snapper under his arm came to be worshiped and the belief in Ebisu-gami had pervaded the fishing villages. Perhaps there had already been in existence throughout the country a belief in a deity named Ebisu, from whom arose the entire Ebisu complex, including Ebisu-sama. We are not certain whether or not the worship of Ebisu, as described in the *Yoshu-fu Shi,* a geographical record of Yamashiro province, Kyoto, compiled during the late seventeenth century, was actually widespread throughout Japan; however, it is evident that at that

period this deity was already worshiped by some fishermen
of the Kinki (Kansai) area. There is need to study this matter further, since the name has now become identified with
the power which grants good catches. If one were to ask a
fisherman what he means when he cries, "Che! Ebesu!"
while he is fishing, he would probably answer that he is
praying to that Ebisu-sama who is one of the Shichi Fukujin
(Seven Deities of Good Fortune) for a good haul. This same
answer seems applicable in reference to the Ebesu-sama
enshrined on the beaches of fishing villages, regardless of
what the objects of worship are in the shrine or what may
be the religious practices there. Indeed, the Ebisu-sama enshrined in the Ebisu altar in each fisherman's household,
even when appearing merely as a float in the shape of
eboshi,[4] is surely worshiped as the old familiar deity of good
fortune. In short, we surmise that the majority of Ebisu
worshiped by Japanese fishermen today either assume the
conventional image of the god of prosperity and happiness,
or take the form of some object, like the float, that is identified with him.

There are localities where stones picked up from the sea
have been consecrated as the images of Ebisu. A famous
Ebisu-sama at Wakamatsu-shi in northeast Kyūshū is a
sacred stone in whose guise the kami is said to have come
ashore entangled in a fishing net.[5] Also, the Ebesu on Meki
Island in the Inland Sea is a piece of rock shaped like a man.[6]
Ebisu is not, however, the only power associated with stones
picked up from the sea and worshiped. The above examples
are only two among the numerous *hyōchaku-jin* (drifted
deities) found all over Japan. In both cases, however, the
extant descriptions are much too brief. Whether the stone
is said to have landed by the will of kami, or whether it was

actually brought ashore by men—and if the latter, how—
are questions as yet unanswered.

The Ebisu-kami at a small village named Seze-no-ura, on
Koshiki Island, Kagoshima-ken, which I visited some years
ago, is a mere stone. This rock is roughly pear-shaped and
was said to have floated ashore. The rock is so enormous that
not even two men could lift it and is definitely not a pumice
stone, which is light. A certain villager who saw this rock
drifting toward the beach made a shrine for it on top of a
hill behind the village, deeming it an irreverent act to leave
the stone in the water. Immediately, however, the rock began to roll back down the hill and halted at the spot where
it is now enshrined. This shrine is located beside a road
leading from the beach to the center of the hamlet. It is
further told that the stone had been very light before it was
installed there, but that it has since become quite heavy.

Such legends of floating stones, which are only one of the
many kinds of hyōchaku-jin that drift ashore and are worshiped, are not rare. Yet if this sacred stone of Ebisu-kami
at Seze-no-ura was truly a stone from the sea as traditionally
told, it could not (because of its weight) have been washed
ashore like a boat or like driftwood. We may assume, then,
that the stone was picked up by some means from the bottom of the sea or from the shore.

At Goka-mura, Oki Island, Shimane-ken, there is a custom of revering stones which come ashore from the west.
Whether they pick them up from the sea or catch them in
their nets, people display such stones on their altars as
Ebisu-sama. Wherever Ebisu-sama is honored, a successful
catch is granted, they say.[7] Judging from the history of various Shinto shrines, this reverence for unusual stones caught
in fishing nets is common in every area of the country.

A slightly different instance may be found at Uchinomura, Kimotsuki-gun, in Kagoshima-ken. Here it is the practice for a blindfolded fisherman to dive into the sea; whatever stone he grabs under water is then brought back and made the object of Ebisu worship. Some time later when good hauls become less frequent, another stone is sought from the sea to replace the old one.[8] I have heard of a similar practice at Seze-no-ura, a village mentioned above. There, at the opening of the tuna-fishing season, a fisherman of a highly respected family whose parents are still alive dives into the sea, his eyes covered with a hand towel. With this he picks up a stone, which is then worshiped as Ebisu-sama, and is called Ebisu-ishi (Ebisu stone). This ritual takes place on the shore near the spot where the fishermen set their nets.

At the neighboring village, Kawakōchi, the people will expect a big haul if the stone picked up is shaped like a man. In this village they use the same method of obtaining the stone as in Seze-no-ura; and throughout this part of the country, the old Ebisu stone is replaced with a new one every year at the opening of the fishing season.

While in the area of Uken-mura on Amami Island, Kago-shima-ken, I heard of an instance of a blindfolded fisher-man's obtaining Ebisu-gami from the bottom of the sea in each haul of the dragnet. This case differs from the few examples of finding sacred stones by chance, whether on the beach or in the fishing net. Although the description was brief, it deserves special attention for the fact that the acqui-sition of the stone from the bottom of the sea was made a definite part of the ritual in the course of the fishing cere-monies. Particularly in the village of Kawakōchi, the shape of the stones used in the ritual is apparently an augury of the size of the catch. Further evidence that various merits and omens are attached to the shapes of the stones can be in-ferred from the examples of Ebisu-ishi, on Meki Island in

the Inland Sea, and at Seze-no-ura, as well as at Kawakochi.
This ritual of procuring a stone from the sea bottom as
the symbol of the fishing god is no longer performed, save
for the three cases in southern Kyūshū mentioned earlier.
From evidence in the legends of drifted-stones and stones
caught in fishing nets, it can, however, be assumed that some
sacred stones were originally obtained during fishing ceremonies. If so, we must conclude that, in such cases, the original form of the fishing ceremony has somehow been
changed or transformed and that only the stone remains as
the symbol of the deity.

In contrast to the worship of Ebisu by the fishermen of
southern Kyūshū, the custom along the coasts of the Sea of
Japan and the Inland Sea is to honor Ebisu-aba as the fishing kami for each fishing net. The Inland Sea is the center
of the distribution area of the custom. This Ebisu-aba is an
unusually large float which is in the middle section of the
fishing net. As soon as this form of fishing ceremony, centered around the Ebisu-aba, came into usage, the old ceremony of picking up the Ebisu-ishi might well have become
unnecessary or outmoded.[9] But there are no clues as to how
these two incompatible practices of Ebisu worship are related to each other or how they originated in the fisheries.

Along the coast of the Sea of Japan there is a ceremony
still observed on the occasion of a ritual feast called
Gokuizake, which is celebrated at the laying of the dragnet.
In this ceremony, the people of Fujitsuka-hama, Kitakan-
bara-gun, in Niigata-ken, place a big float (comparable to
Ebisu-aba) on one of the two net stands and a stone, which
is the central sinker of the net, on the other. In this way
they worship the net and pray for a good haul. I particularly
noted the fact that there they call this stone sinker Ebisu-
ishi. Villagers told me that no taboo is attached to this stone,
and yet one is struck by the thought that the stone and the

big float are treated as the central objects of the ceremony. This subject should receive attention in the future.

Thus, examples of Ebisu-ishi and Ebisu-aba regarded as kami of the fishing net are found only in the large-net fisheries which employ more than twenty or thirty fishermen. Instances rarely occur in the small-scale fisheries operated with gill nets, hand purse seines, long lines, and involving the use of angling techniques, since these fishermen employ several kinds of implements according to the different fishing seasons. Accordingly they enshrine Ebisu-gami permanently at the Ebisu altar in their houses and do not worship him at sea for each small fishing venture. Probably on many of these altars, Ebisu stones, such as are found in Goka-mura on Oki Island, are installed; but on many altars other forms of Ebisu are seen.

In short, stones from the sea, which symbolize Ebisu-gami, are mostly related to hyōchaku-jin legends. However, as in the case of Ebisu-ishi in large-net fisheries, some stones are acquired ritually from the sea bottom at regular intervals. This latter ritual is connected with the ancient belief that the sea bottom or the province beyond the sea is a divine realm. Consequently the fisher folk revere any object that comes from across the sea or rises from the depths of the sea.

Whales and sharks are also called Ebisu. When they approach the shore chasing shoals of fish, and thus bring these shoals nearer the beach, they appear to be Ebisu bringing the catch to the fishermen, who therefore revere these creatures.

There are additional reasons for the manifestation of Ebisu in the guise of marine animals or as the power behind a big catch, and these explain why this belief is so common. One is the fishermen's belief in the surging tide of fish on festival days. For example, the festival of Izou Shrine at Isobe in Ise province on June 25 and 26, called Gosai in the fishing villages of Shima peninsula in Mie-ken, is associated with the legend that a *shichihon-zame* (seven-tailed shark, a sacred fish) will come up the river from the sea to visit the shrine and that anybody who sees it will die. June twenty-sixth in particular is known as Kaeri-Gosai (Returning Gosai), and fishing is halted on both these days.[10] This type of tradition about fish visiting the village on the festival day most frequently involves salmon. One example among several recorded in a local publication, *Noto Meiseki Shi* (*Noted Places of Noto Province*), is the story of a shrine called Shinmei on the riverside at Besshodani-mura up the river from Nawamata-mura. In the river was a stone called *manaita-ishi* (chopping-board stone). On November 15, the festival day of the shrine, a salmon leaped on top of the stone, died, and was swept down the stream; and it was said that those who ate this salmon were attacked by a plague.[11] There are two further legends of salmon climbing on chopping-board stones in Noto (e.g., the salmon at Yamakura Shrine in Chiba-ken), and both are interpreted as instances of offerings made to deities.[12] However, the shichihon-zame of Ise is not to be construed as an offering to the deity of the Izou Shrine. Rather it seems that of its own will this sacred shark makes visits to the shrine on festival days, as in the case of whales whose regular approach to the shore was considered to be a visit to the Ise Shrine or to Daiho on Goto Island. Furthermore, when we consider the fact that the seven-tailed shark was called a sacred fish and that people who saw it were believed to die (for in the old belief those who saw the figure of a god must die), doubts arise as to whether the shichihon-zame was originally thought of as a mere visitor to the shrine or whether its appearance revealed the actual presence of a deity.

As indicated in the above examples, fish which appeared on festival days might have been regarded either as offerings to deities or as the deities themselves, visiting their shrines. Legend tells us that in the shrines bearing the name of *kara-sake* (salty salmon), a number of which are found in Noto province, the objects of worship were actually kara-sake fish.[13] In the examples of Ōsuke-Kosuke[14] legends which are especially prevalent in the Tōhoku area, the deity itself is regarded as being present in the fish. One such instance is found in the Shōnai district in Yamagata-ken. Fishermen in the villages along the river finished their salmon fishing on November fifteenth of each year. That night, Ōsuke-Kosuke, the festival king of the salmon, swam up the river calling "Ōsuke-Kosuke is coming upstream!" Then tens of thousands of salmon, small and large, swam upstream after him. The villagers said that if a man heard the voice, he would die on the spot, so they passed the night by pounding rice into cakes, lest they inadvertently hear the salmon calling, and remained at home all night long.[15] A similar tradition from the same area is that those who heard the voice were destined to die within three days. And so, laying their work aside, fishermen went on an eating and drinking spree with their ears covered to prevent them from hearing the voice.[16] At any rate, we understand that people kept to their houses and celebrated the presence of the god that night. Also at Kawaguchi-mura, Kitauonuma, Niigata-ken, on October twentieth, the day of Ebisu-kō,[17] when Ōsuke-Kosuke is believed to come upstream, the villagers even today suspend their salmon-fishing.

All these stories have developed in communities engaged in river fishing, but similar legends about the ocean still endure. For instance, at Magari on the island of Tsushima, the Gion festival of June 15 is called the fishermen's festival; and a legend is told there that a fisherman who went to sea on that day, thereby violating the taboo, saw the evil omen of a horned shark.

These traditions of sacred fish are not entirely based on the hope of good fortune from the sea. Rather they reveal the belief in Ebisu, which underlies the custom of revering the big fish which chase shoals of small fish toward the shore. Thus the legends have been presented in this paper as descriptions of *yori-gami* (visiting deities) who make regular appearances at festivals.

As we have seen, Japanese fishermen believe that Ebisu-gami frequently appears from the sea. In short, Ebisu-gami is worthy of note not simply as the patron of fishing, but also as a visible deity emerging from the sea, and most striking of all, as a visiting deity. What makes this study of beliefs in Ebisu all the more important is the fact that, while the other hyōchaku-jin survive today only in the form of legends, the Ebisu beliefs are being perpetuated in the fishing villages by traditional rituals deifying drifted objects. Details concerning the original manner of identifying, enshrining, and worshiping these objects are no longer precisely known, but these rituals provide us with information that may lead to plausible reconstructions.

Notes

1. Ebisu is a deity who is believed to protect occupational groups and to bring wealth to his worshipers. Ebisu worship is widespread among Japanese folk in general; in towns and cities Ebisu is thought to be one of the Seven Deities of Good Luck. The pronunciations Ebisu and Ebesu vary according to locality.

2. The deity is usually personified as Ebisu Saburō in the guise of a fisherman. Saburō is a common male name.

3. *Aba* means "float." Usually a fishing net has a float on one side and a sinker on the other. A big net has a correspondingly large float of rectangular form, usually made of paulownia wood, which floats on the water to indicate the center of the net.

4. Eboshi are the headgear worn by nobles in court. The Ebisu-aba is shaped like an eboshi.

5. "Wakamatsu-shi," *Chikuhō Enkaishi (History of the Coastal Districts in Northeastern Kyūshū)* (Prepared by the Chikuhō Fisheries Association [Fukuoka-shi, 1917]).

6. *Seto Naikai Tosho Junpō Nisshi (A Diary of a Travel around the Islands in the Seto Inland Sea)* (Prepared by the Attic Museum [Tokyo, 1940]), p. 177.

7. Shizuo Yawata, "Stones in Oki Island," *Kyōdo (The Province)* (Tokyo), Special Number on Stones in Folklore, 1932, p. 170.

8. Buntarō Takahashi, "Notes on the Research Trip to Uchino-ura in the Province of Osumi," *Minzokugaku (Folklore)* (Tokyo), Vol. V, No. 6, 1933, p. 516.

9. Katsunori Sakurada, "Anbasama to Amidama" ("Anba-sama and the Net-spirit"), *Minkan Denshō (Folklore Journal)* (Tokyo), Vol. V, No. 3, December, 1939, pp. 1–2.

10. Jun'ichi Iwata, "Women Divers' Work in Shima District," *Shima (Islands)* (Tokyo), II (1934), 97–98.

11. Yorisuke Ota, *Noto Meiseki Shi (Noted Places in Noto Province)* (MS dated 1777; reprinted by Kanazawa City Library, 1931.)

12. Shunen Yoshihara, in *Kyodo Kenkyū (Local-Life Studies,* (Tokyo), Vol. III, No. 2, 1915, field-reports section, p. 120.

13. *Kara* means "salty," and *sake* means "salmon." According to the explanation in *Honchō Shokukan (Japanese Foods),* a book published in 1837, kara-sake is a salmon gutted and dried in the cold winter sun. For the legend see Ota.

14. The salmon which is said to appear on the day of the festival is often called by the name of Ōsuke-Kosuke. The leader of the salmon in the legend that follows is regarded as an actual, not a mythological, fish.

15. Yusuke Hashiba, in *Kyōdo Kenkyū (Local-Life Studies)* (Tokyo, Vol. IV, No. 6, 1916, field-reports section, pp. 366–73.

16. Mitsuo Onoda, "Shōnai-chihō no Nōson Gyōji," ("Annual Celebrations armong the Farmers in Shōnai District"), *Tabi to Densetsu (Travels and Legends)* (Tokyo), Vol. IX, No. 2, 1936, p. 61.

17. Ebisu-kō is the day when Ebisu-gami is worshiped. There are two great Ebisu-kō days during the year, January twentieth and October twentieth.

Drifted Deities in the Noto Peninsula

BY MANABU OGURA

On the western side of Central Japan is the Noto Peninsula, which folklorists regard as a veritable treasureland of Japanese folklore. The Noto district, extending into the Sea of Japan whose rough waves pound its shores, possesses a tradition which extends back in time to a mythical stage of history. Although civilized at an early date, the peninsula has only in the present century been influenced by the modern currents of civilization which entered the adjacent districts earlier. Surviving within its confines are a wealth of traditional observances based upon the original beliefs of the Japanese people. The collector of these old traditions and customs finds it toilsome work to travel around the long coast of this isolated peninsula, but his hardships are fully rewarded with an abundant harvest.

i

When we inquire into the origin of the *ubusuna-gami* shrines in the villages scattered along the coast of the Noto Peninsula, we learn that many of them are dedicated to deities said to have drifted ashore in ancient times from the far region beyond the sea.[1] From 1947 to 1957, I collected sixty-eight occurrences of the drifted-deity tradition in the Noto district.[2] Although Japan is surrounded by water and consequently more prone than most countries to preserve its native traditions, the Noto Peninsula may well be unique in the abundance of folklore that lies within its narrow bounds. In the peninsula there can be found, for example, every known type of the drifted-deity tradition of Japan.

There are two principal ways in which deities reach the shore: Either they are brought there by the waves, or they are brought to land by fishermen who find them in their nets. In the first general tradition, each deity from the land beyond the sea arrived on the waves. I have collected fifty-eight examples of this type in the district. Usually these deities are said to have been transported over the waves by some object, but a few of them are believed to have drifted ashore by themselves. In seventeen examples the deities arrived in canoes, in boats fashioned from the wood of the peach tree or in boats made of stone. In other examples, they journeyed to land upon an octopus, a *shiritaka-gai* (a kind of shellfish), a shark, a deer, a tortoise, a mass of *hondawara* (a species of seaweed), or a daikon (a long radish with green leaves).[3] There is also an account in which a deity is supposed to have traveled in the stomach of a whale; and in the most fanciful of all the versions, a wooden image of Kotoshironushi-no-kami emerged on the shore of Minatsuki sitting upon a *saka-daru* (*sake* barrel).

Explanations can be given for some choices of the objects upon which deities traveled. For example, seaweed and radishes are often washed ashore along the Noto Peninsula. The whale is worshiped by fishermen of the district as being related to Ebisu-gami (see preceding article).[4] And the story involving the *sake* barrel may have arisen from the association of saka-daru with the name Sakadaru-jinja (Shrine of Sakadaru). At any rate, there is a regular pattern beneath the stories of deities arriving upon particular objects: An object such as an octopus or shellfish is found on the beach by certain individuals who believe it has brought a deity. These individuals enshrine it, and the entire village soon begins to worship it as the deity's symbol.[5]

. In the second general drifted-deity tradition, fishermen raise the god from the sea. I have collected ten examples of this type within the area. Village informants usually tell of a fisherman who found in his net a large stone or some other object on which the deity was resting. A story of this kind is told concerning the Issaki Hachiman Shrine in Nanao-shi. In ancient times a fisherman named Magojirō went out to sea at Kaki-ga-ura and cast his net in the water. Finding a stone in the net, he hurled it back into the sea. But to his wonder, each time he drew the net up, the same stone rested within it. Some nights later an oracle appeared to Magojirō in a dream and told him it was the deity that rested on the stone. Struck with awe, the fisherman went again to Kaki-ga-ura, caught the same stone in his net, and enshrined it in his house. Later, the stone was placed in the middle of the village as the village tutelary deity. The sea basin at Kaki-ga-ura was eventually filled in with soil, and the villagers marked the spot where the divine stone had been caught by planting a sacred tree. The descendants of Magojirō the fisherman still live in the village of Nanao-shi, and their house is called *kami-sama no osato* (the home of the deity). At festivals in the spring and fall of each year, the deity is carried

MAGOJIRŌ'S HOUSE, which is called "the home of the deity"

KAKI-GA-URA, where the deity is said to have appeared

in a mikoshi[6] around the village. The procession always begins in the eastern part of the village where the home of the deity is located. It is believed that were it to begin from the western side, the mikoshi would not move an inch, and some calamity would occur.

We have seen that deities arriving from the sea upon some object are worshiped symbolically through a veneration of the object itself. The same can be said about deities which are raised from the sea by fishermen. Noto Peninsula tradition reveals that a stone is most often the object on which the deity rests when it is lifted up in a net. Hence stones are often worshiped as symbols of the deities.[7] The origin of this symbolic worship may be traced to the ancient Japanese belief that stones are the vehicles which transport all deities and spirits coming to visit this world from the other. A stone used for this purpose is called *kami-kata-ishi* (symbolic stone of the deity). One of the best examples in the Noto Peninsula of a kami-kata-ishi symbolizing a drifted deity is found at Sukunahiko-no-kamikata-ishi Shrine at Kurosaki-cho, Nanao-shi.[8] This Sukunahiko is a deity (kami) believed to have drifted ashore in a little boat at Kurosaki beach long ago. After this deity had accomplished the great feat of subduing the wilderness and developing the district, it was enshrined at the spot where it first landed. Though it had arrived by boat and had not been lifted from the sea, its presence was symbolized at the landing place by a large stone which the people placed there. This stone, standing 1.7 meters high, is still found within a simple hut among the bushes on the top of the precipice at Kurosaki beach. According to the old people of Nanao-shi, grasses still grow there bearing fruit in the shape of little boats, just as they first grew from the little boat in which Sukunahiko had traveled. This deity is one of the popular heroes in Japanese myth, and is recorded in the *Kojiki,* the *Nihon Shoki,* and other classics, under the name of Sukunahikona-no-kami, the dwarf deity, as a legendary figure who helped open up the land of Japan and who originated the art of medicine.

ii

The drifted-deity tradition may have emerged from the ancient Japanese belief that on certain occasions the gods visit this world from their own world far beyond the sea.[9] The people who encountered these kami honored them and celebrated the meetings through rituals. In these rituals we may see the original forms of the drifted-deity legends. Careful observation of the traditional festivals and customs performed at *hyōchaku-gami* or yori-gami shrines supports this theory.

Scholars considering these festivals and customs must first inquire where the drifted deity is said to have arrived, for the landing place is usually revered almost as much as the deity itself. At Noto-machi, for example, the villagers revere a triangular pond as the place where the deity of Sakadaru-jinja arrived on a *sake* barrel and rested for a while before going ashore. Strict measures are enforced to keep the pond unpolluted, and even childbirth is forbidden at the homes around the shrine. In this manner places connected with legends of drifted deities are often honored by the inhabitants of Noto Peninsula.

The spring and fall festivals are often begun by carrying the mikoshi to the landing place of a drifted deity. Each May the villagers at Maenami in Anamizu-machi still perform rituals that begin on the shore facing the sea. The legend accounting for these rituals, which are attached to Hiyoshi Shrine at Maenami, states that in ancient times while three fishermen from Maenami, Ukagawa, and Okinami were working together, a deity came floating ashore. The Okinami fisherman first noticed the divine figure; the Ukagawa fisherman lifted it up; and a place in the third fisherman's village, Maenami, was selected as the site of the rituals to be held in the deity's honor. Every May the descendants of the old families in these three villages gather together, and the families that have come from Ukagawa carry the mikoshi to the spot on the beach where the yori-gami first appeared. The mikoshi is placed on the shore, and rites are conducted with the people from Ukagawa seated to the right of the mikoshi, those from Okinami to the left, and the families from Maenami directly in front. When the rites at the landing place are over, the people from Ukagawa carry the mikoshi back to the shrine.

These rites follow the regular form of Shinto rituals. Consecrated food offerings of rice, rice cake, *sake,* fish, fowl, garden and wild vegetables, fruit, and seaweed are placed on a plain wooden table. Kagura, the sacred music of flute and drum, is played. *Norito,* an address to the deity, is read by a priest in order to praise the deity's name, to state the manner of celebration, and to pray for the country's peace and the worshipers' prosperity.

The fall-festival rites of Sugawara Shrine at Ukawa in Noto-machi also begin at the legendary landing place of the shrine's tutelary deity. Every November the mikoshi is carried to a distant place called Sakuragi where the deity in ancient times is said to have arrived and been temporarily enshrined. After a ceremony is performed at the landing site, the mikoshi is returned to Sugawara Shrine where the main rites, with more elaborate offerings and more persons in attendance, are then conducted.[10]

What can the folklorist infer about rituals performed in the Noto Peninsula at spots particularly connected with legends of deities drifting ashore? It may be that these traditional rituals, performed at annual festivals, are derived from an ancient but similar form of religous ritual—one that existed before the origin of the drifted-deity tradition. In ancient Japan a religious ritual may have developed in which people welcomed and worshiped the deity who had come from the land of deities beyond the sea. It is possible that the drifted-deity tradition is composed of many localizations of this much older belief.

Even if there were no localized rituals, the existence of many traditions and customs possibly associated with an ancient rite of welcoming the deity from the other world may certify my position. For example, in the festival of Issaki Hachiman Shrine previously described, the procession always begins near "the home of the god" so that the mikoshi can quickly be carried to the home as a symbolic commemoration of the god's arrival. Other facts which may point to an ancient welcoming tradition are the agreement of dates for the festival days of shrines with the legendary dates for the arrivals of drifted deities, the existence of a traditional belief that the northeast or the northwest wind blows on every festival day because these were the winds which brought the deities to shore,[11] and the existence of another belief that on the annual festival day at some shrines, shiri-taka-gai gather along the shore because the deity first arrived astride one of these creatures.[12]

The observances attached to Atago Shrine at Notojima-machi and Tsurugiji Hachiman Shrine at Monzen-machi may also reveal an ancient welcoming tradition in the Noto Peninsula. Atago Shrine was originally dedicated to the *uji-gami* (family tutelary deity) of an old family called Saburōsuke. In the family legend, however, the shrine is dedicated to a deity which arrived from the sea astride an octopus. A member of the Saburōsuke house, finding the deity on the kitchen furnace, honored it, and to this day the

ISSAKI HACHIMAN SHRINE

Saburōsuke family honor the octopus as the deity's servant. Their taboo against eating any part of an octopus has never been broken, for they believe that breaking the taboo will make their family collapse. Every year on November third, the Shinto priest of this village shapes the head of an octopus from cooked rice and secretly places it at dawn on the kitchen furnace of the Saburōsuke home.[13] When the day breaks, the people of the house divide this rice into small balls and give them to their neighbors. A similar ceremony is held on the morning of June twelfth at Tsurugiji Hachiman Shrine at Monzen-machi. On this festival day, *sake* mixed with *wakame* (a kind of seaweed) is offered to the tutelary deity and drunk by the worshipers. The legend is that in ancient times a deity wrapped in seaweed drifted ashore at Monzen-machi on the morning of June twelfth.

Some Japanese historical scholars untrained in folklore may say that the people of the Noto Peninsula present these traditional festival-day performances in order to commemorate the arrivals of drifted deities and that the celebrations have their source in the legends connected with these beings.

However, after surveying sixty-eight legends in the Noto Peninsula,[14] I believe the proper folkloristic view is probably that both the drifted-deity tradition and the observances connected with it developed from the original form of the Shinto rituals. In these rituals the ancient Japanese people honored the deities or the ancestral spirits who visited them annually from the other world beyond the sea. The traditional stories of drifted deities, which modern scholars identify as folklore, should then properly be studied as valuable oral records derived from the much simpler beliefs of the ancient Japanese.

Notes

1. *Ubusuna-gami* is a generic term for tutelary deities. One subtype is hyōchaku-gami, the deity drifted to shore; and another is yori-gami, the deity that floats ashore. These terms are used by students of folklore; the folk call the drifted objects *kami-sama* (deities) or *hotoke-sama* (Buddhas).

2. The number has increased since this study was made. When I revisited the Noto Peninsula during the summer of 1957, I collected five more legends of drifted deities. Hyochaku-gami or yori-gami legends are also told about Buddhist images. There are more than ten Buddhist temples where such legends are preserved. Because the Japanese have regarded Shinto deities and Buddhist saints in similar ways, drifted-deity legends about Buddhist images might well be included in the same category with those discussed in this essay.

3. Since ancient times the Japanese people have considered hondawara a symbol of happiness. Consequently it is used as an ornament at New Year's time. Hondawara and daikon are washed ashore all over Japan. The daikon, commonest of vegetables grown by Japanese farmers, frequently floats downstream into the sea.

4. Ebisu-gami is a deity which presents an interesting problem in Japanese folklore. While fishermen throughout Japan worship this deity as the god of wealth, fishermen in some districts worship the whale and call it Ebisu. The latter may be a localized symbol of Ebisu-gami.

5. According to an ancient tradition the deity of Ikakeyama Shrine at Iori-machi, Nanao-shi, floated ashore from the eastern sea in the shape of two white hens. When a hundred-year-old man scooped them up with an *ikake* (a scooping implement made of bamboo), the two hens immediately turned into Yakushi-nyorai and Kanzeon-bosatsu. (Yakushi-nyorai is a Buddhistic deity in charge of medicine, and Kanzeon-bosatsu is a Buddhistic deity of mercy.) These images were installed in a mountain shrine; the mountain was named Ikakeyama, and the shrine was named Ikakeyama Shrine after the tradition that the images were scooped up in an ikake. The idea that the hens were transformed into Buddhistic deities reveals the old Japanese belief that drifted objects are deities or sacred images of them.

6. A mikoshi is a portable shrine which is carried on the shoulders of many people. At festival time the deity, seated in the mikoshi, travels around the area which it protects.

7. The size of the stone is irrelevant. Sometimes the stones are very big; for instance, the divine stone at Tadatsu Hachiman Shrine in Nanao-shi is 1.5 meters in height, 1.7 meters in length, and 1 meter in width. It is said to have been caught in a fisherman's net.

8. This is an old shrine recorded in Volume X of *Engishiki* (*Institutes of the Engi Era*), a register of important shrines, compiled over 1,000 years ago.

9. The land of deities is called Tokoyo-no-kuni (Land of Eternal Life), and the ancestral spirits of the Japanese people are still thought to reside there. The ancient Japanese believed that deities voyaged back and forth between that world and this one. Their belief poses the interesting question of what geographical ideas of the relation of this world to the land of deities were held by the ancient Japanese people.

10. A man named Dembei first discovered the deity of Sugawara Shrine when it drifted ashore in ancient times. His descendants still live at Ukawa in Noto-machi. According to traditional custom, the ceremony at the annual festival on November seventh does not commence unless one of his male descendants is present.

11. For instance, it is said that on March seventeenth (now April

seventeenth), the festival day of Sakadaru Shrine, the northeast wind is sure to blow.

12. When the spring and fall festival days of Hiyoshi Shrine at Enotomari-machi in Nanao-shi draw near, many octopuses gather near the shore. The people of the area say that "octopuses have come to attend the festival," and the people never try to catch them.

13. The rice figure is called *tako-no-mamma* (boiled rice for the octopus).

14. The following are my previous publications on this subject: "Noto no Kuni Hyōchaku-gami Kō" ("Observations on Drifted Deities in Noto Province"), *Kokugakuin Zasshi* (*Kokugakuin University Journal*), Vol. LV, No. 3, 1954, pp. 30–43; and "Noto no Hyochaku-gami no Kenkyū" ("A Study of Drifted Deities in the Noto Peninsula"), *Nihon Minzokugaku* (*Journal of Japanese Folklore*), Vol. I, No. 4, 1954, pp. 91–94.

鍛治屋

PART FOUR | IRONWORKERS

Japanese Metalworkers: A Possible Source for their Legends

松本信広

BY NOBUHIRO MATSUMOTO

The legends of Japanese metalworkers, like the metallurgical and casting arts these laborers practice, owe their origin to countries other than Japan. Whether these countries are in northern or southern Asia, however, is a difficult question to answer, for the available evidence points in both directions.

Korea seems at first the most likely source from which the Bronze Age may have been introduced into Japan. There are several grounds on which to choose Korea as the birthplace of Japanese metallurgy, casting, and metalworkers' legends. First, the word *tatara* (originally foot bellows, later a forge) is found as a place name both in Japan and Korea. Second, the Chinese *History of the Wei Dynasty* mentions that the ancient Japanese crossed the sea to Korea in the third century A.D. in order to obtain iron. Third, it is also said in the ancient Japanese chronicle, the *Kojiki*, that a Korean nobleman named Ame-no-Hihoko and his followers brought many treasures to Japan.[1] Among these treasures was an ancient instrument known as a sun mirror which the Koreans probably used to make fire from the rays of the sun. If these immigrants from Korea did bring with them such prerequisites for the establishment of a metal industry, it can be inferred that they also brought new forms of beliefs to Japan.

On the other hand, the Japanese art of tatara (the production of iron from iron sand) reveals greater affinities with Fukien and Cambodian metallurgy than with the metal industry of northern portions of Asia.[2] But it might be advisable to assign the origin of metal-goods production in ancient Japan to a time still earlier than the period in which influences from Korea and neighboring areas were incorporated in Japanese metallurgy. The art of metal production in Japan seems, in fact, to be traceable to an earlier tradition which is common to many parts of Asia.

This tradition involves the relationship between the Asiatic mainland and the Japanese islands, which in ancient times was much like that between civilized nations and the Pacific islands in recent times. When immigrants from the highly civilized nations of mainland Asia first came to Japan, the people they found there presumably still possessed a Stone Age culture. The aboriginal inhabitants were so awestruck at the superior culture of these newcomers that they respected them, worshiped them, and even formed myths about them during the period of initial culture contact. By virtue of being the culture heroes of the native Japanese people, these immigrants from the Asiatic mainland were able to organize themselves into special occupational groups, and thereby to increase their own authority and power over the populace.

These newcomers, who brought with them the occupations they had practiced on the Asiatic mainland, also established new systems of beliefs and cycles of legends in Japan. Each occupational group perhaps had its own ancestral god to whom a separate belief system and a distinctive set of legends were attached. At any rate, this was true of the metalworkers, who worshiped Ame-no-me-hitotsu-no-kami (the One-eyed Deity of Heaven), and believed that this deity took charge of their industry. In a manuscript of the *Nihongi* (*Chronicles of Japan*, completed in A.D. 720), for example, we read that Ame-no-me-hitotsu-no-kami was made "a professional metal-worker."[3] Survivals of the worship of this deity were found until recent times in Japan, although he had become Hitotsu-me-tatara, the one-eyed and one-legged monster of the ironworking industry.

i

When folklore materials of this kind are studied comparatively, it becomes evident that they are not peculiar to Japan. The traditions of Ame-no-me-hitotsu-no-kami and Hitotsu-me-tatara, for example, are seen to be related to the ancient southern and central Chinese association of the foot bellows with a legendary one-legged ghost bird;[4] the Chinese belief in this creature is seen to be an antecedent of the later belief of Japanese blacksmiths that Kaneyako-gami, their ancestral god, first appeared riding a white bird. Similarly, the traditional practice among these metalworkers of setting up a corpse in the fireplace while they blow the bellows has some connection with certain of the legends of South China.

One of the oldest Japanese references to this traditional corpse worship appears in the *Arcane Book for the Iron-*

workers, written in the fourth year of Tenmei (1784). In this description of iron-production methods in the San'in and San-yō districts, the following legend about the origin of corpse worship appears:

Bringing *murage* (among the ancient Japanese, a chief of the blacksmiths) with her, Kaneyako-gami descended from the sky upon a white heron. First the deity and her companion flew over the province of Harima; then they alighted on a *katsura* tree (Japanese Judas tree) at Hida-mura in Izumo province. There, they were barked at by a dog and entangled in hemp thread, and the *murage* fell from the tree to his death. The *murage*'s corpse was set up in a forge by Kaneyako-gami, together with a *pile*.[5] And when the deity began to work at the forge, the result of her preparations was the production of an abundant quantity of iron. Other versions of this legend, however, indicate that the *murage* was Kaneyako-gami herself, or that the *murage*'s corpse was placed in a shrine and worshiped as the image of Kaneyako-gami.[6]

The assumption that this ironworkers' legend has its roots outside Japan is based on the fact that corpse worship does not accord with the general Japanese view of death as a pollution. Where, then, are these roots located? The answer may be that the custom of corpse worship sprang from the legends of a particular immigrant occupational group, one which gradually developed the art of metalworking. Iron production is closely connected with the industry of charcoal-making, since both require the use of intensely hot fires. The legend of Kogorō the Charcoal-maker, distributed in various parts of Japan, already has been studied in detail by Kunio Yanagita, who suggests that it has a definite connection with the ironworkers' belief in the god Hachiman.[7] For these reasons, the legend of Kogorō and its analogues on the Asian mainland are of utmost significance to scholars who seek the origin of the ironworkers' legends.

ii

The outline of the Kogorō legend is as follows. Heeding
the instructions of the Buddhist deity Kannon (or in some
versions those of a Shinto tutelary deity), a lady journeys
from the capital city to a country town, in order to become
the wife of a poor young charcoal-maker. One morning,
after their wedding, the wife sends the husband out to buy
some rice. But the young man throws the gold pieces his
wife has given him at the water birds in a pond, and returns
home empty-handed. When his wife reproaches him for this
wasteful deed, the young man replies that if gold pieces are
treasures, they can be found in abundance around the place
where he makes his charcoal. Then he and his wife go there
together, find plenty of gold, and overnight they become
wealthy.

Although this legend appears to have no direct connection with the ironworkers' tradition of corpse worship,
occasionally in South China, and less frequently in Japan,
it is combined with the aetiological legend of Kamado-gami
(the hearth deity). In this tale, a woman of good luck marries a man of poor luck, who soon divorces her and drives
her away from the house. After she wanders about for a
time, she marries a young charcoal-maker, with whom she
finds great wealth in the same manner as in the story above.
Then the ex-husband loses his wealth, and in a miserable
condition passes by his former wife's house. He dies there
of shame, and his corpse is deified as a god of the hearth.
This tale, combined with versions of "Kogorō the Charcoal-
maker," has many analogues on the mainland of Asia.

One of the most striking of these analogues is a Miao tale
from South China. According to the tradition the Miao people have handed down, there was once a wealthy man whose
daughter was much sought after as a bride. Yet her father

refused every one of the marriage offers made to her because he was dissatisfied with the amount of property each of the suitors owned. At last the girl argued this matter with her father, and as a result she decided to leave home. She rode away on a horse which was her father's only farewell gift to her, and her last words to him were that a man's wealth depends upon his lot in life and not upon what he has inherited.

Allowing the horse to take her in whatever direction it wished, she was brought to the thatched hut of a charcoal-maker. There, she asked the old woman in the hut for a cup of cooked rice and for permission to marry her son who was away from home at work. But the old woman refused to let her son marry, because they were too poor. When the son returned from work, however, the girl gave him several pieces of silver with which he was asked to buy some rice. At the front entrance of the rice-dealer's house, a dog attacked the young man. To protect himself, he threw the silver at the animal and returned home empty-handed. Reproached by the girl for his carelessness, the young man retorted that if the pieces of silver really were such precious treasures he could replace them with many more of the same kind; plenty of them were to be found at the place where he made his charcoal. The next morning the young couple went to this place, brought home an abundant quantity of silver, became husband and wife, and used the silver to purchase wet rice fields which soon made them even richer.

But in the meantime the girl's father had become poverty stricken and was reduced to beggardom. When he happened to come as a beggar to his daughter's house, the girl offered him something to eat, including a piece of bread in which she had placed a silver coin. Not noticing the coin, however, the father exchanged the bread for something else. This act was repeated several times; each time the daughter placed a coin in an item of food, her father exchanged the item for a different kind of food. Then, when he realized what had happened and how foolish he had been, he became filled with regret for his bad luck, threw himself into the fireplace, and was burned to death. His remains were deified as the god of the hearth.

According to a different Miao version, the son of a rich man married the daughter of a poor man, but the husband became ashamed of the poverty of his wife's family. Deciding to get rid of his wife, the husband gave her five hundred silver coins, put her on horseback, and chased her away from their home. The horse took the woman to the home of a firewood-gatherer, whose son she married. As in the other Miao version of this story, the young man threw his wife's silver coins at a dog, and countered her reproaches with the statement that such things were found in abundance around his house. He and his wife gathered the silver and soon became wealthy. Then the ex-husband who had, meanwhile, lost his fortune, came as a beggar to his former wife's home and burned himself to death in a moment of shame and remorse. He is said to have become the deity of the hearth.[8]

A similar story is told in China's Canton province. An unlucky man exchanged a piece of bread, in which his ex-wife had placed a gold coin, for an entire loaf of coarse bread and as a result did not receive the hidden piece of gold which she had intended to give him. When he discovered his misfortune, the unlucky man killed himself in distress and was thenceforth worshiped as the hearth god.[9]

iii

Immigrants from the Asian mainland may have brought these aetiological legends to Japan with them. Archaeological evidence shows that the Yayoi culture, which thrived in Japan during the first century A.D., is indebted to the ancient civilization of the Asiatic mainland for techniques of rice cultivation. The ironworkers' practice of corpse worship and their tradition about its origin could have evolved from legends introduced by people of southeast Asia. Numerous Japanese variants of these hearth-deity stories seem to support this theory of migration and its corollary that distinctive Japanese folk beliefs were generated within traditional Asian forms. Variants are presented herein from Chiba-ken and Shiga-ken.

In Chiba-ken people still tell the story of how a human corpse came to be worshiped as a deity of the home. One version of this tale may be summarized as follows. Once upon a time there were a head family and its branch family, both of them prosperous. One day a man of the branch family took shelter from the rain in the shrine of Dōroku-jin (a guardian deity at the village boundary). Shortly thereafter another person wet with rain took refuge at the same shrine. The second man began to talk with Dōroku-jin and to prophesy that children would be born that night in the houses of both families. He predicted that the boy who would be born to the head family and the girl who would be born to the branch family some day would become a fine couple. Having overheard this conversation, the man from the branch house hurried home to find that a baby girl had indeed been born; then he hastened to visit the head family, and saw that a baby boy had been born to them. When he informed both families about this conversation of the gods which had come true thus far, everyone was quite excited. Happily both families waited for their children to grow up.

When both children reached maturity, the remainder of the prophecy was fulfilled. The couple married, but soon the husband grew to dislike his wife because of her unattractive appearance. One day, he prepared for her a meal of rice boiled with red beans,[10] gave her a red cow to ride on, and drove her out into the fields. Weeping with sorrow, she let the animal take her wherever it would. At last the cow brought her to a solitary house on the slope of a mountain. There she stopped, and married the house's male occupant.

Together with her new husband, the woman became rich enough to live in comfort. Her former husband, on the other hand, met with successive misfortunes, and was reduced to earning his living as a bamboo-basket dealer. It so happened that one day, having lost his way on the mountain, the basket dealer stumbled upon his ex-wife's home. Not knowing her real identity, he sold her several baskets on this and on later occasions. When he learned, however, that this generous mistress of the house was none other than his former wife, he was so shocked that he died. Filled with pity, his ex-wife buried him behind the fireplace in order to deify him as Kōjin (the deity of the hearth).[11]

A similar legend concerning the origin of a household deity is recorded by the Buddhist priest Taichu in *Memoir on Shintoism in the Ryūkyūs* (although this tale actually came from the mainland). The legend is as follows:

A farmer who lived in the village of Yura, Kōga-gun, in Ōmi province [now Shiga-ken], once spent the night under a tree on a mountain. At midnight a light appeared from the east and came to rest upon this tree. Then a voice from the root of the tree asked, "What has happened tonight?" And the light answered, "Children were born in neighboring houses at Yura within this district. The boy was born with characters written upon his hands to tell that he will become a winnow-maker and peddle his wares from door to door. The girl has characters in her hands which reveal that good luck will come to her."

When the farmer returned home at daybreak, he found that

a baby boy had been born in his house and that a baby girl had been born in the home of his neighbor. When these children grew up, they became husband and wife. The husband, however, began to lead a dissolute life. At length he drove his wife away, and with a servant maid for company the weeping woman set forth on a long journey to her relatives' home in a distant region.

On her way she stopped at a house for shelter from the rain. There she met the place's only occupant, a twenty-four- or twenty-five-year-old man who had lost his wife and his parents. Taking pity upon each other, the man and woman married. They lived together in comfort, for the wife had been born under a lucky star.

Meanwhile the former husband had dissipated his fortune, and consequently was reduced to peddling the winnows he had made. Visiting his ex-wife's home, he failed to recognize her, but she immediately recognized him. The kindly woman bought many winnows from him. When he visited her house again, she—still keeping her knowledge secret—put him up for the night in her maid's room. That night she peeped in at him, and just at that moment he happened to glance in her direction. The man now recognized his ex-wife, and, filled with shame, he fell to the ground and died. The woman ordered her servant to bury the corpse secretly behind the fireplace. This is said to be the origin of the hearth deity.[12]

Various tales of this sort have been collected in Japan, and compared with one another.[13] Perhaps the oldest one is from Miyako-jima in the Ryukyus, for this variant agrees in its essential details with those of the first Miao tale presented above. As in the Chinese story, so too in the Miyako version the second husband of the divorced woman is a charcoal-maker who eventually becomes a rich man. The ex-wife in this story places, on the spot where her husband died of shame, a stone on which she pours a cup of tea in his memory every time she drinks tea herself. Other Japanese variants are found in the Tohoku area (the northeastern districts of Japan) where an ancient custom of worshiping an ugly mask as the hearth god still survives. In one Tohoku version, after the poor husband is discovered by his ex-wife, he stays at her house as a servant for the rest of his life.

iv

Further evidence that the legend of Kogorō the Charcoal-maker evolved from similar stories known on the Asiatic mainland is gleaned from a comparison of the legend with tales from Burma and Korea. Identical motifs, for example, are discernible in the tale of the water-snail prince told among the Palaung of Burma:

To the wife of a king who prayed for a child a baby was born in the form of a water snail. The king placed it on a raft, and sent it floating down the river. The raft floated on and on until it reached the kingdom of Naga, where the dragon queen found the child and took it to her husband. But the dragon king refused to take care of it because it belonged to the world of humans.

Placed upon the raft again, the water-snail prince continued to float downstream until he came to the land of the demons. There, a female demon picked the child up and began to take care of it. Seven months later the water-snail prince turned into a human boy. He remained in the land of the demons for ten years, until the day when he happened to open the door of the forbidden storeroom. Finding the room full of the bones of animals and human beings, he knew for the first time that his foster mother was a demon. Taking her clothes from the storeroom, he put them on with great haste, stole the elements of water, fire, and wind from the garden, and fled from the land of demons.

Soon he reached the kingdom of Chambanagō, where the king had just posted an important announcement. The announcement was that the king had commanded his daughter to throw down a hood from the top of a tower and that the man on whose head the hood dropped would receive the princess as his wife. On the day set aside for this event, a crowd of people assembled beneath the tower. In the crowd's midst was the water-snail prince, upon whom the hood fell. Then, as he had agreed, the king gave the princess to the lucky man; but because the demon's clothes in which the prince was dressed had a bad smell, the king disliked his new son-in-law and drove him away with the princess.

At the time of the newlyweds' departure the princess' mother gave jewels to her daughter as a farewell gift. When the prince and princess had settled themselves in a valley, the princess gave one of these jewels to her husband, and told him to use it to purchase food. But the prince looked at the jewel and claimed that if it were such a treasure, he could find many others like it near their dwelling place. The couple gathered these jewels, became extremely wealthy, and built a splendid palace in which to live. When the prince removed his demon's attire the bad smell left him, and he appeared as a fine young man. The princess' father heard about this change in his son-in-law, effected a reconciliation, and gave the happy couple half of his kingdom in which to live in comfort for the rest of their days.[14]

Stories with the major motifs of this Burmese folktale and the Japanese tale of Kogorō the Charcoal-maker are found in Korea also. One such story is told about Yam Boy, the thirtieth king of Pekche. Extracted from the *Memoir on Three Kingdoms: Silla, Pekche, and Kokuryo*,[15] this tale is as follows.

A woman who lived by a pond married the dragon of the pond and gave birth to a boy. When the child grew up, he earned his living by digging up and selling yams; therefore, everyone called him Yam Boy. One day Yam Boy heard of a beautiful princess, the third daughter of the king of Silla, and went to the capital city to see if he could win her hand. There he won the friendship of a group of boys by giving each of them part of his yam lunch. Then he taught them to sing a song telling of a secret love affair between the princess and himself.

Upset by this false rumor, the princess' parents decided to send her away to a remote land. When it was time for her departure, her mother, the queen, gave her an abundance of pure gold as a farewell gift. Then the girl set forth on her journey, unaware that Yam Boy had joined the party as an attendant. But when the party had almost arrived at the land of the princess' impending exile, Yam Boy made his presence known, dared to ask her to marry him, and obtained her ready consent. The couple went to Pekche to live, and there the princess gave her husband the gold her mother had presented to her. When the princess told Yam Boy that they could use the gold to live on, he laughingly replied that he had been familiar with gold from childhood but had not known it was such a precious substance. He told her that it was plentiful around the place where he used to dig yams. So the two of them went there and obtained great wealth.

Although the legend of Kogorō the Charcoal-maker and its Burmese and Korean analogues do not agree with one another in every detail, these stories nevertheless do have two important motifs in common. First, the heroine in each story chooses her husband by her own free will; and second, the hero in each of these tales informs his wife nonchalantly that he has access to plenty of treasure. Because of these striking similarities, the possibility that the Kogorō legend emerged from the tales of Asian immigrants to Japan is not weakened at all by minor variations from one story to another. Thus it is of little importance that the hero of the Burmese variant is an adventuresome traveler rather than a charcoal-maker, that he discovers jewels instead of gold, and that he is born as a water snail rather than as a human being. Yet it is interesting to note that the heroes in both

the Burmese and the Korean variants issue forth from
the world of water. One is born as a water snail, while the
other is the son of a water dragon. Both heroes, too, meet
with eventual good luck. Stories of this kind, which deal
with lucky beings connected with the water world, not only
are related to the Japanese legend of Kogorō the Charcoal-
maker, but also to a cycle of Japanese stories which are based
upon the notion that the water world itself is the source of
wealth. In this cycle, for instance, is found the well known
Japanese tale of "The Little Boy from the Dragon Palace
Under the Water."[16]

v

All of the tales presented in this paper deal with men
who are the recipients of good or bad luck. In the blacksmiths' legend about the descent of Kaneyako-gami from
the sky, for example, the murage's misfortune is his fatal
plunge from the tree. Kaneyako-gami, on the other hand,
capitalizes upon the murage's death to produce an abundant
supply of iron. In the legend of Kogorō, the Charcoal-maker
becomes aware of his good luck when his wife reveals to him
the value of gold. The Miao, Cantonese, Ōmi, and Miyako-
jima variants of the hearth-deity legend all deal with a
young man's rise in fortune and the subsequent misfortunes of an older man. And the Palaung and Pekche analogues to the legend of Kogorō the Charcoal-maker focus
upon the steady increase in good fortune of their youthful
heroes. Finally, a remarkable point of resemblance among
most of these tales is that the husband's good luck is revealed
to him by a woman.

The women in these tales all choose their own husbands,
a cultural trait observable wherever women enjoy social predominance and particularly common in southeastern Asia.

Hence, in the Burmese story of the water-snail prince, the
episode in which the princess chooses her husband by throwing a hood from the tower may be connected with the custom current among the aborigines of South China, in which
young people gather at a spring festival to throw balls at
the persons they wish to choose as mates.[17] It seems reasonable to presume that this custom is a primitive precursor of
the more advanced method of choice which the princess of
Chambānagō employs. It likewise seems reasonable to infer
that the idea of a woman's marrying a man of her choice, in
the manner of the heroine in the Charcoal-maker story, is
derived from the less advanced manner of choice described
in this Burmese folktale. These suppositions lead me to
believe that stories of the Charcoal-maker, which are distributed continuously over the Pacific coast of the Asiatic
mainland and throughout the Japanese islands as well, reflect the idea of maternal authority prevalent in southeastern Asia. This indicates that the legends were probably
carried from the continent to Japan and helps to support
the theory that the Japanese ironworkers among whom
these tales are told owe the origin of their occupation, their
system of beliefs, and their legends to an ancient immigra-
tion of artisans from the Asian mainland.

Notes

1. From the *Kojiki,* compiled in A.D. 712, we learn that Ame-no-
Hihoko was the son of a lord who lived in the Korean kingdom of
Silla in ancient times. The *Kojiki* states that Ame-no-Hihoko came
to Japan in search of his wife, who had left for Japan earlier. She
had deserted him because he had become too haughty, and had returned to Japan, which she claimed was the land of her ancestors.

2. This fact was pointed out by Kuniichi Tawara, in his *Korai no*

Satetsu Seiren-hō (Traditional Methods of Iron Refinement) (Tokyo: Maruzen Kabushiki Kaisha, 1933), pp. 132–46.

3. *Nihon Shoki* (Nihon Koten Zensho [Series of Japanese Classics] [Tokyo: Asahi Shinbun Sha, 1948]), I, 149. Another mythical culture hero from Korea who followed Ame-no-Hihoko to Japan was a potter who settled in Ōmi province and became the ancestor of Japanese potters (*Nihon Shoki* [Tokyo: Asahi Shinbun Sha, 1953], II, 105). For further discussion see the author's article, "La Légende de Kokoro le Charbonnier," *Bulletin de la Maison Franco-Japonaise* (Tokyo), Vol. II, Nos. 3–4, 1930.

4. Marcel Granet discusses this association in his *Danses et Légendes de la Chine Ancienne* (Paris: Librairie Félix Alcan, 1926), II, 516–37.

5. *Pile* is the technical term for a bundle of pieces of wrought iron to be worked over into bars by being rolled or hammered at a welding heat.

6. Shigenaka Shimohara (ed.), *Tetsuzan Hisho* (*Arcane Book for the Ironworkers*), pp. 3–11. MS dated 1784; published as a supplement to *Korai no Satetsu Seiren-hō*.

7. See Kunio Yanagita, "Sumiyaki Kogorō ga Koto ("On the Stories of Charcoal-maker Kogorō"), *Kainan Shōki* (Some Notes on the Southwestern Islands) (Tokyo: Ōokayama Shoten, 1925), pp. 233–312. This study by Yanagita is explained in detail in my article "La Légende de Kokoro le Charbonnier."

(TRANSLATOR'S NOTE: Hachiman was first worshipped at Usa in Kyūshū, hypothetically as a god of the forge. Later [in the ninth century] he was enshrined in Kyoto, the capital city, and revered as the protecting deity of the city. Then he became the tutelary deity of the powerful warrior clan of Genji and was subsequently worshiped as a god of war. Still later, he became enshrined in many farming and other villages throughout the country. The name Hachiman means, literally, "eight banners." Yanagita's explanation of the Kogorō legend is summarized as follows. The story of Kogorō the Charcoal-maker developed into its present form at the time when charcoal-making was generally considered to be mean work. Yet it can be inferred that this story has its roots in the belief associating charcoal burning with the mysterious power which controls fire. Charcoal-making required a special technique, and the chief use of charcoal was for melting metal. It must have been the group of metalworkers, that is to say the itinerant blacksmiths, who originated the Kogorō legend and carried it to various places. This story has been told as a part of the cycle of Mano Chōja [The Rich Man Mano] which flourished in Bungo province (present Oita-ken in Kyūshū), where until recently a large number of charcoal-makers resided. This version of the legend tells that Kogorō the charcoal-maker was in a former life the Mano Chōja who prospered in this province. The story of this rich man appears to have a special relation to the famous Hachiman Shrine of Usa located at a place adjoining Bungo province. According to a version of the tale which appears as an episode in a medieval ballad, Mano Chōja had a graceful daughter named Tamayo. Enamored of her outstanding beauty, the emperor disguised himself as a humble mower and traveled alone to the province where she lived. One time when Mano Chōja was presiding at the celebration of Hachiman Shrine, he announced that whoever could perform the traditional rite of arrow-shooting should marry his daughter; the mower came forward and successfully shot two arrows. As he was about to shoot the third arrow, the shrine began to tremble, and the great deity Hachiman appeared to pay his respects to the emperor in the guise of a mower. Filled with reverence, the rich man offered his daughter to the emperor.

Now, the heroine's name, Tamayo, is derived from *tama-yori* which means "the one possessed by a spirit or deity," a term used to designate female deities. Most of the shrines where the female deities of this name are worshiped, for example the famous Kamo Shrine in Kyoto, perpetuate the legend of the marriage between the great divinity and a human virgin, or of the mythical birth of a child deity from a virgin. One of the three divinities enshrined at Hachiman Shrine of Usa, which is the birthplace of the cult of Hachiman, is called Tamayori-hime [Princess Tamayori]; and, although no story has been transmitted which tells of her, the fact that the belief in a young or princely deity has been very conspicuous in the cult of Hachiman suggests that there once existed a legend of a mythical marriage of this female deity and the resulting birth of young Hachiman; furthermore, the stories of the unusual marriage of Kogorō and of the daughter of Mano Chōja are probably derived from this no longer extant legend. Moreover, it may be inferred that the cult of Hachiman was generated on the basis of belief in the god of tranquil fire, represented by charcoal fire. This cult stands in contrast to that of the Kamo Shrine, in which flashing fire is venerated as the thunder god, a child of the great sun god, born of a human virgin.)

8. Both Miao tales have been summarized from Ling Shun-sheng and Ruey Yih-fu, *The Miao Tribe of Western China* (The Institute of History and Philology of the Academia Sinica, Monograph Series A, No. 18 [Shanghai, 1947]), pp. 257–65.

9. Wolfram Eberhard, *Chinese Festivals* (New York: Abelard-Schuman, 1952), p. 22.

10. This sekihan (or red rice) is an uncommon food, which is cooked only on special days or upon ceremonial occasions, such as festival days and anniversaries.

11. This tale is paraphased from Kunihiko Uchida's *Nansō no Rizoku (Folk Customs from the Middle Part of Chiba-ken)* (Tokyo: Ōsetsu Shoten, 1915), pp. 100–103.

12. Taichu, *Ryukyu Shindo-ki (Memoir on Shintoism in the Ryukyus)* (Tokyo: Ōokayama Shoten, 1936), pp. 95–96. First published in Kyoto, 1648. Quoted in Yanagita. Taichu was a Buddhist priest, 1552–1639, who used the pen name Benrensha Ryotei.

13. See, for example, Yanagita, "Ashikari to Kamado-gami" ("Reed-Reaper and Hearth Deity"), *Kainan Shōki*, pp. 140–44.

14. This story is retold from J. Przyluski's "La Princesse à l'Odeur de Poisson et la Naga, dans les Traditions de l'Asie Orientale," *Etudes Asiatiques* (Paris), I (1925), 269.

15. *Sangoku Iji (Memoir on Three Kingdoms: Silla, Pekche, and Kokuryo)* (Edited and published by Chōsen Shigaku-kai [Korean Society of History] [Seoul, 1929]), II, 34–35. This work was originally compiled by Ichiren, a Buddhist priest during the era of King Churetsu of Kokuryo (1275–97). These kingdoms existed from the beginning of the fourth to the middle of the seventh century.

16. See Yanagita, "Kaijin Shōdo" ("The Little Boy Sea Deity"), *Momotarō no Tanjō (The Birth of Momotarō the Peach Boy)* (Tokyo: Sansei-dō, 1942), pp. 54–119.

17. The Miao custom is described in Hu P'u-an (ed.), *Chung-hua ch'uan-kuo feng-su chih (Customs in all of China)* (Shanghai: Ta-ta t'u-shu kung-ying she, 1935), Vol. VI, Book 2, p. 30. For the similar Thai customs as found in Yunan province see An Ko-ming (ed.), *Chung-kuo shao-shu min-tsu feng-kuang (Customs of Minority Peoples in China)* (Hong Kong: Hsueh-wen shu-tien, 1955), p. 122.

信者

PART FIVE | WORSHIPERS

The Double-Grave System

BY TAKAYOSHI MOGAMI

Discovery of the obscure custom of double burial has thrown some light on ancient Japanese ideas of death and the soul. The double-grave system in Japan first received the attention of scholars in 1919, when a report on burial customs appeared in the journal *Minzoku to Rekishi (Ethnos and History)*. Two more papers concerning burial customs were printed in this journal in the next four years,[1] and in 1929 Kunio Yanagita published an article, "The Development of Funeral Customs," in which he attempted, for the first time, to discover our ancestors' ideas concerning the spirits of the departed.[2] The next year, Kōtarō Tsujii published a discussion of the double-grave system as practiced in the whole area of the Iga basin.[3] From 1934 on, as surveys into remote areas and mountain villages were carried out under Yanagita's superintendence, the double-grave system found in various regions became the object of much folk-loristic interest.[4] Tokuzo Omachi, who had worked on the mountain-village study, wrote several articles on the custom.[5] During the war years the study of this and other subjects was necessarily discontinued. At the close of the war, however, the research was renewed, and such investigations as those by Kaoru Ishikawa, in the Mino district in Gifu-ken,[6] and Isamu Isogai, around the Tamba district in Kyōto-fu,[7] covered fairly wide areas.

While the above-mentioned field studies in the mountain villages were being carried out, I visited the districts of Ise and Iga, where the double-grave system is conspicuously evident. Since 1949 I have undertaken a special inquiry into the double-grave system in many regions of Japan. The results of my study were first published in a summary article,[8] and subsequently appeared in book form. In the following paragraphs I would like to summarize the subjects treated in those studies, to discuss what has been accomplished up to the present time, and to suggest what remains for further inquiry.

In the so-called double-grave system two tombs are erected for the same person, one where the dead body is buried and the other where memorial services are offered for the departed soul. The Japanese terms are *ume-baka* (burial grave) and *mairi-baka* (memorial tomb where the dead person is revered).[9] The mairi-baka, to all outward appearances, resembles the ume-baka, for both possess the same type of burial marker, which is generally a tombstone. The term *mairi-baka* is used by scholars to distinguish the memorial tomb from the ume-baka, but the local terms used for the mairi-baka vary in the different regions where the system is practiced. In many areas, the term is made by adding a qualifier to the stem *baka* (the combining form of *haka,* "grave"); for example: *kiyo-baka* (consecrated grave) and *matsuri-baka* (ritual grave). In other locations the word *haka* or *bochi* (graveyard), without further qualification, is used for both the burial grave and the memorial grave, which is visited. Formerly, scholars considered the double-grave system to be a rather unusual practice found only in a few areas, but thorough investigation has shown its wide distribution extends over a large part of the country, save for the urban centers. Particularly in the Kinki district, center of the earliest civilization in Japan, and the neighboring areas, evidence of the existence and spread of this custom is quite clear. In the western halves of the Chūgoku and Shikoku districts, in all of Kyūshū, and throughout the northeastern part of Japan (all far removed from Kinki) the double-grave system is, however, rarely found.

The forms of the ume-baka and mairi-baka, and the practices connected with them, have gradually become known to scholars. In regular burial practice, the haka is the place where the corpse is buried, where ritual performances for the dead are carried on, and where the spirit of the deceased is believed to repose. In the double-grave system these functions are divided between ume-baka and mairi-baka, but the precise function assigned to each differs according to local custom. Through the study of these practices we may find a clue to our forefathers' belief in the spirits of the dead, and in particular, to their ideas on the relationship of spirit to the dead body.

There appear to be three separate types of the double-grave system presently functioning. In the first of these, visits to the ume-baka may completely cease after the burial ceremony is held. In most cases, however, the mourners will visit the ume-baka on certain special occasions when services are to be performed, until a prescribed period of mourning has expired. The length of this period will vary according to locality. After the termination of this period the people will wholly refrain from visiting the ume-baka.

In the second type of observance, visits to the ume-baka occur even after the termination of the mourning period, on special occasions such as Bon and Higan.[10] In one variation of this type, only those directly involved in the services for the departed spirit—close relatives and the Buddhist priests—visit the ume-baka after the expiration of the mourning period. (There is yet another case in which the people, while they continue to visit the ume-baka, also visit the mairi-baka on special occasions, such as Bon, Higan, and Buddha's birthday, April eighth.[11] This would seem to be a reverse form, but its pattern is basically that of the second type of practice; for in this case, too, the ume-baka is visited during the period of mourning for the new spirit that has just departed from the buried body.)

In the third form of the double-grave system, the people continue to visit the ume-baka even after the period of mourning has expired and the mairi-baka is established. In other words, the ume-baka and the mairi-baka are treated in the same manner on all occasions.

These three types of the double-grave system appear to indicate three successive stages of deterioration. In the earliest or fundamental stage, all visits to the ume-baka cease after the time for mourning has ended; in the second stage, visits to the ume-baka occur on special occasions after the mourning period has come to a close; and in the third or degenerate type, no distinction is made between the observances involving the ume-baka and those involving the mairi-baka.

Various opinions have been expressed concerning the origin of the double-grave system. Most scholars agree that this system originated because of the abomination felt for the unclean corpse. Our ancestors intended to honor the purified spirit on clean ground some distance from the grave where the corpse was interred, hence the institution of the mairi-baka. However, it seems that the early Japanese considered the soul purified only when the body was completely reduced to a skeleton. When the period of purification had passed, the soul was worshiped at a new and undefiled place removed from the corpse.

The question arising at this point is why a separate, new ground is required for the memorial service when the purification of the corpse itself is recognized with its skeletonization? One important factor bearing on this question is the use of a common burial cemetery in a community. In rural areas, it often occurs that each buraku, or kinship group, has its own small burial ground. In the earliest civilized districts, the ground available to the common people for such an unproductive purpose was extremely limited. In these circumstances an old burial plot was used, after a period of time, for the burial of a new corpse. Variations of the custom exist: The common cemetery may be loosely divided among the village families, or the apportionment to each family can be marked out, with each individual grave distinguished from the others. These practices may be the result of later developments. The ancient cemetery was intended for common use; accordingly, an old burial ground had to be dug up again for a new corpse in the course of time. Such a grave had only a transitory mark on it, such as an earth mound or a stone from the river bank, which was usually reduced to nothing or lost after a short period of time. Hence, the burial ground could not long be identified as the resting place for any individual corpse. Although an individual corpse was purified after a proper lapse of time, the burial plot itself remained polluted because other corpses were constantly being buried nearby. For this reason a new, unpolluted ground distant from the actual cemetery was required as a place to honor the spirit.

On the other hand, the nobility and the propertied class, who had emerged by the early Middle Ages ar d who possessed large areas of land, could provide sufficient ground for each individual grave and could use the true grave as the site for memorial services. In studying the burial systems in Japan, historians have so far dealt only with the tombs of those individuals who belonged to the noble class and consequently have ignored the existence of the double-grave system. Further, among the common people in the districts of comparatively recent development, where the people have been allowed to make use of larger tracts of land, each family has secured its own cemetery, and each individual grave has been separately marked by a tombstone. This is one of the primary reasons why the majority of the villages in the northeastern and southwestern parts of Japan, which were settled much later than the Kinki district, have only the single-grave system.

In the second type of double-grave system discussed, wherein visits to the ume-baka occur on special occasions although the mourning period has ended, the ume-baka is believed to be the place where the spirit of the deceased stays even after the mairi-baka is established. Thus, the mairi-baka does not become the permanent home for the departed spirit. The mairi-baka is visited at ordinary times for the purpose of worshiping the spirit at a clean place. On special occasions, such as Bon and Higan, when the spirits of the forefathers are invited to the home, the family goes to the ume-baka to meet the spirits at the beginning of the festival and leads them back to it at the end of the celebration. In other words, although the site of the memorial service is moved from the ume-baka to the mairi-baka, the spirit itself is thought to remain within the ume-baka.

As for the third type of the double-grave system, the degenerate form in which both graves are treated in the same manner on all occasions, a more detailed explanation is hardly necessary. Clearly, it is unreasonable to build two graves which are treated in the same way; therefore, the emergence of this third type may have been caused by the collapse of the original form. As the burial yard in the original, communal form came to be divided among individual households, and as permanent tomb-markers were erected for individual persons, it became a custom to pay visits to those burial graves as well as to the mairi-baka on every ceremonial occasion.

Furthermore, the importance of the mairi-baka diminished as the site of the memorial service was gradually neglected, and finally the double-grave system was supplanted by the single-grave system. Another degenerative process appears in the tendency to bury the corpse in the mairi-baka. The result is that the ume-baka is forgotten in the course of time. A rare example is available in which the ume-baka and the mairi-baka are both utilized for the same purpose. In this case, the two tombs are used alternately for burial, both serving as permanent graves. Hence, each household is in possession of two graveyards, but only one grave is allotted to each person.

As has been stated, the custom of visiting the ume-baka during a certain prescribed period of mourning after the burial cermony is always observed. The length of this period may vary considerably from one part of the country to another. In some locations the burial grave is visited only on the day of the burial or the day following. In other areas, the mourning period may range from three to seven, thirty-five, forty-nine, or a hundred days or even to a year, four or five years, thirteen years, thirty-three years, and fifty years.

There are two theories concerning the original length of the mourning period. According to one theory, the earliest practice was to visit the ume-baka only at the time of the burial and to confine all subsequent visits to the mairi-baka. This is suggested by the ancient belief in the immediate separation of the spirit from the body after death, as demonstrated by the surviving custom of calling out the name of someone who has just died to keep his spirit from leaving the body. Furthermore, the corpse itself was regarded as something unclean, and this feeling is reflected in certain local terms for "burial" (*nageru,* "to throw away"; *suteru,* "to abandon") and "burial grave" (*hafuru,* "to throw"; *nagesho,* "a place where things are thrown out"; *suteba* "a place where things are abandoned"). Thus, according to the first theory, the period of mourning originally lasted for a very short while; as time passed, this period was prolonged more and more, the length of time varying according to the district in which the custom was practiced.

There is a second theory which seems to me to be more valid. The old practice of *mogari* among the nobility,[12] the custom of confinement in the mourning house which was practiced among the common people up to recent years, and the custom of *chūin,*[13] a mourning period of forty-nine days, which still prevails over wide areas, support the idea of a quite opposite transition, namely, from a long to a short observance of the mourning period. All of these customs, current in ancient times, called for the close relatives of the dead to avoid physical contact and intercourse with other individuals while they were waiting for the soul of the dead one gradually to become purified and go to eternal repose. During this time, the relatives were considered to be in an unclean and unsafe condition, since they had been in contact with the polluted corpse. It appears that the period of mourning, or waiting for the soul to be purified, has been reduced in more recent years, and the taboos have been moderated. The common people, due to their daily working requirements, cannot remain in seclusion and confinement for such long periods. Except where the controlling force of the community has been so great that the household under confinement is looked after by the other members of the community, this custom has seldom been preserved. The forty-nine-day mourning period of chūin was shortened to seven days, then to three, and at last to merely the day of the funeral.

The introduction of the custom of cremation also influenced the reduction of the mourning period. This custom is particularly prevalent in the urban areas and in the regions where the Shin sect of Buddhism is current. The purification of the corpse, which is attained after a relatively long time in the case of interment, is completed in one night in the case of cremation. Since the purification is accomplished in a short time, the mourning taboo is also quickly relaxed. The site of the cremation has the same character as the ume-baka, in that both are places where the purification of the corpse is accomplished. The ashes of the dead are usually buried at the location in the graveyard where the cremation has taken place, and it is here, rather than at a mairi-baka, that the memorial services are held for the spirit after the short period of mourning. These practices suggest that the custom of cremation has taken on characteristics of the single-grave rather than the double-grave system.

The custom of reburial is another case which supports the theory that originally a comparatively long mourning period was observed. Faint survivals of reburial can still be seen scattered throughout the country, particularly in the Satsuma Peninsula, in several villages on the eastern coast of Kyūshū, and on the island of Tsushima. It is also found sporadically on the coast of Kishū and Bōshū, on Hachijō-jima, and very rarely in the inland area of the mainland. According to this custom, the corpse is removed from the original burial grave after it has been reduced to a skeleton, and is reburied in a new ground where the memorial services are thereafter performed. This practice resembles the double-grave system in the point that two graves are used for one individual, but in the case of reburial both graves are given the functions of ume-baka and mairi-baka. The necessity of reburying the purified skeleton in a new place probably arises, as in the double-grave system itself, from the use of a common community cemetery.

A variation of the reburial system is the carrying of a handful of earth taken from the ume-baka to the mairi-baka when the latter is established. This custom is found over a wide area. In some areas, incorruptible pieces of the body, such as teeth or bones which have been kept for this purpose, or some other matter closely connected with the corpse, are buried in the mairi-baka, and the body itself is left in the ume-baka. Consideration of these traditional customs has led me to the following conclusion: The tendency to regard the spirit as immediately separated from the dead body and to ignore the corpse quite soon after burial is not part of the original burial practice, but results from the shortening of the mourning period.

A question often discussed is when and in what way the double-grave system actually appeared in Japanese history. It is not easy to find an accurate answer to this question through the study of folklore materials. We can only point out that the custom of erecting the mairi-baka, as found today, seems already to have existed somewhat before the sixteenth century, when the mairi-baka was a monument type of tombstone—one for each individual in each household—placed in sacred ground, such as the compound of a temple. The monuments called *itabi* and *gorin-no-tō*,[14] which were probably put up for departed souls in earlier times, may have been erected also in such a sacred cemetery.

The most primitive form of burial ground found today is

an area used in common in one community. Earth mounds, stones from the river bed, or bamboo sticks are used to mark the burial spot, where close relatives may come during the mourning period to pray for the dead. At the present time, one can see stone monuments exhibiting carved phrases from the Buddhist sutras, stone statues of Jizō, or small temples called Kannan-dō or Jizō-dō, standing adjacent to the common burial cemetery.[15] These monuments were probably worshiped in memorial services by the people who visited the cemetery. In this sense these monuments corresponded to the mairi-baka of the present. In fact, as it became customary to build a permanent monument for each departed soul of each household on the ground around such a monument or temple, the monument also assumed the function of the mairi-baka.

The community monument was not necessarily built next to the burial ground. One supposes that, during ancient times, the unclean communal ume-baka was naturally located in a desolate place—on a mountain, in a waste field, on the river bank, or on the seashore. On the other hand, the site of the common memorial ceremony is believed to have been always a plot of ground selected for reasons of purity and convenience. Sometimes a small temple or pagoda was established, and, if the region were not under the influence of Buddhism, probably a small shrine was built. In earlier times, trees were planted to form a grove, which then became a shrine.

The idea has spread widely that the spirits of the dead become tutelary deities when the series of Buddhist-style memorial services is completed in the thirty-third or the fiftieth year after death. In many places these are considered to be the particular deities of the household and are enshrined not far from the house. In ancient times, before the mairi-baka appeared, these deities were probably worshiped on the same sacred ground where the spirits of the dead, which had been purified in due course of time, were honored. In later days, some of these sacred areas may have developed into the cemeteries which accommodated many mairi-baka. This might have been the beginning of the second form of the double-grave institution in which the ume-baka and the mairi-baka are located at some distance from each other.

There are some villages where the double-grave system appears to have developed rather recently. One such case is a buraku which had formerly possessed a single common cemetery at some distance from the village. As the buraku expanded, new homes were built near the cemetery. A new cemetery—for ume-baka—was established at a more distant place, and the old cemetery came to be used as the site for mairi-baka. There is another case in which the double-grave system had been practiced in a buraku, with the ume-baka and the mairi-baka lying side by side; but a new burial cemetery came to be needed farther away, owing to an increase in population, and both of the old graveyards were then used as mairi-baka cemeteries. In such recent developments, the modern regard for sanitation rather than the taboo against the pollution of death has been the compelling motive in the separation of the ume-baka and the mairi-baka.

Notes

1. Katsuzo Takeda, "Tsushima Kisaka Chihō no San-goya to Rinbo" ("Concerning the Hut for Childbirth and Round Stonepile Tomb in Kisaka District in Tsushima Island"), *Minzoku to Rekishi (Ethnos and History)* (Tokyo), Vol. II, No. 3 (September), 1929; Yoshinaga Tamura, "Rantōba" ("Graveyard"), *Minzoku to Rekishi*, Vol. V, No. 3 (March), 1921; Keika Takahashi, "Bochi Igai ni Shitai

o Hōmuru Fūshū" ("The Custom of Burying Corpses in Other Places than the Graveyard"), *Shakai-shi Kenkyū (The Story of Social History)*, Vol. X, No. 1 (July), 1923.

2. "Sōsei no Enkaku ni tsuite" ("The Development of Funeral Customs") *Jinruigaku Zasshi (Journal of the Anthropological Society of Tokyo)*, Vol. XLIV, No. 6, 1929, pp. 295 ff.

3. "Iga-bonchi ni okeru Bochi no Chiri-teki Kosatsu" ("Geographical Observations on the Graveyards in Iga Basin"), *Chikyū (Earth)*, Vol. XIV, No. 6 (December), 1930.

4. The survey of mountain villages throughout Japan was undertaken by the members of the Institute of Local Life Study, under the leadership of Kunio Yanagita, from 1934 to 1937. The result of this investigation was published in Tokyo in 1937 and was translated and edited by Masanori Takatsuka and George K. Brady as *Studies in Mountain Village Life* (University of Kentucky Press Microcards Series A, *Modern Language Series*, No. 2 [1954]).

5. "Ryobo-sei no Shiryo" ("Report on the Double-Grave System"), in Kunio Yanagita (ed.), *Sanson Seikatsu Chōsa (Studies in Mountain Village Life)* (Tokyo: Hajime Shuzui, 1936), II, 72 ff.; and "Bo-sei Oboe-gaki" ("Notes on the Grave System"), *Kōzu no Hana-shogatsu (The New Year Festival in Kōzu Island)* (Tokyo: Rokunin Sha, 1934), pp. 265 ff.

6. *Chu-No no Minzoku-gyoji ni tsuite (On the Traditional Customs in the Central Part of Mino Province)* (Mimeographed pamphlet, Gifu City, 1951).

7. "Tanba Chihō oyobi sono Shūhen ni okeru Ryōbo-sei ni tsuite" ("On the Double-Grave System in Tanba Province and its Vicinity"), *Ayabe Kōkō Kenkyū Kiyō (Bulletin of Ayabe High School)* (Ayabe City, Kyoto Prefecture), 1955.

8. This article "Ryōbo-sei ni tsuite" ("On the Double-Grave System") appeared in *Minzokugaku Kenkyū (Studies in Folklore)* (Annual Report of the Folklore Society of Japan) (Tokyo), II (1951), 1–34.

9. The grave is not the only place where the spirit of the dead is honored. There are the Buddhist altars in each house, regular shrines and temples, and temporary altars at Bon time, where memorial services for the departed spirits are performed.

10. Bon is the period of several days before and after the fifteenth of July, when each household honors the ancestral spirits, setting an altar called Bondana in the principal room or verandah. The ancestral tablets are placed on the altar and various foods are offered to

the spirits. Higan is the week including either the vernal or autumnal equinox. Generally it is the occasion when Japanese visit the family graves.

11. In some districts, for instance in a part of the Kansai area, people visit the family graves on April eighth, Buddha's birthday.

12. Mogari is an old custom no longer observed, which was practiced by the nobility in ancient times. During a fixed period following a death, the close relatives of the dead person were secluded in a ceremonial place watching the body. The body was buried after this period expired.

13. The forty-nine days following the death of a person is the mourning period called *chūin*. During this period close relatives of the dead live under social restrictions and devote themselves to the services for the dead, making offerings and praying for the peace of the soul.

14. *Itabi* means literally "board monument," although actually it is a monument made of a flat stone resembling a board. A gorin-no-tō is a kind of five-storied stone monument, constructed of five differently shaped stones which symbolize sky, wind, fire, water, and earth.

15. Kannon is a Buddhist deity of mercy, who is sometimes represented as many-handed; Jizō is also a Buddhist deity of mercy, who especially helps the souls of the dead; a *dō* is a small temple or a hut honoring the deity.

The Concept of Tamashii in Japan

BY NARIMITSU MATSUDAIRA

Tamashii (soul or spirit) is the nuclear idea of the early Japanese religion. In the organized creed of Shintoism the kami (deity or spirit) is the central concept; however, when we investigate the folk beliefs and traditional rites practiced among the common people of Japanese villages, it becomes clear that, in fact, they presuppose a supernatural entity resembling but yet distinguishable from kami—that which is called *tamashii*. Through studies synthesizing the data reported by ethnologists and folklorists, the Japanese idea of the universe can be dimly reconstructed. This idea has probably been transmitted from primitive times, although an abstract idea of this sort cannot be attributed to a certain fixed period. It existed before, and now coexists with, the diffusion of scientific knowledge. This concept might not have been supported wholly by all the people in the past, and it is not thoroughly extinct in present-day Japan. Japanese scholars have tried to discover the pattern of such popular beliefs, and in this paper I am going to describe the concept of tamashii, as determined by those investigations.

What is tamashii? According to Japanese belief, everyone has a tamashii within his body. Senses, judgment, thinking, feelings of joy, resentment, pleasure and sorrow—all of these may be considered the operations of the tamashii. The tamashii is, so to speak, a force which brings about the psychological reactions in man.

A tamashii, moreover, often has the same attributes as a kami. *Kami* may be translated as "god" or "goddess" (although the Japanese conception of kami is far different from the Western conception of God). A kami, a higher and purer spirit, is neither visible nor tangible. Tamashii can assume a definite form when it so desires; usually it becomes an appalling monster or a frightening ghost. When tamashii does not take such a specific form, it moves in the air in the shape of a small ball and shines in the darkness. This is called *hito-dama* (man's tamashii). It also resembles a kami in that it may take possession of a man or an object it meets along the way.

The greatest difference between tamashii and kami is that the former, although able to move about independently, always dwells in a living body for a certain period. During this time, it commands the body at will and attains its own desires. At the same time, tamashii is greatly influenced by the flesh. When the flesh feels hungry, the tamashii feels hungry; when the flesh is gratified, so is the tamashii. The action of a man is decided by the operations of both the tamashii and the flesh. When a man dies, his tamashii will sorrow over any mistreatment of the corpse. This shows the lingering influence of the relationship between the tamashii and the flesh. As a rule, only after the death and the disintegration of the body does the indwelling tamashii leave and begin its own activities. There are many such floating tamashii in the universe, which have been separated from bodies. They are waiting for the opportunity to enter the bodies with which they meet, to dwell in and act on them. As a result, a person may be possessed with many tamashii at one time. In this case, several spirits do not dwell separately in a man but are fused into one, just as the water in two vessels becomes one entity when one vessel is emptied into the other. If the tamashii that are blended have different natures, the nature of the new tamashii is derived from the mixture of all of them and acquires so strong a power that it may not be easily affected or overpowered by another tamashii it encounters.

Tamashii is imperceptible, dwells in an object or in a man, gives it or him its own nature, and has the liberty to appear, disappear, transform itself, and fly. Moreover, it has a power that no human being can resist. A tamashii upsets the laws of nature, interferes with the movement of the universe, influences the fate of men, and foresees all phenomena in the future. An evil spirit can inflict injury, exhaustion, or even death on a person who passes his haunts; he can change the weather, perhaps even raise a thunderstorm that lasts a month. Thus, a tamashii appears to have much the same nature and substance as a kami. In fact, the action of transferring a kami to a sacred tree such as the sakaki is called *mi-tama-utsushi* (literally, "transferring of a spirit"), and the thing to which a kami is transferred is called *mi-tama-shiro* (a thing on which the tamashii rests). The people sometimes speak of *nigi-mi-tama* (a gentle or benevolent spirit) or *saki-tama* (a spirit which blesses, *saki* implying happiness) as kinds of kami. (*Tama* and *tamashii* are synonymous.)

The spirit that dwells in a living body is usually a tamashii, not a kami, because the influence of the flesh upon the spirit is too great. However, the tamashii inhabiting a human body is in the process of becoming a kami. There seems to be a continuous cycle of spiritual development and change, in which spirit in its two aspects circulates between heaven and human bodies on earth. Under favorable conditions, the spirit that has fully matured within a body will ascend to heaven after the death of the body and eventually become a kami. When these spirits prosper and overflow heaven, they descend to earth, enter bodies of newborn babies, and repeat the life of this world as tamashii.

In general, the nutritious elements which promote the growth of spirit are the very elements that a person employs for his food, clothing, and housing. Especially effective are those materials which contain divine elements, such as consecrated food prepared by clean persons, or water drawn from a purified spring. While a spirit dwells in a man, and after it leaves him, as well, an important opportunity for partaking of divine food is provided by a festival or a ritual: an occasion when the spirits of the dead and the living meet and feast together. People attend a festival to nourish the tamashii that dwells within them.

The different attitudes toward age groups stem from this idea. Aged people are respected not only because they have lived long, but also because their spirits have accomplished a satisfactory growth and come to resemble kami after taking nourishment at many festivals. Until the end of World War II the Japanese used to add a year to their ages after the New Year festival in the winter. This custom also proceeded from the idea that spiritual growth occurred after the festival. Anyone, regardless of his age, who served kami more frequently than did an ordinary person possessed a spirit that had grown to be almost a kami itself, because he had taken so much divine nourishment.

A tamashii that has been freed from the body through

death becomes either a raging spirit or a calm spirit, de-
pending on the psychological state of the man at the moment
of death. When such passions as resentment, jealous love,
and melancholy have kept burning in a man up to his last
breath, his spirit becomes a very dangerous being, for the
spirit that has lost its body must remain forever in the pas-
sionate state it was in at the time of death. This spirit strug-
gles to flee from the incessant convulsion of its passions. As
a result, the spirit wields its special power against, and does
injury to, anybody whom it meets in its path, and forces him
to cooperate. It then becomes a foe of society.

The tamashii of a person who died in the melancholy
state of solitude is comparatively calm; but when it learns
of the mistreatment of the body in which it used to dwell,
it grieves greatly and frightens someone in order to exact
his help. If this request is rejected, the spirit dares even to
injure him.

Raging spirits are considered very dangerous to society by
the mass of the village people and need to be placated, paci-
fied, or appeased by any means. One way to accomplish this
end is to subdue the angry spirit through the help of a strong
deity, who can neutralize its evil character. The purpose of
harai (a type of purification ceremony in Shintoism) is not
only to honor the deity with divine utensils and divine food,
but also to subdue dangerous spirits. People attempt to
store the power of kami in various places, such as at the
family altars, in the foods offered at altars, and even in their
own bodies through the eating of the ritual food and
through ritual purification. The kami make their visitations
in numbers on the occasion of public festivals and private
rituals. If the living, through the power obtained from the
kami, can drive away the evil spirits continually thronging
about them, they may indeed achieve peace of mind and a
sense of security.

The best means of protection, however, is to console and

soothe the raging spirit, and let it ascend to heaven. For that purpose the people often hold a banquet and dedicate the feast to evil spirits. Thus the evil spirits are deified as kami. How many shrines have been built for such revengeful spirits! The people enshrine the spirit that rages too dangerously as a *waka-miya* (young deity) or as the son of a strong deity, just as they put mischievous children into the custody of a great teacher. After the lapse of many years, the spirit's evils are forgotten, and it comes to be revered as a benevolent deity. Tenjin-sama[1] is the best example of this sort.

It sometimes happens that the raging spirit escapes a living body and vents its special violence. This happens when a person's emotions become aroused to such an extent that they cannot be soothed. Such a spirit is feared as *iki-ryō* (the spirit of the living); its action does not differ basically from that of *shi-ryō* or *shi-rei* (the spirit of the dead), except that it is transitory and will re-enter the body when its violence has subsided.

What will happen to the spirit of a man whose last moment is peaceful? It ascends to heaven and becomes one of the tutelary deities. But this requires further explanation. The spirit of a man who dies young writhes as much as an evil spirit. Its agony is all the stronger because it is still immature, is bound by various desires and passions, and is reluctant to give up the things of this world. On the other hand, the spirit of a baby, which is still godlike, and the spirit of an old man, which becomes godlike again through having reached full maturity, are not disturbed by passions, and they are not particularly discomposed at the time of their death. Such spirits ascend to heaven most easily and become members of the society of tutelary deities.

So long as the phenomenon of death is so abominated by man, a spirit of the dead cannot visit a person without caus-

ing agitation of mind. Every such spirit is therefore considered dangerous to society. People must be on special
guard against these spirits, and they should provide some
assistance to both the dying and the bereaved. The readiest
way is to console and soothe the spirit of the dead by offering up an abundance of nourishments. When somebody
dies he is offered rice and many other kinds of food beside
his pillow and before his tomb. All the relatives and ac-
quaintances gather together and hold a wake for at least
a week to console his spirit by reciting sutras, singing chants,
and staging festive banquets every night. All of these practices are intended to assuage the spirit and to pray for its
smooth ascent to heaven. Sometimes a sedge hat, a pair of
sandals and a stick are placed in the coffin for the preparation of the journey of the dead. In some extreme cases people put these traveling outfits in front of a half-opened door
one night during the wake, and sweep them out of the house
with a broom. Sometimes the mourners destroy objects
cherished by the dead, such as the cup he used in daily life.
This action serves to cut off the lingering affection that the
spirit might retain towards this world, to precipitate its
ascent to heaven, and to guard against its straying back to
this world.

Those relatives who are near the corpse need to take special precautions. They should take in a part of the spirit of
the dead, blend it with their own spirits, and transmute the
nature of their spirits into the likeness of the spirit of the
dead. Then the dead can accept their offerings and services
with ease, just as a kami is pleased with the service of a man
who is, himself, like the kami. The spirits of the dead will
not attack another spirit of the same nature. This blending
of spirits may be accomplished if the close relatives partake
of the same food that is offered to the spirit of the dead. Not
only the relatives of the dead but also those who work near

the corpse are required to take such food. Also, it is said that those who eat the rice which is served at the time of the funeral will not become ill.

Those who have had contact with the corpse, however, are then regarded by other men as being fully as dangerous as the spirit itself, and are shunned accordingly, for their spirits have already been transmuted into the likeness of the spirits of the deceased. This is why those who serve deities avoid the unclean fire in the house of a person who has recently died. The *tōya* and *toshiyori* of a *miyaza*[2] do not cease to perform their holy works even when their relatives die, but they are prohibited from attending the funeral of any man, even a close relative, or from taking food with a bereaved family. Only if they are mindful of these prohibitions will they be unaffected by the uncleanness of death. A priest who is engaged in dealing with corpses—sitting by the bed, burning incense, chanting sutras, praying for the soul's peace—is abhorred by kami even if he is not a relative of the dead.

The spirit that has undergone a severe shock at the time of death is gradually soothed and then continues to grow. Having parted from flesh, it is a free spirit. But it can hardly sever the strings of attachment to the body in which it dwelt for a long time. So it often lingers around the corpse, lamenting over the perishing body and thus hindering its own appeasement and growth. The attachment extends also to the house where it once lived. It is commonly said that the spirit of the dead does not leave the house for forty-nine days.

Consequently, the ritual nourishment is supplied both at the house and at the tomb of the dead. The food to be offered is basically the same as that for the living. The spirit is supposed to eat rice, drink *sake,* wear kimonos, appreciate music, and enjoy dancing. People hope the spirit of the dead will be soothed by these pleasures and ascend to heaven.

The food offerings for the dead differ in some ways from the regular repasts of the living; for instance, the Japanese thrust a pair of chopsticks into the bowl of boiled rice prepared for the dead, an act tabooed for the living. Similarly, a bedside screen is erected upside down near the head of the deceased, and hot water is added to the cold, not vice versa as is usually done, to moderate the temperature of the water with which the body of a dead person is washed. All these reversals of regular custom are intended to emphasize the contrast between life and death.

Many of these practices may have been the products of Buddhist influence.[3] The most striking among them is the omission of *sake* and meat from the offerings to the dead.[4] It is difficult to know how the spirits were treated before the coming of Buddhism to Japan. To my great regret, the only thing I can say positively is that the forms of the memorial service for the dead have not been entirely changed by Buddhism.

It is generally supposed by scholars of the subject that the life before death corresponds to the life after death as regards the growth of the spirit. In both cycles, the spirit passes through similar stages. In the past, the following rituals celebrated the stages of growth during a given person's lifetime. The *ubu-yu* ritual (in which a newborn baby is given its first bath) is held right after the birth of the baby. *Miya-mairi* (to go to the shrine of the tutelary deity) is performed a week after the baby's birth. The *umare-go* ritual (the ritual for the newborn baby) is held at the first winter festival following its birth. *Kodomo-iri* (to join the company of children) is held when the child reaches the age of seven. When the youth becomes fifteen, he passes through the initiation ceremony called *genpuku,* which is also known in the villages of *wakashū-iri* (literally, "to join the company of adolescents"). *Chūrō-iri* (to join the company of the elderly) is a rite administered to a man around the age of forty, and *otona-iri,* "to become one of the headmen or leaders," the final rite of passage, comes when he has reached sixty.

A second set of rituals is observed during the thirty-three years following death. *Yukan* (to wash the body of the dead) takes place right after death; *sōsō* (the funeral) is held within several days after death; *kuyō* and *furumai* (a service to console the spirit, and a ritual banquet) continue for a week after death; *kengu* (to offer up food) and *bosan* (to visit the grave) continue for forty-nine days after death; *hōyō* (memorial service in which a Buddhist priest recites sutras and in which a feast is held for the invited relatives of the dead) is held seven times during the first forty-nine days; the first Bon[5] festival after death includes special entertainments for the spirit of the dead; *hone-arai* and *kaisō* (washing of bones and reburial) are carried out three years after the death.[6] In addition to these special rituals, memorial services are regularly observed. Within thirty-three years after death, the spirit achieves full maturity; and after that date individual memorial services are no longer held, because from that time on, the tamashii ranks with perfect kami.

If one studies the rituals and festivals carefully, one notices that the people cease to treat the tamashii individually after the first summer festival following death, and begin to treat it as one of the ancestor spirits. This change in attitude means that the spirit has ceased to be dangerous to human society after the service held during the first summer festival following death. From that time on it is a mem-

ber of the group of *so-rei* (the spirits of ancestors) which
cherish offspring and protect them.

At the Bon festival, the so-called *nii-botoke*,[7] the spirit
of a man who died after the preceding Bon, receives special
treatment. When the families make fires at gates and on
nearby hills to invite the spirits of the dead, each family
which has lost a member in the past year lights an especially
big fire for the spirit of the newly dead. Also, in many places
the households of the newly dead erect a wooden or bamboo
pole at the gate and hang on it a lantern as a sign. At the
time of the Bon dance, too, they set the *ihai* (a memorial
tablet) of the newly dead prominently on the dancing stage,
and let it fully enjoy the summer night. Such special treatment ceases entirely after the second Bon following death.
Thereafter they dedicate to it only the same rituals that are
due the spirits of all ancestors at household altars and in
temples.

One can draw the same conclusion from the treatment of
the corpses in the practice of hone-arai or kaisō, which is
carried out in the second or third year after death. This
practice survives only in the Amami and Okinawa Islands,
but in former days hone-arai may have been observed
among the folk in keeping with the custom of *fūsō*.[8] The
people of these islands regard the burial immediately after
death as temporal. So the relatives disinter the corpse after
two or three years, pick up the bones from which the de-
cayed flesh has dropped, wash them well, and take them to
their final burial ground. The place for the burial of such
bones should be a site where all the ancestors have been
buried. At the time of this burial, the relatives and the
neighbors of the dead hold a magnificent banquet, at which
they drink *sake* and dance boisterously, praying for the
spirit's safe ascent to heaven. From this example, too, one
may presume that the dead join the group of ancestors two

or three years after death and become members of a spiritual society which consists of all the ancestors since the formation of the kin group concerned.

Thus the Japanese concept of life presumes two correlative social lives: one the social life of this world on earth, and the other that of the spiritual world in heaven. Spirit grows in both of these worlds and has a tendency to ascend to the upper world. When heaven overflows with these prosperous spirits, they drop upon earth one by one, dwell in new bodies, and begin the social life on earth again. Only at the transient periods when it shifts from the one society to the other, namely at the time of birth and death, is spirit treated as a completely separate entity.

When a spirit is confined within the bounds of society on earth, it is regarded as a safe and trustworthy being. But when it becomes independent, and lacks intimate relation with society, spirit is looked upon with unusual fear and anxiety. The spirit of a baby at the time of its birth, as well as the newly freed spirit of one recently dead, are then independent. If a spirit of the dead is unquenchably bad, it remains outside the bounds of society and is feared as an untrustworthy, evil spirit. It can be soothed only through the dedication of special rituals. Those tamashii who will never compromise with the society of *so-rei* (ancestral spirits) live eternally as independent beings. Such spirits are in the end revered as new, independent deities.

The spirit of one who dies in peace lives alone for a time after it leaves earthly society. After receiving consolatory services for several years, it joins the society of ancestral spirits, although it is not completely qualified to do so, and begins the life of the celestial society. What then is the celestial society? I suggest it is the society of uji-gami or tutelary deities.

In a kin group of simple patrilineal structure, the members worship the spirit of their mythological first father as their tutelary deity. There are many examples which bear this out. The Fujiwara family worshiped the spirit of their first father, Amano Koyane-no-mikoto, a semi-mythological being. A kin group which is believed to descend from a dragon worshiped the dragon as its tutelary deity. A kin group whose members regarded a kappa[9] as its first father worshiped the kappa as its tutelary deity. In these examples, the members of a kin group not only have the same surname, but also are believed to have the same physical features or to bear certain distinctive marks. Lineal descendants of a kami, as superior members of the group, preside over the festivals and rituals of the tutelary deities. Sometimes they become so exclusive that they do not permit the people outside the kin group to attend rituals.

However, *uji-gami* may sometimes mean not only the first father of a clan but the spirits of his offspring as well. From the representation of kami in divine dances, from the data in *Shinmei-cho*,[10] and from examples of *saimon* (ritual invitation recitals to deities)[11] one can infer that a Japanese kami is never alone and independent, but is followed by many spirits of his offspring. It seems that the prestige of a kami exists in proportion to the number of his subordinate spirits, in other words, his blood relatives and subjects in the celestial world. They have ascended to heaven after death and are carrying out the same communal life in the world of spirits.

So there are three different interpretations of the tutelary deities of a kin group of simple structure. First, *uji-gami* signifies the spirit of the mythological first father of a kin group. Second, it also refers to the spirits of the offspring of the first father. Third, it means a spiritual community organized under the control of the spirit of the first father.

In spite of these varying interpretations, one essential

point is widely recognized. That is, the tutelary deity protects with parental affection the organized body of offspring who worship him, and the latter serve him with filial affection and reverence. One sees that the earlier the historical period, the stronger is the belief that every community of men must have a protective deity. Further, it is believed that among animals, plants, and even among instruments and utensils, those who belong to the same species form a tribe and are controlled by a protective deity of that species. In *Shinmei-chō* and in the saimon are lines which suggest this interpretation.

One may say that the tutelary deity is a prototype of the general conception of kami. Any major kami must be followed by the spirits of offspring, and the latter must belong to the same species as the ancestor and have grown to be minor kami themselves. From this thought, one can draw two corollaries. The essence of a kami is, in the end, tamashii. Kami and tamashii have almost the same attributes. The difference between the two is that kami is ranked higher, is more powerful and more trustworthy than tamashii. From this point, one may infer that tamashii becomes kami when it is fully nourished and purified through effective rituals and festivals, but that it does not cease to be tamashii even when it becomes kami. A kami is only a tamashii nurtured through the mystical means of offerings and rituals until it attains a power beneficial to its proteges.

Bibliography of Pertinent Works

Higo, Kazuo. *Miyaza no Kenkyū (Study on Miyaza, Cult Organization in the Community)*. Tokyo: Kōbundo Shoten, 1941.

Inoue, Raiju. *Kyoto Koshu-shi (Old Religious Customs in Kyoto).* Toyonaka-shi: Chigin Shokan, 1940.

Matsudaira, Narimitsu. *Les Fêtes saisonnières au Japon (Province de Mikawa).* Paris: Librairie orientale et américaine, G. P. Maison-neuve, 1936.

———. *Matsuri (Festivals).* Tokyo: Nikko Shoin, 1943.

———. *Matsuri: Honshitsu to Shoso (The Festival: Principles and Aspects).* Tokyo: Nikko Shoin, 1946.

———. "Le rituel des prémices au Japon," *Bulletin de la Maison Franco-Japonaise* (Tokyo), nouvelle série, Tome IV, No. 2, 1955.

Motoyama, Keisen. *Nihon Minzoku Zushi* (Illustrations of Japanese Folk Customs). Tokyo: Tokyō-dō, 1955. Vol. I, *Festivals*; Vol. II, *Folk Religious Practices.*

Origuchi, Shinobu. *Kodai Kenkyū (Studies on Japanese Antiquities).* 2 vols. Tokyo: Ōokayama Shoten, 1929–30.

Tsujimoto, Yoshitaka. *Washu Sairei-ki (Festivals in Yamato Province).* Tanbaichi-machi: Tenri Jiho Sha, 1944.

Yanagita, Kunio. *Nihon no Matsuri (Japanese Festivals).* Tokyo: Kōbun-dō, 1942.

———. *Shin Kokugaku Dan (On the New Study of Japanese History).* Tokyo: Oyama Shoten, 1946–47. Book 1, *Festival Days*; Book 2, *Shrines in the Mountains.*

Notes

1. Tenjin-sama is the deified spirit of a famous statesman, Michizane Sugawara, who was exiled from Kyōto, the capital, to Kyūshū in 901. After the latter's death, so much damage was inflicted on the capital that the Emperor had a shrine built, in an attempt to appease the spirit of the statesman.

2. A miyaza is a special religious organization concerned with the ceremonies of worship connected with shrines. It is organized by the heads of the families in a village, and often only families with special qualifications can join it. The tōya is the head or the chief representative of a miyaza. Toshiyori (literally, "old men") are the aged males who take central positions in a miyaza.

3. For instance, the custom of placing objects needed for travel-

ing, such as a hat, a walking stick, money, rice, and sandals in the coffin or on the grave, derives from the Buddhist belief that the deceased must start on a long journey to the other world. A cup of cooked rice offered the dead immediately after death is intended for his trip to Zenko-ji Temple, a central Buddhist temple, whence he will depart for the other world.

4. Buddhist mourners do not offer *sake* to the dead. In Okinawa, however, where Buddhist influence has not penetrated, mourners offer *sake* instead of water even today.

5. Bon is the "All Souls Day" of Japanese Buddhism, and the best known of all Japanese festivals. It is celebrated in July or August.

6. The custom of bone-washing and reburial is now found in the Okinawa and Amami Islands. While such a custom, especially as regards grave construction, has been partially elaborated by the cultural contact with southern China where similar burial systems prevail, the beliefs themselves seem to be basically common to those found in Japan proper. The existence of the so-called double-grave system in various localities of rural Japan might be suggestive in this connection. On the other hand, the custom of cremation, presumably derived from Buddhism, is not so widespread in rural Japan, where simple burial is usual.

7. *Nii-botoke* means literally "new Buddha," implying the spirit of a person recently deceased.

8. Fūsō (literally "wind-funeral") was a method of burial practiced in ancient times in Japan. According to this method, a corpse was covered with straw, clothes or a box, and left on the ground in the open air. In the Amami and Okinawa Islands, up to a hundred years ago, the body was placed in a cave, and the bones washed and bleached after the lapse of several years.

9. The kappa is a goblinlike water spirit—usually, although not always, malevolent.

10. *Shinmei-cho* is the primary list of all the names of the kami in Japan to whom official divine paper cuttings were offered at the beginning of a year, when ritual prayers for a rich crop and the security of the state in the ensuing year were held by the government of the time. The number of the kami on the list was 3,132, and they were ranked higher than other kami. We cannot clearly know the year when the list was completed, but it was already in existence in A.D. 743. (The ceremonial practices described above have ceased since the end of World War II.)

11. *Saimon* means literally "ritual sentences," and as a generic term refers to a written text in archaic language read at a Shinto festival and addressed to kami; it begins by invoking the names of many deities. The reference here is to the saimon inviting kami to earth.

A Study of Yashiki-gami, The Deity of House and Grounds

BY HIROJI NAOE

Yashiki-gami is essentially the family tutelary deity whose additional characteristics vary with each different locality. Yashiki-gami is enshrined at a corner of the yard or in a distant field or forest owned by the family. If the significant problems concerning this deity could be solved, various aspects of the original beliefs among the Japanese people would be clarified. These problems are too complicated for brief discussion; hence I will here limit myself to studies on this subject undertaken up to now and will only suggest the points remaining for future investigation.

I. THE NAMES OF THE DEITY AND THEIR DISTRIBUTION

Yashiki-gami is the term generally used by folklore scholars when speaking of this deity. The names actually employed by the people vary according to locality. In the northern part of Japan, from the northeastern Tōhoku district to the northern Kantō district, this deity is called *uji-gami* or *uchi-gami*. The similar appellation *utsugan* (*utsu* = *uchi*;——*gan* = *kan*=*kami*) is found in the southern half of Kyūshū. The fact that virtually the same names occur in both the north and the south of Japan is noteworthy. At present, nearly half of the 45,000 Japanese village shrines are uji-gami shrines. To differentiate the two kinds of uji-gami, the deity which belongs to the family is in some places called *yashiki-ujigami* or *sedo-ujigami* (*sedo* means "back yard"), and in other places where the house or family deity is called *uji-gami,* the village-shrine deity is called *ubusuna* (native soil) or *chinju* (protector and peace-bringer). Why the village-shrine deity and the house deity are both now called *uji-gami* is an important question. Within the areas where the designation *uji-gami* is used for denoting the household or family deity are scattered a number of localities in which the household or family deity is called by the generic name of "deity of the earth," with dialectal variables such as *ji-gami, ji-no-kami, chi-jin* and *ji-nushi.* These names are found intermittently in a wide sweep from central Japan, including Miyake-jima and Mikura-jima which belong to the district of Tokyo-to, down to northern Kyūshū. Also in these areas there occurs the term *kōjin*, meaning "rough deity." This name is diffused in and around Okayama-ken and Shimane-ken, in central Kyūshū, and in Chiba-ken in eastern Japan. Another name for the house deity, *iwai-jin* (or *iwai-gami*), is found mainly in Yamanashi-ken and Nagano-ken and also in the western part of Hyogo-ken and in Saga-ken. However, this name is not distributed widely.

In addition, the household deity is often called by the proper names of particularly well known deities worshiped in a locality, such as Inari, Gion, Akiba, Shinmei, Kumano,

Yashiki-gami Shrines*

JINUSHI-SAMA'S SHRINE, at Yashiro, Yubara-machi, Okayama-ken. People of the house get and use water at the pond in front of the shrine.

JI-GAMI'S SHRINE at Shimokarato, Arima-gun, Hyōgo-ken

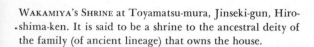

WAKAMIYA'S SHRINE at Toyamatsu-mura, Jinseki-gun, Hiro-shima-ken. It is said to be a shrine to the ancestral deity of the family (of ancient lineage) that owns the house.

*Erected by village families on their private grounds

JINUSHI-SAMA'S SHRINE at Kawakami-mura, Makabe-gun, Okaya-ma-ken. Five stones, piled one on another, symbolize the deity.

KŌJIN'S SHRINE at Yoshihama, Katsu-ura-machi, Chiba-ken. Go-hei is placed in the middle of the hut.

JINUSHI-SAMA'S SHRINE in Tsushima, Nagasaki-ken. Under an old tree are three small shrines with the stones of each arranged to form three sides of a rectangle; a round stone is placed in the center.

Tenno, Hakusan, Atago, Hachiman, Wakamiya, Yama-no-kami, and so forth. It may be noted that yashiki-gami worship is observed throughout the Japanese islands, regardless of the local name given the deity.

II. THE MANNER OF YASHIKI-GAMI WORSHIP

The way in which yashiki-gami is worshiped also varies according to each locality. By comparing these variations we can partially reconstruct the changes that have occurred in the original form of yashiki-gami worship. First, we must consider the shrine of yashiki-gami. Some of the deity's shrines are handsome, permanent buildings erected from wood or stone, while others are simple, temporary structures made of straw, which are rebuilt each year with new straw. These are associated with traditional sayings, such as "Don't make too magnificent a shrine lest your house should decline," or "If you erect a permanent shrine you will be cursed." The custom of building a permanent shrine for a deity is based on the idea that the deity establishes himself, and perpetually remains, in the shrine. However, this idea is not considered by scholars to be the original folk conception. Deities and spirits, invisible to human eyes, were believed to visit this world on festival occasions and to leave with the termination of the festival. So it was necessary only to mark the spot where a deity stayed during such a period.

Displays such as *go-hei* (sacred paper strips), sacred branches, or round stones are often seen in the smaller shrines, whether these are permanent or temporary. These displays throw light on the ancient custom of worshiping gods without shrines. In some localities the rituals for yashiki-gami are held in a clean corner of the yard, where sand is sprinkled and go-hei are put up. The go-hei symbolize the sacred object upon which the god descends and rests. In earlier times when paper was not yet popular, the *kezuri-bana* (a stick, half of which is shaved into thin strips which are curled up to give the appearance of a flower) took the place of the go-hei. This kezuri-bana came into use following the popularization of sharp-edged tools. In a much earlier era, people probably held rituals for gods around a growing tree or stone selected as the sacred object upon which the god descended. In fact, in Kumano province in Wakayama-ken, in the northern part of Okayama-ken, and in Iki-no-shima, Nagasaki-ken, the animistic custom of worshiping a stone or an old tree is still observed.

When we compare the different conceptions of yashiki-gami that exist in various regions, we find that they may be classified into two types: (*1*) a yashiki-gami who is enshrined only by a certain head family or old family in a kinship group or in a community, and (*2*) a yashiki-gami who is enshrined in each family house in a community. Whether these two types of yashiki-gami worship coexisted from the beginning or whether one has developed from the other remains an unanswered question; however, the recent researches into this subject have proved that the first type prevails in remote, conservative villages. Furthermore, these researches have also shown an ancient origin for this form of worship among the kinship groups centering around a head family. Therefore we may presume that originally only the main families maintained yashiki-gami shrines where the other members of the group worshiped the deity. The social changes following the medieval period weakened the unity of the kinship group (which is called *dōzoku* by Japanese rural sociologists). This decentralizing tendency resulted in the establishment of branch families and the eventual independence of each family. Under such circumstances, the individual family has advanced in prestige in the community. The conclusion can then be drawn that the original mode of yashiki-gami worship has developed into the present form in which each house has its own shrine on its own lands. Between the yashiki-gami of the kinship group and the yashiki-gami of the individual household can be distinguished an intermediate form of worship in which the deity is enshrined by both the branch families and the head family. Examples of this intermediate form may be seen in several districts at the present time.

In the original form of the yashiki-gami ritual, the head family takes the lead in performing the regular ceremony of the yashiki-gami which belongs to that family. All the branch families then join in the service. Only a few examples of this pure form exist today, and in its place we find that some families in a kin group take turns in conducting the rituals for their yashiki-gami, enshrined with the head family. This change may have been brought about by the decline of the head family, the rise of the branch families, and the dispersement of the kinship group. For example, in Tobi in Ibano-mura, Hikawa-gun, Shimane-ken, there are nine families which belong to the Oka family line. They celebrate the head family's yashiki-gami by turns, and six families among them have their own yashiki-gami as well.[1] This intermediate type may show the form in transition from worship of the yashiki-gami of a kinship group to worship of the yashiki-gami of an individual family. As the unity within a kinship group dissolves, each individual family comes to build its own yashiki-gami shrine.

The establishment of a yashiki-gami in each family surely developed in modern times. We cannot overlook the rising tendency of households to regard yashiki-gami as the protective deity of an individual family and its grounds. An example of this trend may be found in a village in western Shizuoka-ken: When a man is building his own house, he brings there a portion of earth from the grounds of his natal home as an offering to the earth god.[2] In a village in the eastern part of Shimane-ken, twelve families worship the *ji-nushi-gami* as their yashiki-gami, and three among them state that they separated their yashiki-gami from that of the head family when they originated their new households.[3] These instances may clarify the connection between the yashiki-gami of the individual branch families and that of the head family.

There is another change detectable in the mode of worship, namely the worship by a whole community of the yashiki-gami of a specific head family or an old family. For instance, the *chinju-sama* (tutelary deity) of a village in the eastern mountainous portion of Aichi-ken is said to have been formerly the yashiki-gami of a family that has declined. According to legend, the deity caused the downfall of the family because they sacrilegiously cut down the trees in the shrine grove and then moved the shrine to their own lands.[4] Another example is found at Yugi-machi in Jinseki-gun, Hiroshima-ken, where there are three village shrines of kōjin, the rough deity—Shigetomo Kōjin, Akazuka Kōjin. and Zenitsubo Kōjin. At the present time fifty families worship Shigetomo Kōjin as their tutelary deity, and they take turns every year holding the ritual services. It is said that there was once a Shigetomo family which was called Kōjin-moto (literally, "the center of the kōjin cult group").[5] From this tradition we may suppose that the deity, which was formerly a yashiki-gami, was once the tutelary deity of a powerful family and later became a tutelary deity of the village. There are many similar instances in other villages.

Another variation may be seen in areas where the power of the yashiki-gami of an influential family was extended over other families, and the cult organization centering around the original family was gradually enlarged. As this trend developed, and the idea of a kin-group tutelary deity was weakened, the family yashiki-gami came to be recognized as the village tutelary deity. It is also possible that certain powerful yashiki-gami were united and enshrined as the village deity. Whatever the case may be, the yashiki-gami of a kin group centering around a head family has two characteristic tendencies: to become multiplied as the yashiki-gami of individual families, or to develop into the village tutelary deity. We may conclude that the changes in kinship yashiki-gami worship, coupled with the new deities introduced since medieval times from foreign cultures, have led to the complicated forms of yashiki-gami we see in various regions today.

The yashiki-gami rituals are generally held twice a year, in the second month of the lunar calendar when the farmers celebrate the deities at the commencement of the preliminary agricultural work of the year, and in the tenth or eleventh month of the lunar calendar, during the harvest festivities. In some localities, the ritual may be held only in the autumn. These two occasions in spring and autumn correspond with the seasonal alternations between two deities, ta-no-kami (deity of the wet rice field) and *yama-no-kami* (deity of the mountain). Kunio Yanagita recently suggested that ta-no-kami might be identified with the ancestral spirit. If his hypothesis is accepted, we can assume that the ancestral spirit is invited, as the deity of the rice field, at the commencement of the spring festival and that it returns to the mountain after the harvest. On these two occasions yashiki-gami is also honored.

III. THE CHARACTERISTICS OF YASHIKI-GAMI

It is usually taken for granted that yashiki-gami has a tutelary character, but from region to region a considerable variation in his character and functions can be detected. Our recent research into this subject is moving in the direction of studies relating to ancestral spirit worship. For example, in Shizuoka-ken, yashiki-gami is called *ji-no-kami* (earth deity). And there is a tradition in some villages that the ancestral spirit stays in the earth deity's shrine.[6] In the mountainous region in Aichi-ken, shrines of ji-no-kami are found near the houses of the old families, and the explanation of their origin says that the shrines once served to deify the ancestor who founded the family. In Hyōgo-ken the ji-gami is customarily interpreted as an ancestor deity. From the Kumano region to Shikoku, the word *ji-nushi-sama* is used for *yashiki-gami,* and in many villages it is said that the ancestor who opened the land was deified as ji-nushi-sama. In the Oki Islands, a part of Shimane-ken, the shrines of ji-nushi-sama are often found beside the wet or dry rice fields. Islanders say that these shrines were first built to honor the ancestors who bought the lands.[7] From Okayama-ken to Shimane-ken there is an area where kōjin worship is widely observed, and kōjin, revered as yashiki-gami, is often said to have first been worshiped as an ancestral spirit. Iwai-jin, who is worshiped as yashiki-gami in the area from Yamanashi-ken to Nagano-ken, is usually believed to be the deified ancestor. In all these instances, an ancient ancestor or founder has been deified as yashiki-gami.

Another example illustrating the close relationship between yashiki-gami and the ancestor spirit is the practice found in some areas of deifying an ancestor of each generation as yashiki-gami. For instance, in Kodama-gun, Saitama-ken, there is a tradition that after the last anniversary service (according to Buddhist practice celebrated in the thirty-third year after death), the spirit of the dead relative becomes a ji-no-kami and is revered as a yashiki-gami by the family concerned.[8] There are some villages in Shizuoka-ken where the spirit of the dead ancestor is thought to become a ji-no-kami and to function as a yashiki-gami for his house after the fiftieth anniversary of his death.[9] In southwestern Fukui-ken[10] and southeastern Hyogo-ken, every kin group has its own ji-gami shrine, and when a kinsman dies his spirit is deified as a ji-gami after the fiftieth anniversary of his death.[11] An analogous custom in Iwaki-gun, Fukushima-ken, places the necessary passage of time at 100 anniversaries after the death of every ancestor, whereupon each is deified as a yashiki-gami.[12] At Iino-machi, Miyazaki-ken, it is observed that the memorial tablet for the dead is moved from a Buddhist ancestral altar into a little shrine called *uchigan-dō* (uchi-gami's shrine) on the thirty-third anniversary of the death.[13]

The custom of erecting a *toba* (the wooden symbol of a tomb), with cedar boughs attached to it, on the burial spot to mark the ending of Buddhist services for the soul of the dead on the thirty-third anniversary of the death, is widely observed throughout the Japanese islands. This custom is based upon the idea that the soul of the dead is gradually purified until it loses its individuality and is merged into the complex of ancestral spirits in the thirty-third or fiftieth year after death. Up to the present, the data for identifying this complex of ancestral spirits with yashiki-gami is somewhat restricted to the foregoing examples. Nevertheless, they are quite widely distributed, and their similarities cannot be dismissed as coincidences. We presume that there formerly existed a common belief among the Japanese people that the purified spirits of the dead became yashiki-gami, family tutelary deities.

As can be seen from the foregoing, there are two concepts of the relationship between yashiki-gami and ancestor spirits. One holds that only the remote ancestor or ancient founder of the family is deified as yashiki-gami, and the other that the ancestral spirits of each generation are so deified. Whether these two ideas originated together in a prehistoric time, or whether one preceded the other, is our next question. My opinion is that the older form of belief is that in which the first ancestor or founder of the family (in most cases the traditional founder) is deified as yashiki-gami. A number of instances clearly show the connection between yashiki-gami and the grave of the founding ancestor. For example, at Sasagawa, Miyazaki-mura, Shimoniikawa-gun, Toyama-ken, seven old families, whose ancestors are said to have first settled the land, worship the graves of their own ancestors as *ji-shin-sama*. All these graves are located at the corner of the yard under big trees and are generally on a hillside behind the house.[14] At Tōgō-mura and Iso-mura on Oki-no-shima, Shimane-ken, a stone pile in the yard is worshiped as the symbol of ji-nushi-sama.[15] This is said to be the grave of the first and second ancestors. The old family of Abe at Aso-dani in Kumamoto-ken has a kōjin shrine adjacent to the ancestor's graveyard;[16] and we have other examples of similar cases. To sum up, I consider that the custom of honoring the ancestral spirits through the medium of the burial or monumental grave of the first or superior ancestor led to the idea that the spirit of the dead relative becomes a yashiki-gami after the thirty-third or fiftieth anniversary of his death.

Another important consideration in the relation of yashiki-gami to the ancestral spirit is the worship in many places of the deity Inari as yashiki-gami. It is known that in the Tōhoku district the two are identified. In Shizuoka-ken, ji-no-kami in the form of yashiki-gami is often merged with Inari, so that we find earthen statues of Inari in some ji-no-kami shrines. On the fifteenth of November, the festival day of ji-no-kami, the children go through the village saying "Kon, Kon," in imitation of the fox's voice, and begging for cooked rice, and there is a place where ji-no-kami is called Konkon-sama.[17] Iwai-jin in Nagano-ken and ji-gami in Hyōgo-ken are often connected with Inari. The diffusion of Inari worship is in itself a complex and fascinating problem, which must in large part be left for future studies. From the investigations made up to now, we may conclude that Inari worship has spread over a large area, building upon the common belief in ta-no-kami. If this conjecture is proved, we may postulate the course of development as proceeding from an ancestral spirit to ta-no-kami and then to Inari. Hence the ancestral deity may be connected with yashiki-gami in terms of yashiki-gami's relation to Inari.

If the yashiki-gami emerged from ancestor worship, it might originally have been regarded as a tutelary deity governing the entire life of a kinship group, and consequently could have possessed the character of an agricultural deity. The belief in yashiki-gami as an agricultural deity is widely held in Japan. As previously stated, the festival days of yashiki-gami are generally connected with agricultural labor. The spring festival occurs when the farmers start the farm work of the year, and the autumn festival comes after the harvest. Furthermore, Inari, worshiped as yashiki-gami, is in many places believed to be the agricultural deity. At Saikai-mura, Suzu-gun, Ishikawa-ken, the old families who are said to be the descendants of the first settlers worship ji-gami as yashiki-gami. In one of these families, on the occasion of ae-no-koto rituals for ta-no-kami on the fifth of December, it is customary to visit the shrine of ji-gami on the hillside behind the house and to offer *ama-zake* (sweet *sake*) to the deity. The visit to the shrine is also performed during the ae-no-koto ritual in spring, on the ninth of February.[18] Here again, the close relationship between yashiki-gami and an agricultural deity, ta-no-kami, is apparent. The more restricted concept, that yashiki-gami is simply a deity who protects the house, may represent a degeneration from the older communal belief in yashiki-gami.

Throughout Japan the villagers often regard yashiki-gami as a violent deity, much given to harming and cursing men. There are a great many tales of people being made ill from his curse, because they have not shown the proper regard for the deity, have failed to perform his rites carefully, or have cut down trees in the grove around his shrine. Of course, *yama-bushi* (mountain monks) and shamans were instrumental in the diffusion of such tales. Nevertheless, cursing is considered one of the characteristics which belong to ancestral spirits. The gentleness with which the deity patronizes the family—in other words, the deity's special favor to the family—may sometimes become a fierce power manifested against things outside the family. For example, kōjin, worshiped by a kinship group in Hikawa-gun, Shimane-ken, is supposed to have been in former days the main family's yashiki-gami;[19] and it is said that if someone of another kin group cut down a tree in the grove around the shrine, he would receive a curse.[20] A similar story is told concerning iwai-jin, who is worshiped in the vicinity of Matsumoto-shi, Nagano-ken. So this disposition of yashiki-gami to curse and cause harm to men is thought to be a derivation from the violent aspect of the ancestral spirit.

IV. THE REMOVAL OF THE SITE OF THE RITUALS FOR YASHIKI-GAMI

As we have said, yashiki-gami is presently enshrined at a corner of the yard or in a forest or field which is owned by the worshiping family. In the course of time, the site of the shrine has undergone changes. In Yamanashi-ken and Nagano-ken, iwai-jin shrines are quite often erected in areas distant from the residence, such as a field, a forest grove, or the foot of a hill. The same changes can be observed in the locations chosen for the shrines of ji-gami and kōjin. It may be that in former days people celebrated their own ancestral deities on a selected spot in their fields or forests. As time passed, the site of the rituals was gradually moved nearer to the residence and finally into the residential grounds. This change in site may have been effected for the convenience of people attending the ceremonial banquet, or perhaps determined by the repartitioning of the fields.

When we inquire into the original form of yashiki-gami worship, including the question of the ritual site, we must notice the worship of Niso-no-mori (the Grove of Niso) in Oshima-mura, Oii-gun, Fukui-ken. We find there twenty-four households, said to be the descendants of the first settlers, each of whom has a grove surrounded by bamboo bushes and centered around an old tree. On November twenty-third, each family gathers in its own grove and performs rituals in honor of their ancestors. We should also notice the worship of Kōjin-mori (the Grove of Kōjin) in the San'in district and in northern Kyūshū, where the grove belonging to the head family is considered sacred to the ancestral deity worshiped by the people of the same kinship group. All our evidence indicates that the present widespread form of family worship of a household deity is quite recent in origin.

Notes

1. Yoshishige Oka, "Izumo Hikawa-gun Shohō Kōjin Kikigaki" ("Note on the Kōjin Cult in Hikawa District of Izumo Province"), *Izumo Minzoku (Izumo Folklore)*, No. 18, 1953, pp. 19–20.

2. Sakuji Nakamichi, *Enshū Sekishi-mura Minzoku-shi (Folk Life of Sekishi Village in Tōtōmi Province)* (Tokyo: Kyodo Kenkyu Sha, 1933), p. 72.

3. Takatoshi Ishizuka, "Chū-San'in no Yashiki-gami" ("Yashiki-gami in the Central Part of San'in District"), *San'in Minzoku (San'in Folklore)*, No. 5, 1955, pp. 9–15, 25.

4. Kōtarō Hayakawa, *Sanshū Yokoyama-Banashi (Stories from Yokoyama in Mikawa Province)* (Tokyo: Kyōdo Kenkyū Sha, 1921), p. 4.

5. I visited this village and collected data in January, 1956.

6. Takeshi Uchida, "Ji-no-kami-sama (Shizuoka-ken)" ("Earth Deity [Shizuoka-ken]"), *Tabi to Densetsu (Travels and Legends)* (Tokyo), Vol. VII, No. 4, 1934, pp. 49–57.

7. From the author's unpublished field notes, taken after a visit to these islands in August, 1951.

8. Hisako Maruyama, in a report given at a monthly meeting of the Folklore Society, 1952.

9. Uchida, loc. cit.

10. Kidō Saitō, "Mie no Ji-no-kami" ("Ji-no-kami Cult at Mie"), *Nihon Minzoku-gaku (Journal of Japanese Folklore)* (Tokyo), Vol. II, No. 4, 1955, pp. 68–72.

11. Katsuya Nishitani, "Mura no Kōsai" ("Social Life in the Village"), *Minkan Denshō (Folklore Journal)* (Tokyo), Vol. XIV, No. 1, 1950, pp. 14–18.

12. Toshio Iwasaki, "Uji to Uji-gami" ("The Lineage and Its Tutelary Deity"), *Nihon Minzokugaku no tame ni (For the Study of Japanese Folklore)* (Tokyo), IV (1947), 90–91.

13. Arimitsu Kashiwagi, "Uchigan-sā" ("Tutelary Deity") *Minkan Denshō*, Vol. X, No. 1, 1944, pp. 80–82.

14. Motozō Kunori, "Sasagawa no Ji-gami Dozoku-shin" ("Ji-gami and the Ancestral Tutelary Deity"), ibid., Vol. XIV, No. 11, 1950, pp. 14–15.

15. Ishizuka, loc. cit.

16. Takayoshi Mogami, *Mairi-baka (The Memorial Grave)* (Tokyo: Kokin Shoin, 1956), p. 227.

17. Nakamichi, p. 71. The fox is believed to be the servant of Inari, or sometimes this animal is identified with the god himself. Country people felt a mystery in the clever or shrewd actions of foxes and readily associated them with spirits or deities.

18. Ichiro Hori, "Oku-Noto no Nōkō Girei ni tsuite" ("On the

Farming Rituals in the Inner Noto District"), in *Niiname no Kenkyū (Studies on the Niiname Festival)* (Edited by Niiname Kenkyū-kai [Tokyo: Sōgen Sha, 1953]), II, 96–97.

19. Oka, loc. cit.

20. Oka, p. 20.

The Village Tutelary Deity and the Use of Holy Rods

BY TOSHIAKI HARADA

Although folk Shintoism has undergone a series of trans-
formations since the Middle Ages, its core remains the beliefs and rituals traditional among the common people and
maintained in their community life. Each village is strongly
independent and, without exception, has its own uji-gami,[1]
the tutelary deity or deities whose guardianship extends
over every aspect of the village life. The villagers, called
collectively the *uji-ko*[2] of the deity, are regarded as the
descendants of the uji-gami, and are all considered to be in
a state of equality beneath him; hence, scarcely any dis-
tinctions of class or status are found among the village
people. This concept of the villagers' relationship to the
tutelary deity has been retained until the present day.

No special person in a farming village is entrusted with
offering services to the uji-gami. Only in the community

where life has become complex are hereditary professional priests to be found. In some localities there is still practiced the institution of tōya, which does provide for a systematic appointment of services to the uji-gami. This system does not follow the principle of selection based on hereditary family lineage. Rather, the responsibility is assumed in turns by members of the uji-ko who are chosen by age, by residential sequence in a row of houses, by lottery, by divination, and so forth. The individual so selected, who is called *tōya* or *tōnin*,[3] is not required to possess any conspicuous religious experience or talent. His term of duty is usually. one agrarian year, beginning with the time of sowing rice and ending with the harvest period.

The character of the tōya, however, has undergone modification in many localities, due to the increased complexity of village institutional organization and ritual performances. Besides the tōya, village elders and young men's associations came to perform some subsidiary though often important parts in the rituals of the community. But these groups, too, rotated their services each year, and no person has claimed a permanent or hereditary position. The position of hereditary priest is a later development in larger and more important shrines having a large uji-ko, and in the bigger cities.

Any priest, whether he was the tōya on duty, a village elder, or a hereditary priest, was considered as assuming to some extent the character of the uji-gami.[4] He consecrated his own house to the uji-gami and offered services to the deity every morning and evening. He honored the uji-gami in a specific place or room, the original site being presumably the front or side entrance to the house and grounds. In certain instances, the uji-gami was honored at some appropriate place in the house considered clean and undefiled, such as the *toko-no-ma*[5] or the ceiling. These latter cases seem to be later divergences.

Presumably, the original procedure called for the priest to worship the uji-gami at his house in some fashion, and such a procedure can still be observed in various localities. At present, the uji-gami whom the priest worships in his house is usually considered a manifestation of the "primary" uji-gami revered in the village shrine, and the coincident ways and manners of worshiping the uji-gami support such an idea. Today uji-gami worship generally involves performing services in the village shrine of the uji-gami, and it would be natural for the house of the priest, consecrated to the uji-gami, to be regarded as a branch office, so to speak, of the village shrine. But I am skeptical as to whether this practice represents the original form of uji-gami worship. I believe that the rotating system of the tōya, the one-year priest, preceded the establishment of the village shrine and hereditary priesthood, which modeled its services on the tōya, and not that, as is customarily believed, the former system developed from the latter.

In any case, the hereditary priest is now charged with offering services either at a "branch shrine" traditionally maintained in his house or at a *kami-dana*,[6] a special altar located on a shelf near the ceiling of his house. The tōya or village elder who, as a temporary priest, serves for only one year also celebrates the uji-gami in his own house during his tenure of office.

Ceremonies for the uji-gami vary according to region. In this regard, attention should be called to a relatively wide distribution of the holy rod known as *o-hake*. The o-hake is erected at the entrance of the priest's premises or of his house at the time of the village community festivals. As both library work and field surveys reveal, the term *o-hake* is found over nearly the entire country. It appears in villages closely juxtaposed in southern Hyōgo-ken, in the eastern part of Kagawa-ken, and in northern Ishikawa-ken and is found scattered elsewhere throughout Japan. In the

north the rods are seen at Tenno-mura in Akita-ken and at
Shizu-mura in Ibaragi-ken, and to the west they are found
on the east coast of Oita-ken in Kyūshū, and in the southern
part of Ehime-ken in Shikoku; a shrine in western Yamaguchi-ken has records showing that the rod was displayed
at one time in this vicinity. Other records of ancient shrines
at Kamo, Yasaka, Ise and Atsuta reveal the use of the term
o-hake before the Middle Ages.

The rods vary in form and size according to region, often
deviating from the normal o-hake. The *hei,* ordinarily used
in Shinto rituals, seems also to represent such a deviation.
A hei (sometimes *go-hei*) may be made from the leafy
branch of the sacred sakaki tree *(eurya ochnacea)* or from
a *kushi* (bamboo skewer); both are decorated with paper
strips and are usually a foot or a foot and a half long.
Throughout Japan, Shinto priests use the hei to bless or
purify the people. In some localities where an outside altar
of earth or a simple hut is consecrated to the deity, the hei
is the center of rituals. For instance, at Kawanishi-mura in
Nara-ken, a temporary shrine is erected, within which the
so-called o-hake is raised. The people call this practice the
o-hake-tsuki, tsuki implying "to build up." Nevertheless,
the o-hake in this case is nothing but a small *sakaki-hei* and
hei-gushi (gushi=kushi), which suggests a close connection
between the o-hake and the hei. At the present time the hei-
gushi is used on the eve of the festival and the composite
sakaki-gushi at the main festival on the following day. This
is an example of the ritual use of what may be called a
small-scale holy rod.

In other localities where the people emphasize the idea
that the deity descends from on high, a bamboo hei is ele-
vated in the air, as in southwestern Shiga-ken, where the rod
is called *takama* (a high heaven). Such an idea, either manifest or latent, is widely found in various localities of western

Japan such as Hyōgo-ken, Okayama-ken, Kagawa-ken and Kōchi-ken, in all of which the term *o-hake* is prevalent. In these localities the tallest bamboo in the village is often used as the o-hake, or a bamboo hei is raised up high and ornamented with smaller hei made of sakaki and paper strips. A special cult group, Sengen-kō, extending over a group of villages, plants a tall bamboo on a mountainside, and even ties the bamboo to a large tree. The worshipers do this not only because they believe the deity descends from high above, but also because they worship the holy summit of Mount Fuji.

Elsewhere the same kind of holy rod is found under other names than *o-hake*. The sacred bamboo is called *taihō* (a great treasure) at Kashima Shrine in Ibaragi-ken, and *bonten* in Dewa-gun, Yamagata-ken, where a bamboo rod beautifully adorned with paper strips is used in the worship of three mountains.

In sum, the holy rod is one widespread symbol of divinity in uji-gami worship suggesting a possible common ancestry for the present diverse forms of village Shinto services. In the primary form existing before recorded history, the o-hake may have served to welcome the descending deity, particularly at agricultural rituals. If this hypothesis is correct, then o-hake and tōya customs would have preceded the Shinto institutions of the hereditary priesthood and the village shrine.

Notes

1. The term *uji-gami*, originally designating the deity of a lineage or clan, is now used mainly to indicate the tutelary deity of a village as a whole.

2. The term *uji-ko* is applied to those affiliated with the cult group of uji-gami, *uji* being "clan" or "lineage" and *ko,* "children."

3. The tōya is the head or the representative of the miyaza, a special religious organization for worship centered around shrines, organized only by the male heads of the families in a village. *Tōya* implies "the house or family in charge." *Tōnin* means "the person in charge" or "the person concerned."

4. As the representative of the whole uji-ko, the priest constantly pays reverence to the uji-gami, often representing the uji-gami himself before the uji-ko. On the other hand, as the head of the whole uji-ko he takes on the character of an administrator over them. Under such an atmosphere of uji-gami worship, religious performance and secular administration tended to fuse with each other in the popular ideology. This fusion seems to be reflected in the etymology of ancient Japanese terms: the matsuri signifies "a religious performance or festival," and *matsuri-goto,* "festival affairs," i.e., administration or political control on both the village and national level.

5. Toko-no-ma is an alcove, originally perhaps a place to receive an honorable guest in the best room or drawing-room, but now used as an ornamental recess for flowers and hanging scrolls.

6. From *kami* (deity) and *dana* (a form of *tana*), meaning "shelf."

The Position of the Shinto Priesthood: Historical Changes & Developments

BY TATSUO HAGIWARA

I. GENERAL CONCEPTION OF THE SHINTO PRIESTHOOD

Shinto shrines abound in mid-twentieth-century Japan and vary in size and importance from nationally known to very obscure shrines in small villages. Some of the smaller village shrines or *jinja* are under the supervision of priests at larger ones which are centrally located, but many of them are run independently. Such independent jinja date from the end of World War II, when the state administration of shrines was abolished. The rescinding of state regulations abetted the reaction against the uniting and combining of shrines, a movement which was provided for by law in the late nineteenth century and which had continued unchecked until the end of World War II.[1]

Professional priests are not attached to all of these numerous shrines. Most of the small country shrines have no contact with professional priests; and in their place old, influential families take charge of the ritual performances at the jinja. Even many of the larger village shrines are without professional priests, and their rituals are regularly performed by priests having permanent appointments at the central shrine of each district. Only a few of these central shrines have more than two permanent priests; and even they, although professional priests, rely upon an additional occupation, such as schoolteaching or civil service. Since the abolition in 1945 of national laws to administer the Shinto shrines, it has become difficult for priests to live on the scanty income provided them.[2] In short, the Shinto priesthood is not a paying profession, unlike the Buddhist priesthood, whose close association with Japanese ancestral-spirit worship has provided a source of income. Besides these local Shinto shrines, however, there are several large and famous ones which support many priests under a hierarchical system.

The professional character of a Shinto priest is also markedly different from that of his Buddhist counterpart. Notwithstanding that both are religious men, they differ widely in their means of religious expression. Whereas the Buddhist priest devotes much of his time to missionary work and to prayer, the Shinto priest concentrates upon the maintenance of his shrine and the duties of presiding at the shrine's annual festivals. None of his time is devoted to missionary work and very little of it to religious supplication. His primary endeavors are to maintain a friendly advisory relationship with the villagers, to remain indifferent to personal material considerations, and to arrange for someone to succeed him in his holy profession in a manner which is suitable to the divinity. A priest (Mr. Kiyama) whom I interviewed at his mountain home in Okayama-ken in 1947, and whose forefathers had followed the same profession for centuries, made the following typical observations:

1) Shinto priests have traditionally been called by the familiar name Kannushi-san[3] because they have always been good friends and advisors to the villagers and because the villagers have always taken an enthusiastic part in their shrine's annual festivals.

2) Shinto priests have traditionally maintained a disinterested attitude toward their own lives, because they know that it is wrong to be mercenary. In addition, they have always recognized that the more indifferent they are to material considerations, the greater support they will receive from the villagers for maintenance or reconstruction of their shrines.

3) Shinto priests feel that property inheritance should not be taken into account when they arrange for succession to their holy profession. Thus they are not necessarily succeeded by their eldest sons as is usual among laymen.[4] Instead, if they have many sons, Shinto priests decide on their heirs by looking for omens indicating divine favor. In Mr. Kiyama's family, a mole on a particular part of the arm was often regarded as the needed sign.

Characteristic of the regulations governing the duties of the Shinto priest are those contained in a document written in 1767, which is kept at Katsura Shrine.[5] Among the document's specific articles are three which stipulate (*1*) that the priest should not cut down a tree in the compound of a shrine except to fulfill the need for everyday fuel; (*2*) in the case of financial need the Shinto priest should consult his uji-ko[6] (congregation); and (*3*) even if a *kannushi* (priest) has many sons, only one should succeed him. The other sons should be treated as ordinary villagers. These and other regulations contained in the document of

1767 presumably have been obeyed by Shinto priests and villagers in the region around Katsura Shrine.

In spite of the existence of basic attitudes and regulations to which all Shinto priests must adhere, a considerable degree of local variation in priestly functions seems to prevail. In the Tsugaru district of Aomori-ken in northeastern Japan, for example, which is rich in folk traditions, the villagers insist that their Shinto priests should excel in religious dance.[7] The fact that such skill is required of ordinary priests—and not of professional dancers or female priests—indicates that the people expect them to become possessed by a kami and thereby to play the role of godlike beings in the festivals. Accordingly, the religious dances are usually performed by several priests who are invited for the occasion from neighboring parts of the region in which the Tsugaru district is located. This practice of inviting additional priests suggests that originally the rites might have been performed by a permanent body of priests attached to one Shinto shrine; however, in the San-yo and San'in regions in western Honshu, *mai-dayū* (male dancers) perform the religious dances, leaving the Shinto priests free to pursue their traditional functions.[8]

II. HISTORICAL CHANGES IN THE SHINTO PRIESTHOOD SYSTEM

The first great change in the history of the Shinto priesthood took place in the late sixteenth and early seventeenth centuries, when the Japanese feudal system was finally established. At that time the villages completely gained their independence from the ancient aristocratic regime and were reorganized by the feudal lords. The feudal lords replaced the old village organizations with a new communal system which gave Japanese villages the character of peasants' organizations. Whereas prior to this reorganization the Shinto priests had been included in the *shōen* system[9] controlled by the governing nobility, the priests now came to be regarded by the common people as "the priests of our village." Each village, with the destruction of the old order, felt that it had a right to its own shrines and priests. Unfortunately many of the smaller villages could not afford to keep their own permanent priests and instead had to share them with other villages.

The shift of political power from the aristocrats to feudal lords also resulted in the decline of large and powerful groups of Shinto priests attached to privileged shrines. The chief factor in the decline was the collapse of the shōen system. The eminent groups attached to Hie, Kasuga, and Kehi Shrines (respectively in Otsu city, Shiga-ken; Nara city, Nara-ken; and Tsuruga city, Fukui-ken) were disrupted by Oda Nobunaga (1534–82), a hero who paved the way for the unification of the feudal lords into a single political power. Nobunaga deprived these shrines of their prerogatives maintained by the power and prestige of the aristocrats. When he attacked Enryaku-ji, a great temple on Mount Hiei, Hiei Shrine, which was closely connected with it, also suffered.

The removal of the aristocrats from control over the Shinto priesthood assisted the rise of a systematic school of Shintoism called Yoshida Shinto, founded by a priest belonging to the Yoshida family. Capitalizing on the trend of the age toward unification, the Yoshida Shinto made a successful appeal to the central government, and in 1665 the Tokugawa Shogunate recognized Yoshida Shintoism as embodying the principles most suitable to the Shinto priesthood under the new regime. These principles emphasized the unity of Shintoism, Buddhism, and Confucianism, and the presence of kami in the individual soul. The shogunate announced that all priests should follow the regulations prescribed by the Yoshida Shinto in performing religious ceremonies. The Yoshida family was also given the privilege of issuing licenses for the Shinto priesthood and of appointing priests to their posts.

In the 1870's the new Japanese government of the Meiji Restoration dealt the traditional Shinto priesthood further severe blows. In 1871 it issued the following proclamation:

Shrines are public institutions and should not be owned privately. With the decline of the Shinto spirit, most priests, taking it for granted that their appointments were personal privileges, have up to the present time considered their positions as hereditary. And under the assumption that the shrines were their personal properties, these priests have regarded themselves as different from ordinary people. These attitudes, however, go against the spirit of the new government and will lead to grave evils if they continue unchecked. Accordingly, this government, which believes strongly in the unity of politics and divine service, has decreed that all Shinto priests must be newly appointed through a national examination.[10]

This was the second setback suffered by the Shinto priests in the late nineteenth century, as the new government had already deprived them of their land tenure. Through the national examination given in 1872, many priests from old families of high social standing were weeded out of the profession. At the great Ise and Kasuga Shrines, large groups of Shinto priests lost their traditional occupations and were literally thrown out into the streets.

The Japanese Shinto priest system now underwent a fundamental change. The prevalent idea that priests must inherit their positions gave way to a new view that the priesthood was bureaucratic in character. Of course, not all of the priests who passed the government examination lacked family ties in the priesthood. Surviving the great upheaval of the Meiji era (1868–1912) were some priests whose families had followed this profession for more than ten or twenty generations. And even in mid-twentieth-century Japan, shrines exist which have maintained and still maintain priestly families who have resided there for centuries. For instance, Kamo-Ikazuchi Shrine in Kyoto maintains more than 150 priests and their families. However, these families do not depend solely on the priesthood for their livelihood but instead have subsisted mainly by farming. Kamo-Ikazuchi is one of the few shrines at which we can still trace the traditional system of jinja and their hereditary priests—a system which in most other cases was crushed during the Meiji era. The priests at this shrine have kept accurate genealogical records to prove their descent, in marked contrast with priests elsewhere who either have not kept such records or have done so in an unreliable manner. Elsewhere, records of this kind cannot be trusted as historical documents because they partake of the character of legend or of fabrication designed to trace a nonexistent ancient lineage.

In the first decade of the Meiji era a group of priests who had combined Shinto and Buddhist religious practices into a unique cult received a heavy blow when the government prohibited religious mixtures of this kind, with a view to reviving the religious purity of the Japanese spirit, to be found presumably only in pure Shinto. Prior to the establishment of the Meiji government, Shugendō, a sect of Buddhism, had spread widely throughout the Kantō and Tōhoku areas. In the pre-Meiji period Shugendō had arrived at a peculiar synthesis by combining old Shintoistic rituals of mountain worship with Buddhistic formulas and incantations. Although they dreaded the Shugendō priests as magical practitioners, the villagers had respected them as leaders of rituals and relied on them to help heal diseases. The Shugendō sect was officially abolished in 1872 and its form of worship has been lost. Most of the Shu-gendō priests, however, entered the ordinary Shinto priest-hood, and within its framework have handed down some survivals of the old form of mountain worship.[11]

For instance, the most important rite practiced by Shu-gendō ascetics is that of *mine-iri* (seclusion in the moun-tains). This practice is believed to have originated in the old folk custom of climbing the mountains at the beginning of rice-planting rituals and the feast for ancestral spirits. Mountain-climbing also served as an initiation rite for boys. Another annual Shugendō rite, *saitō-goma,* the rite of burn-ing specially prepared firewood, is held at certain shrines when prayers are offered for peace and a good crop, and when priests purify polluted persons and places.

III. THE ORIGINAL AND MODERN FORMS
OF SHINTO PRIESTHOOD

The functions of the kannushi (Shinto priest) have slowly become specialized over a long period of time. Whereas the term *kannushi* may have in ancient times been applied loosely to people performing widely different com-munity functions, in modern Japan it applies only to the Shinto priest whose task is to perform a specific set of duties effectively. The present-day obligations of the kannushi, and their ancient derivations, can be divided into the fol-lowing six categories:

1) Abstinence or purification. Purity is the essential qual-ity of the kannushi. In ancient times, the idea might have arisen spontaneously within each community of choosing a person to be purified who would thenceforth preside over the rites necessary to ensure the community's safety and prosperity. The modern idea that a kannushi is one who purifies people may stem from this ancient custom.

2) Possession by deities and divine revelation. Possession by a deity, an occurrence in which some Japanese people still believe, is likely to happen to a kannushi. In ancient Japan, on the occasion of religious festivals people actually saw—or imagined that they saw—their deity appearing before them. As we have noticed already, this primitive belief survives in parts of modern Japan, such as the Tsugaru district, where the villagers still envisage their deity appearing before them in the body of their kami-possessed dancing priest. It is possible that the term *kannushi* may have originally designated only those persons considered most likely to become possessed.

3) Reciting Shinto prayers. Offering prayers to his shrine's deity is another obligation of each Shinto priest. In ancient times, the Japanese people believed that the language a deity uttered through its chosen medium was unintelligible to ordinary people. Consequently it was necessary for a particular person to sit face to face with the divine being and converse with him. Naturally a kannushi was chosen to perform this service. Many years later though, priests forgot the original significance of this service and inverted it into offerings and prayer to the deity.

4) Superintendence over divine offerings. The kannushi is required to preside over the handling of the deity's food and sacred vessels. In ancient Japan worshipers realized that a Shinto deity would be pleased only if these things were handled by holy men. Therefore, this duty too was assigned to purified people. Even in mid-twentieth-century Japan, the kannushi is obligated to superintend the preparation of divine food and manipulation of divine paraphernalia—a service which is sometimes attended with complicated, esoteric rites.

5) Taking responsibility for the community. The supreme power to preside at a community's annual religious festivals is entrusted to a person who possesses an intuitive ability to understand the normal cycle as well as the vicissitudes of the people's life. Under the enlarged kinship system of ancient Japan, the chief of the kinship group presumably assumed this responsibility, he being the person most likely to perceive the deity's will. However, as the religious function became differentiated from the political function in later days, presiding at festivals became more and more an essential duty of the kannushi. The kannushi therefore replaced the chief as the person expected to indicate the deity's will through divination.

6) *Financial maintenance of shrines.* In ancient Japan a kannushi was expected to take charge of financial affairs relating to the upkeep of the shrine's buildings and estate and to raise the annual funds necessary for festivals. Later, as the kannushi's functions became specialized, laymen were permitted to have a hand in these affairs.

The development of these six major functions of a Shinto priest is illustrated by a rich vocabulary of Japanese terms often applied to members of the priesthood. For example, the priest's function as a purifier of people is revealed by the old word *hafuri* (or *hōri*), meaning "the one who purifies," even though the term today is applied mostly to the local priests of lower grades or to some assistants in religious performances. The kannushi's traditional ability to become possessed by a kami is illustrated indirectly by many terms in modern usage signifying a dancing female shaman or a child possessed by a deity or spirit. These terms indicate that women and children are regarded as important mediums of supernatural possession and revelation; and yet revelation of kami through male priests also still survives, a fact which may explain why *tayū-san* (male dancer) has become the familiar name for Shinto priests. The kannushi's supplicatory function is reflected by the word *negi,* which derives from a verb meaning to pray and appeal. His superintendence of the deity's food and paraphernalia is suggested by *miya-moto* and *kō-moto,* words signifying a person at the center (*moto*) of a cult group. His responsibility for the community is exemplified also by the archaic words *tone* and *otona,* both of which, in their modern forms, refer to village elders. The Shinto priest's traditional responsibility for the financial maintenance of his shrine is illustrated by the words *gūji* (chief of the shrine) and *kagi-tori* or *kagi-azukari* (keeper of the keys) which are applied to him.

The continued specialization of the functions of the Shinto priest has led to greater emphasis upon certain of them and to the elimination of others. For example, the kannushi's modern duty of offering prayers to the deity seems to be increasingly stressed. Another indication of this changed role may be seen in the altered sense of the word *negi,* derived from this specialized function of prayer, but now used as a general title for the Shinto priest. Meanwhile the priest's responsibility for the financial maintenance of the shrine and his role as the oracle of divine revelation seem to be diminishing. During Japan's monarchic age (500–1191) the emperors gave each Shinto deity a rank which was subject to promotion. With official authorities wielding such an influence over local deities, the implication of the term *gūji* underwent a change. Originally, a gūji was simply the financial officer of a local shrine, but the term came to be applied to the priests of shrines of higher rank which were supported morally as well as financially by the central government. With such support, it is not surprising that until 1945 these gūji gained control of priestly duties over and beyond the management and business of the shrine. Whether the gūji's ascendancy over the kannushi will continue remains to be seen.

Other functions of the Shinto priest traditionally have

been less his exclusive province. Superintendence of the handling of divine paraphernalia and food, and leadership in community festivals have developed more distinctly in the shinji-tōnin system than in the priesthood. In the shinji-tōnin system, family heads of a community rotate the duties of performing Shinto rituals and conducting festivals.[12] If these men form an exclusive and more or less systematized group in charge of holding rituals, their group is called a *miyaza*. The institution of miyaza arose during the fifteenth century, mainly in the Kinki area of central Japan, when the local villages gained independence from their landlords. Whenever a Kinki village became free from aristocratic control, its well united residents formed a practical organization for the allotment of duties pertaining to religious rituals.[13] Remembering that the professional Shinto priests still were part of the aristocratically controlled shōen system, these villagers conducted Shinto rites on their own and balked at any interference from the professionals.

Even when a miyaza does not function according to strict traditional practice, it usually retains some of the major features of the shinji-tōnin system. Customarily, each year a different miyaza elder assumes responsibility for daily care of the shrine, being called a *miya-mori* (keeper of the shrine) when on duty. In some villages, where it is believed that the deity does not always stay in the shrine, the miyaza chooses a member of the group to supervise the service at his home for one year. The individual chosen to be on duty must practice abstention, and his residence must be consecrated and prepared for the festival at which the deity will be revered. For example, divine foods for the kami are usually prepared in the home of the individual on duty. From this practice of rotating ritual duties arose the terms *ichinen-kannushi* (one-year kannushi) and *nenban-kannushi* (kannushi on duty for a year), which were applied to miyaza elders serving at certain local shrines. Whenever these forms of communal religious practices exist, the Shinto priest can play only a secondary role.

With the establishment of the Tokugawa Shogunate, however, the miyaza was transformed, in most parts of Japan, from an autonomous village folk cult into a ritual institution. Under this new regime, powerful priestly organizations had to disband due to the reduction in their land tenures as granted by earlier governments. The high-ranking priests were forced to turn to villages in search of posts. With the downfall of the anti-Tokugawa feudal lords, many samurai lost their livelihoods, and to them the village-shrine priesthood seemed a desirable profession. The office of priest became less and less an hereditary affair, so that even people of the lower classes were able to assume priestly duties. After several generations, the descendants of such lower-class persons often could obtain full priestly status, as authorized by the license of Yoshida Shinto, mentioned above.

Two historical instances may illustrate how the trend toward the open-door system of priesthood still continued to operate, and clashed with the closed system of the miyaza, which excluded non-villagers. In the pre-Tokugawa period, the *otona-shu* (miyaza elders) of a shrine in Shiki-gun, Yamato province (Nara-ken), held complete control not only over the performance of religious rites, but also over the disposal rights of irrigation water and forest land belonging to the community. At the beginning of the Tokugawa era, however, they employed a janitor to look after the shrine, and the janitor some years later acquired the necessary qualifications enabling him to become a regular priest of the village shrine.

On the other hand, the miyaza in a village of Tsuzuki-gun, Yamashiro province (Kyōto-fu) in the middle Tokugawa era was firmly organized and noted for its exclusiveness toward newcomers and strangers. The elders rebuked a new priest who, though not a native of the village, insisted on his right to the shrine by virtue of his being the foster son of the former priest.

As a general rule this kind of exclusive attitude was rare under the Tokugawa government. The position of the Shinto priest became increasingly autonomous and tended to absorb the most essential functions previously exercised by the miyaza, without remonstrance or interference from the community.

Notes

1. After World War II, Shinto ceased to be the official religion of the Japanese nation. When, in 1945, all shrines were freed from government control and began to manage their affairs by themselves, some of the smaller village shrines took advantage of the situation by separating from the larger shrines which had dominated them since the late nineteenth century.

The official statistics for 1938 give a total of 110,238 shrines, broken down as follows: governmental and national, 205; prefectural, 1,098; regional, 3,616; village, 44,823; miscellaneous small shrines, 60,496. This gave a ratio of .88 shrines per 1,000 people, and 1.8 Shinto priests per 10,000. The number of jinja, however, was down to about 80,000 by 1956 (still an average of twenty shrines to one city or village); see *Jinja* in *Basic Terms of Shinto*, compiled by the Shinto Committee for the IXth International Congress for the History of Religions (Published by Jinja Honchō [The Association of Shinto Shrines] Kokugakuin University [Tokyo, 1958]).

2. The income of a shrine mainly depends upon subscriptions and offerings of parishioners and worshipers, and upon their purchase of amulets and tablets. Before World War II, prefectural governments gave a small allowance to regional shrines, and the national government did the same for prefectural and higher-ranking ones. Priests attendant on these governmental shrines were paid according to the

salary scale for all government officials. For instance, the salary regulations of employees in those shrines, issued in 1921, state that the first grade gūji (principal priest) was paid 3,400 yen a year; and the thirteenth grade or lowest-class gūji, 900 yen. (The annual salary of a professor at the Imperial University in those days was about 3,000 yen.) After the war, Jinja Honchō (The Association of Shinto Shrines) prescribed a pay plan for employees, revised in 1954, which gave the first grade gūji 70,000 yen a year and the lowest, the twentieth, 3,000 yen. (The ratio of prices between 1921 and 1954 is about 1 to 300.) However, because the financial conditions differ in each shrine, the actual incomes of the priests are not standardized.

3. Kannushi-san is the title used by villagers in addressing particular priests in their midst. In contrast, *kannushi* alone is used more generally to designate any person employed in rendering services to Shinto deities.

4. The widespread primogenitural inheritance of family occupation and property, however, was to a large extent curtailed by the new Japanese constitution of 1946.

5. Katsura Shrine is in Naka-machi, Taka-gun, Hyōgo-ken. The document referred to is a contract exchanged between the priest and parishioners of this shrine in 1767, which has been kept there with many other papers concerning the shrine's affairs. A portion of it is quoted in *Hyōgo-Ken Jinja-Shi (Book of the Shrines in Hyōgo Prefecture)* (Publication of Hyōgo-Ken Shinshoku-Kai [Nishinomiya, 1938]), II, 583.

6. Literally, *uji* means "clan," and *ko* means "child." The uji-ko are persons under the influence of an uji-gami. *Uji-gami*, originally designating the deified ancestral spirit of a clan, is now the term for the tutelary deity of a village or a smaller division of a village.

7. I discovered this attitude of villagers toward their priests during my field investigations in 1946.

8. *Mai* means dance. *Tayū* (of which *dayū* is the combining form) formerly designated Shinto priests in a sense; however, these terms now most frequently indicate dancers or other types of performers.

9. The shōen was something like a European manor of the Middle Ages. In this system land controlled by imperial families, by noblemen, or by priests of the old aristocracy belonged to important shrines and temples; and the priests of such shrines held a supervisory position over the peasants who lived in a shōen. The shōen system was in widespread existence during the dynastic period (500–1190),

and it continued on a smaller scale until the right to hold a private shōen was abolished completely toward the end of the Muromachi period in the early sixteenth century.

10. *Jinja Seido Hōrei Yōran (A Survey of Laws and Regulations on the Shrine System)* (Publication of Jingi-in Sōmu Kyoku [General Bureau in Charge of Shinto Worship] [Tokyo, 1941]), p. 93.

11. Shugendō priests belonged to Buddhist temples and worshiped Buddhist deities and saints, using Buddhist sutras and doctrine. However, they practiced Shinto rituals, such as religious abstinence, purification, confinement, and presentation of offerings. Unlike the Buddhist priests, they always dressed in simple clothes, with peculiar headgear on their unshaven heads, and wore swords. Disliking pollution and honoring cleanliness, they refused to participate in death ceremonies. They prayed for happiness in this world rather than in the next.

12. The head men are sometimes called *shinji-tōnin,* although they are more usually referred to as *tōnin* or *tōya.* Each is an ordinary villager who, when it is his turn, takes charge of all the services in the regular rituals or festivals of the shrine or cult group to which he belongs.

13. The village of Tokuchinho, Gamō-gun, Shiga-ken (presently Yōkaichi-shi, Shiga-ken), provides a good example of this process. It is a medieval village whose records of the development of the miyaza system have been located in medieval manuscripts and private papers found in old houses of the region. Lafcadio Hearn pointed out the case of Miho Shrine in Yatsuka-gun, Shimane-ken, which had a cult organization similar to a miyaza (*Japan, an Interpretation* [Rutland, Vermont: Charles E. Tuttle, 1955], p. 166). It is interesting to note, too, that upon the annual festival of this shrine the ichinen-kannushi of this group was possessed by the deity, whose divine announcements he revealed.

主
婦

PART SIX | **HOUSEWIVES**

Menstrual Taboos Imposed upon Women

BY KIYOKO SEGAWA

Until the end of the nineteenth century, a custom widely observed throughout Japan required that women live in a special hut or, more recently, in an isolated room, during the menstrual and parturient periods. According to an old woman of Shino-jima, Aichi-ken, a menstruating female withdrew to a special hut called a *kari-ya*[1] to take her meals and to sleep. Since the hut belonged to the community, it was used by all the women of the village during menstruation; and sometimes as many as twenty of them were there at the same time, cooking and eating their meals together.

During the tabooed period the women wore old, unlined garments as a token of abstinence. In the daytime they engaged in their regular work of fishing at sea with the men. At the cessation of the menses the women purified themselves in the sea water, washed their hair, and changed

239

clothes. On the eleventh day they went to the village temple to take meals, each woman bringing her own portion of rice. On the twelfth day they were permitted to return home to live and dine with their families. Thus the taboo forced most women to live apart from their families for one third of the month.

The custom underwent gradual simplification at the end of the nineteenth century. First, the women ceased to pass the night in the hut but continued to cook and eat there. In time the hut was abandoned entirely and the women kept to a straw mat in a secluded corner of the house, where they ate their food (left-over rice) on a special hearth. During a woman's menstrual period, all the fires in her house were extinguished and made anew, and all the pots and pans were washed. A fire taboo was placed upon these women, who were believed to have a pollution that might infect the family fires.

On the island of Himaka-jima, next to Shino-jima, menstruating women passed seven days in a kari-ya containing a hearth. On the eighth day, after simple purification rites, they drank a cup of tea obtained from the village temple or from a neighboring house, before they were allowed to return to their own families. The fact that these localities were the enclave territory of the Ise Shrine, most powerful of all the shrines, may have contributed to the pious attitude of the villagers in keeping abstinence.

In the mountain districts of Kitashidara-gun, Aichi-ken, the menstrual hut was called *koya, bun-ya,* or *betsu-ya.* Only the oldest village women, eighty years of age and over, have experienced the secluded life of the koya. They recall that, in their younger days, during menstruation they worked in the field by day as usual, but spent the night in the koya. The taboo prohibited their entering the main room where the family shrine was placed, going into the storehouse, or touching the well. When menstruating women called at another house on business, they were not allowed inside, but were supposed to stand at the entrance. Pickles and *miso* (bean paste) uncooked by fire could be brought to the menstrual hut, but never boiled food, for it was feared that the fire of the main house would be polluted by any contact, however indirect, with a menstruating woman.

After the period of abstinence, whether in summer or winter, the women would wash their bodies, hair, and clothes at the river in order to purify themselves. Like the women of Shino-jima who ate their meals at a temple for one day before returning to their family tables, so the women of Aichi-ken had to be given a cup of tea at some house other than their own. Otherwise they had to make tea outside their own houses or on the earth floor and share the tea with some children who happened to be playing nearby, before they were permitted to eat at the family table again. This rite, called *ai-bi* (sharing the fire), was necessary as a purification ritual before women could resume ordinary daily life. Personal articles used by the women during seclusion could not be brought into the home, for they too carried the infection. For a week after the women returned, they were prohibited from entering the room of the family shrine.

These customs apply only to the fishing and mountain villages of Aichi-ken, whose old traditions have persisted relatively unchanged. In the lowland farming villages where improved transportation modernized the mode of life, the taboo of abstinence vanished ten or twenty years ago. Some elderly women still remember the old ways, and some fragmental usages also suggest that menstrual taboos once existed there. By comparing the survivals of old customs collected in the remote country villages, folklorists may trace their gradual decline.

Data of this sort on menstrual taboos, obtained from
many districts of Japan, are assembled below. In Mie-ken,
due to the influence of the powerful Ise Shrine, the taboo
has been strictly kept until recent years. Most women on
the coast of this district are engaged in diving for ear shells
and top shells. Formerly during menstruation they left their
homes to live in a hut called *koya* or *taya,* where they
cooked and ate their meals. It was said that when three
women were assembled in the hut, the youngest would become *haramido* (pregnant), whether or not she was married.
These women divers went to work as usual but had to avoid
a sacred region of the sea called Yoroizaki. A local legend
tells that once a ship laden with coin was wrecked on the
rock of Yoroizaki, and all the villagers rushed to retrieve
the coins. A menstruating woman, vexed to lose this chance,
after much hesitation decided also to gather coins; but she
was swept away by the waves the moment her foot touched
the sacred rock.

In Takeno-mura, Kyōto, women in menses are isolated
in a special room and must eat food cooked in a special pot
on a special hearth. In Kasa-gun in the same prefecture,
girls of thirteen years and upward are warned not to have
a hand in rituals during the tabooed period. In Tottori-ken,
a menstruating woman feeds herself at a separate hearth on
the earth floor in a corner of the house. The corner is called
taya-beya (separate hut), a name which suggests the time
when a separate room or hut was set apart for the menstruating women.

Fishing villages along the coast of Shimane-ken are noted
for the piety of their inhabitants. In Kitahama-mura,
Hikawa-gun, unclean women were kept in a corner of a
room or *engawa* (a kind of verandah) and compelled to observe the food taboo. The men of the family had to do the
cooking if no other woman was available. At one time the

village also had a hut where menstruating women lived together. After seven days' abstinence they performed a purification rite, going down to the beach to drink sea water, and then returned home. This custom has died out and the hut has been torn down, but it is said that a house built on the spot where the hut stood will prosper.

An old record of the island of Mishima, Yamaguchi-ken, at the western extremity of the Japanese mainland, states that during the tabooed periods women were isolated in a special room and that childbearing women underwent abstinence for thirty-three days after the birth. Old women on the island have said, however, that they themselves had not experienced this old custom save at the autumn festival. After the preliminary ceremony of purifying the hearth for the grand festival, all the unclean people of the village— those who had recently borne children, who were menstruating, or who had suffered a recent death in their family —were removed into a temporary hut, where they stayed till the end of the festival. Those living in this hut ate food cooked and brought in by their families. To the student it seems unreasonable to make a present of cooked food to a person who has been isolated for fear of contaminating the family fire. Here is a problem involving the relation between ritual abstinence and ritual eating, for this custom of presenting gifts of food is common on the occasions of childbirth and death.

The site on Mishima is now called by a place name, Betsu-ya (Separate Hut). Some people say that women spent the period before and after childbirth in a corner of the barn, and those who were under the death taboo moved to a place near the temple. So the possibility arises that the betsu-ya might have served mainly for the menstruating women.

On the island of Shiga-jima, Fukuoka-ken, villagers followed the custom of using a special hut and hearth during menses and after a death.[2] At Ōshima-ura, Munakata-gun in the same prefecture, the women in menses did not move to a special hut but used special bowls and trays in their homes. In Amakusa, Kumamoto-ken, it is said that formerly the village women spent their menstrual periods in a hut on the mountain.[3]

In Matsumae-machi, Ehime-ken, a fisherman's wife when menstruating used a special hearth under the eaves outside the house. Because it was taboo for her to enter the house, she remained outside until the termination of her menstrual period and returned only after cleansing her hair. In Nishiuwa-gun, in the same prefecture, the isolated meal taken by one in abstinence was called *kiri-bi* (separating the fire). In Gogo-mura, Kagawa-ken, if a woman was menstruating at New Year's time, she was removed to an isolated house and left there to eat alone. On the first day of the new year every woman refrained from visiting other families. In the small islands in the Seto Inland Sea, women also followed the custom of spending their menstrual periods in separate huts provided with hearths.

In various localities near Hamamatsu-shi, in Shizuoka-ken, there are a number of place names which indicate the former existence of such a hut. Some deserted wells still remain in the fields and are said to be the wells used by the women in abstinence. In this district, after the tabooed period expired, the women would invite guests to have *himachi*[4] with them. This may correspond to the custom in Aichi-ken, mentioned earlier, of the women's eating with other people at the end of menstrual abstinence.

In the Izu Islands (O-shima, Miyake-jima, Hachijō-jima, among others) the custom of spending the menstrual period in a special hut has been strictly observed up till recent years. In Ō-shima, menstruating women were forbidden to walk along the roads which were used on the occasions of festivals or rituals. At Tomisaki in Chiba-ken, at the onset of menses the woman would pretend to step over a ditch, and would then retire for her period of seclusion to one of the barns where farmers stored grain and fishermen mended their nets. She would carry with her a bowl of left-over rice to eat during this time. At Chikura, in the same prefecture, the period of menstrual abstinence was usually seven days, extended to eleven days at New Year's time. At the end of this period the woman took a meal called *hatsu-batsuho*[5] before returning to her normal life. (In this district the word *hatsu-batsuho* was also used for the rice offered to new babies at the celebration of their first meal 120 days after birth. It may be an important clue to the origin of abstinence customs that the feast at the expiration of the period was called *himachi* or *hatsu-batsuho,* words which are usually associated with rituals or cults.) During New Year's celebrations the menstruating women assembled in a certain house. Elder ones spent the time spinning thread or darning clothes, and young girls played cards. The women were said to enjoy themselves there, and sometimes they were joined by the young men of the village. The usual daytime work was carried on during menstruation.

By the beginning of the twentieth century this custom had become obsolete, for the villagers were able to simplify observance of the abstinence taboos by getting *o-fuda* (purifying charms) from Kōyasan, the head temple of the Tendai sect of Buddhism in Wakayama-ken. In the villages of Kita-azumi-gun and Nishi-chikuma-gun in Nagano-ken, under the influence of the Mitake Shrine, huts called *hiya* or *hima-ya* were set apart for menstrual and parturient women to stay in during the period of abstinence. Thus in the regions around such influential Shintoistic shrines as Mitake and Ise, the old custom survived till the beginning of this century. In Sado Island, Niigata-ken, a menstruating woman was called "the woman in bun-ya," but she actually lived in a corner of the main house with a special hearth for her own use. The inconvenient custom of living in a secluded hut was eventually simplified, as were the customs attached to pregnancy and death.

The instances mentioned above were all collected from districts west of the Kanto plain. That so few come from the eastern area is due partly to the writer's restricted field investigation and partly to the scarcity of other reports from this district. In fact, examples of secluded huts for polluted people are rarely found in the Tōhoku area in northeast Japan, although the sense of the impurity of menstruation prevails among elderly women of that area. At the same time, we must notice that in Okinawa and other islands south of Kyūshū, where there are many survivals of the old customs, menstrual huts and hearths are rarely found.

The main reason for isolating polluted women has been the fear that they will contaminate the fire. It was taboo for them to touch the hearth and the well lest they should stain the family fire and water. They were not allowed to touch the kegs of miso (bean paste) and *sake* lest they spoil these important foods, and they could not be present before the altars of Shinto deities. At Nagoya-mura in Saga-ken, the custom of seclusion has been gradually moderated to allow the woman to sit at table with her family; however, during menses not only the woman but the whole family must still abstain from going to the shrine. The woman even avoids exchanging words with people who are on their way to the shrine. During the shrine festival, menstruating women live in abstinence in a secluded hut on the mountain. In Seihaku-gun, Tottori-ken, the husband also abstains from going to the shrine.

People engaged in hunting, fishing and charcoal-making require strict observance of menstruation taboos. Throughout Japan impure women may not touch fishing nets and other fishing implements, or get into a boat. In Kuga-shima, an island of Gotō-retto in Nagasaki-ken, where a belief in the deity of the mountain is popular, polluted women were once prohibited from going to the mountain to gather firewood. There is a region there where unclean women are believed to be easily possessed by wolf-spirits. At Minami-zaki-mura, Shizuoka-ken, quarrymen's wives, during the menses, used separate vessels at meals for fear of infecting their husbands. In the same region it was once believed that a polluted person who happened to meet a *tengu* in the mountains would be in great danger. In the fishing villages the peasants feared blood pollution more than the death pollution. For example, at Tomisaki in Chiba-ken, other villagers avoided lending knives to the menstruating women. In no instance were contaminated women permitted to share food or clothes with other people.

In Kōhoku-gun, Shizuoka-ken, it is said that if a women aborted a child or did not keep the menstrual taboo or if a person secretly ate the meat of four-legged animals (breaking the Buddhist taboo), a strange and tragic happening would occur in the village. If an abortion or taboo violation was known to have occurred, the villagers gathered together all their flint stones used for fire-making and had them purified by the local smith, as a protection against the consequences of the illegitimate act. (In the past, people regarded blacksmiths as having special powers and skills.) In a hamlet at Furikusa-mura, Kitashidara-gun, Aichi-ken, the villagers had their flint stones burned by the smith for purification, and also swept their hearths, when they heard evil omens such as a bird's song at night or the fox's strange cry, omens suggesting a fire contamination somewhere in the village.[6]

In the same village, it is told, a Shinto priest who peeped

into a menstrual hut was struck by a village lad and disappeared forever. A hundred years ago, at Kuroiwa hamlet in the same village, a house caught on fire, and a menstruating woman would not break the taboo and enter the room of the family shrine. She watched while the precious genealogical scroll, handed down for many generations in the family, went up in smoke.

Thus women were bound, body and soul, by the idea of pollution. The old women on Himaka-jima told me that in recent years when the culture was changing and they were first allowed to take meals with the family during menstruation, they felt uneasy and were conscious of their pollution.

On the other hand, celebrating the onset of menses is a joyous custom prevalent throughout Japan. The expression "the first blossom" is used in many areas. Girls in "first blossom" are usually feted with sekihan (rice boiled with red beans) and introduced to the village society as grown-up women. In Toba-shi in Mie-ken, on such occasions, villagers laid the sekihan on the altar.[7] At Kitahama-mura in Shizuoka-ken the girl at her first menstruation was presented with rice and beans by her mother. This she boiled, and all the women in the menstrual hut shared the feast. In the Izu Islands of Tokyo-to, the young girls have been elaborately feted. Thus in Hachijō-jima, the southernmost of the Izu Islands, on this occasion wealthy parents sometimes gave a newly built hut to their daughter. Relatives and neighbors sent presents of rice, each gift amounting to about eight quarts. The festivities lasted for a week with village youths as the chief guests and were far more important than wedding celebrations on these islands. The parents made elaborate preparations for their daughters to be feted, for the girls were now qualified to receive marriage proposals. In O-shima, the island near Tokyo, dressed-up parents holding a lighted lantern in their hands sent their daughter off to the menstrual hut. Relatives and friends followed her, and in the hut they all celebrated the occasion with mochi, sekihan, *sake,* and other food brought and prepared by the family. The young men of the village were invited to this feast. On the same day the girl's mother paid a visit to the shrine of the tutelary deity to report the daugher's maturity.[8]

To celebrate the first menstruation is natural enough as it is proof of maturity and marks the commencement of womanhood. But the monthly taboo imposed upon women, the idea of impurity attached to them, and the sense of humiliation caused by sexual discrimination, seemed to females severe and distasteful treatment. Even the women of the cities who knew nothing of confinement in menstrual huts were sensible of their physical impurity during the monthly periods. Since the beginning of the twentieth century, with the rapid change in cultural habits, Japanese people have largely freed themselves from the old pollution taboos and customs.

Notes

1. A similar institution is found in the *ubu-ya,* a hut where a woman spends a certain period of abstinence after she has borne a child. Building a special hut for the parturition was probably a prevalent custom in ancient Japan, and examples of ubu-ya are still found in some villages today. All the data given in the present article, unless otherwise indicated, were obtained on field trips which I undertook from 1935 to 1939.

2. "Shiga-jima no Betsu-gama" ("Separate Hearth in the Shiga Island"), *Shima (Island)* (Tokyo), II (1934), 232.

3. *Fujin Kōron (Women's Review)* (Tokyo), April, 1936.

4. *Himachi* originally referred to the custom of a group of people from the same community assembling in a certain place to spend the

night in abstinence and worship. The original religious meaning has been lost, and the term now often means no more than being off from daily work and having a party or other entertainment.

5. *Hatsu-batsuho* is a dialect word of *hatsuho,* which means "the first crop."

6. *Aichi Kyōiku (Education in Aichi Prefecture),* May, 1940. This same description can also be found in the unpublished field notes on Furikusa Village by Kiyoko Segawa, 1935.

7. This information is found in a short report from Toba, one among several brief reports from various places appearing in the "Shiryō" ("Folklore Materials") column in *Minkan Denshō (Folklore Journal)* (Tokyo), Vol. V, No. 2, 1940, p. 8.

8. Tokuzō Ōmachi, *Hachijo-jima (Hachijo Island)* (Tokyo: Sōgen Sha, 1951), p. 158. The field notes which form the basis of Omachi's book were made in 1938.

Ashiire-kon, Putting-One's-Feet-In Marriage

BY TOKUZŌ ŌMACHI

The earliest known form of social organization in Japan was based on the temporarily or permanently matrilocal marriage. A young married couple would live at the home of the bride's parents for a certain period of time—not infrequently for their entire lives—after the wedding ceremony was performed. With the rise of the military class in the early Middle Ages, patrilocal marriage assumed greater importance. In the feudal society dating from the time of the first military government—the Kamakura Shogunate, established at the end of the twelfth century—this form superseded more and more the matrilocal type of marriage.

In present-day Japan patrilocal marriage is usual, although in certain remote districts vestiges of the old matrilocal system can still be found. A kind of matri-patrilocal marriage is also known to exist, in which the wedding ceremony is held at the bridegroom's home, although the married couple later spend their nights in the bride's natal house. This form appears to be important in the general history of marriage in Japan, and the author has termed it *ashiire-kon*.[1] *Ashiire* literally means "putting-one's-feet-in," and *kon* means "marriage"; the secondary sense of the term is "trial marriage." Ashiire-kon may represent a transitional form from the matrilocal to the patrilocal marriage system and can still be observed in the Izu Islands, especially in To-shima.

To-shima is a volcanic island about seven kilometers (4.5 mi.) in circumference, located about twenty kilometers (12.4 mi.) south of Izu Ō-shima. The Izu Islands are about sixty kilometers (37.3 mi.) south from the coast of the Izu Peninsula, and are part of Tokyo-to. To-shima's volcano, conical in shape, is now dormant. The steep slope on the northern side of this island has been cultivated into a terraced village, thickly inhabited and surrounded by camellia trees. The total number of households in the village is eighty-five. Fifty-eight are the original households, thirteen belong to new settlers, and fourteen belong to retired people. Three hundred seventy-five inhabitants reside in To-shima, according to the register at the village office in October, 1949. In 1840 there were fifty-four households on the island. Thus very little increase in the number of houses has occurred during the last hundred years.[2] Only the eldest sons may inherit property, and all younger sons are traditionally obliged to seek adoption in another family, to leave the island, or to forego marriage.

i

In To-shima the initiation of both boys and girls is celebrated when they reach the age of fifteen. The girls' initiation, called *kane-tsuke-iwai* (the ceremony of dyeing the teeth black), is observed in an elaborate group ceremony

on January second.[3] After kane-tsuke-iwai, the girl will
nèver again sleep in her own house. She must now sleep in
another house or dormitory in the village, called *nedo* ("the
place to sleep in," *neyado* in standard Japanese). From two
to five girls usually sleep together in each nedo, retiring
there every evening after finishing their meals at their own
homes. Sisters must go to different nedo. Generally it is
decided when a girl is born to which nedo she will go. There
is only one sleeping house for the boys of the village, who
spend their nights there after their sixteenth year.

The nedo is an institution primarily designed to unite
the young people. In sending their sons and daughters to
nedo, parents show their indifference to their children's
choice of brides or bridegrooms. The master of the house
used as nedo takes charge of the young people who sleep
there, but they seem to have almost complete autonomy in
their marriage decisions. Lack of parental authority over
the children's mariages can be proved by the fact that *yome-
katagi-kon* (marriage by stealing the bride) has never been
practiced on this island, although it is known in the western
districts of Japan, particularly in Kyūshū. Yome-katagi-kon
can be developed in a society where the authority of the
young men's group and that of the parents over the marriage decision are equally balanced.

So, in the past, the bride and the bridegroom chose each
other, and the marriage ceremony was performed. After the
wedding the couple slept in the same nedo until a child was
born. Following its birth they spent their nights in the
wife's natal house. Such customs died out about thirty-five
years ago, in the late Taisho era (1912–25).

ii

Currently, the actual formalities of marriage begin when
a kinsman of the bridegroom goes to the bride's natal house,

usually at night, to propose marriage. The bride's parents in most cases are expecting him and readily accept the proposal. There is no drinking of *sake* to celebrate the engagement on that occasion. Nor is the man who goes on this errand called a go-between. His duty is finished after this single visit, and he has no special relation with the new couple.

Before evening the next day three to five female relatives of the bridegroom visit the bride's natal house to offer greetings and to take the bride back with them. The bride accompanies them in her usual plain clothes. There is a simple tea party at the bridegroom's house to which the neighbors, usually only the women, are invited. The bride's mother arrives to join the celebration. The only male who attends this rite is the bridegroom's father. The bridegroom himself is not present. There is no special reason for his absence, save that he need not be introduced to the people since he has already been united with the bride, and the couple have begun to sleep in the same nedo. The purpose of this occasion is to celebrate the first formal meeting between the bridegroom's parents and the bride, and to announce the marriage in public. *Yome-nigiri* (bride's rice balls) are eaten around the hearth. The word *yome-nigiri* is the only ritual term used in this ceremony. After the assembled villagers eat yome-nigiri and drink tea the wedding ceremony is over, and the bride and other guests leave for their own homes. With these simple formalities the marriage is completed and acknowledged by the public. Until the time when her husband becomes head of the family, the bride will be called *anei* (sister) a term indicating her social status rather than kinship.

No other ceremony is observed, not even to celebrate the first meeting of the bride's parents with the bridegroom, although this is the most important event in conventional matrilocal marriage. Nor is there any occasion for the drinking of *sake,* the usual accompaniment to any Japanese ceremony. No exchange of engagement gifts takes place. In other islands of the Izu group the same form of marriage is practiced, and in some of these islands the marriage ceremony is called *ashiire,* whereas in To-shima the people had not previously employed that term. In recent years, influenced by the general trend of the times, the marriage ceremony has become more elaborate on most of the islands. This new form of marriage ceremony is called *shūgen.* The word *ashiire* was then adopted by the people of To-shima to signify the older form of marriage. Thus on this island the marriage ceremony was simple, and the girl's initiation held a far more important position in the life cycle. This contrast parallels that between ashiire and *uide-iwai* in Hachijō-shima, another of the Izu Islands. Uide-iwai is the celebration which is held when a girl comes home from the secluded hut after her first menstruation. In Hachijō-shima this occasion was the girl's initiation or rite of passage.[4] In To-shima the bride is now regarded as a member of the husband's family after the simple marriage ceremony described above; and following it she comes to the husband's house early every morning, from the next day on, to work with his family and eat meals with them. In such a residential situation, however, there is a significant problem, which is discussed below.

iii

A wife who works for her husband's family in the daytime returns to her parents' house, after supper, along with the husband. This custom is called *nedo-gaeri* (to return to a sleeping place), a practice which continues until the retirement of the husband's parents. There are many parents who before their retirement live with their daughters' children and whose sons' children live in the daughter-in-law's natal house (see Appendix I, p. 260). On this island, as in many other regions, retirement for elderly parents requires them to leave home and establish themselves in a separate dwelling, called an *inkyo-ya* (house of retirement). Upon the retirement of a man's parents, the man returns to his parents' home, with his wife, as the head of the house. His wife is now called *kakaa* (mistress or mother) instead of *anei,* and her obligations to her parents' home are now terminated.

iv

The bride's marriage portion is customarily kept in her natal house until she becomes the mistress of her married household. To make this subject clear, I will return to the marriage ceremony. The girls of To-shima dress specially for their initiation ceremony. Their parents provide them with a gown and ornaments, whereas for the marriage ceremony they need not prepare anything. As was mentioned above, the bride is married in her everyday costume. Nor do the bridegroom's parents, before the wedding, have an obligation to offer any clothes or gifts to the bride. From the day following the marriage ceremony the bride, in her work clothes, labors for the husband's family. She is not provided with new implements for farming or carrying burdens either by her husband's parents or her own parents. She must bring the old farming tools which she used at her natal house. As her clothes are all kept there, too, she must return to change her garments when she gets wet in the rain during her work. After the marriage ceremony the husband's parents are responsible for supplying the bride with additional clothes, and these too are kept at her natal home.

The bride's parents, at whose house the couple sleeps, supply bedding for their married daughter, son-in-law, and
grandchildren. One woman's portion was reserved in her
natal home for a long time; she was thirty-five years old,
had four children, and performed nedo-gaeri for twelve
years after her marriage. Her clothes were kept in her parents' house until quite recently. When a married daughter
finally does become mistress in the household of her husband, she takes all her belongings from her natal house.

v

The succession of the son, upon his parents' retirement,
is celebrated as the most important event in the household.
The celebration begins with a rite at the ōya (main house).
The sons and daughters, in their best clothes, send off the
parents to their inkyo-ya. As they leave, the new mistress
weeps ceremonially, holding the hem of the mother-in-law's
dress. A scene of departure is enacted. (This ceremonial
weeping is connected with the custom of crying in the funeral ceremony of the Izu Islands—including To-shima.)
Another rite takes place at the inkyo-ya; and this is followed by a feast of seven days and seven nights, during
which time the villagers visit the retirement house to celebrate the occasion. Parched beans are customarily eaten
during these festivities. This great feast is held not only to
honor the retirement of the old couple, but also to honor
the new couple's succession to control of the household. In
addition, it may also serve as the occasion for the couple to
make a public announcement of their marriage. In recent
years, while the marriage ceremony has become increasingly
elaborate, the girl's initiation ceremony appears to be dying

out and the retirement celebration has diminished in importance. (See Appendix II, p. 262.)

vi

In present-day Japan, To-shima is a rare example of a locality where wives give birth to children in their natal houses. Until about sixty years ago, women on this island used to spend their menstruation periods in a hut called *ko-ie* (little house), cooking their meals there on a separate fire. Even at that time, however, this hut was not used for childbirth. In the present day, wives give birth to children at their natal houses while they perform nedo-gaeri, but some wives return to their parents' houses for delivery even after they have ceased nedo-gaeri and have become the mistresses of their husbands' homes. If their parents are already retired, they go to the retirement house. (See Appendix III, p. 263.)

This custom demonstrates that a woman is so tied to her natal home that she does not completely belong to the husband's household even after she becomes mistress of the house. The ceremonies on the third and the seventh days after the birth of a child are held at the mother's natal house. Mother and child go to the father's house for the first time on the fourteenth day after the birth, an occasion called *uchikatari* in the local dialect. From that day on the wife eat meals at her husband's house again. Usually she takes a rest from farm work till the thirty-fifth day after childbirth, at which time a celebration is held. The husband does not usually visit the wife's natal house for forty-five days, or sometimes seventy-five days, after the birth of a child.

As the evidence presented shows, the women of this island have a strong tendency to depend upon their natal houses.

They call this house *oregae* (my own home) and refer to their husband's house by its house name (its *yagō*). This evidence supports our hypothesis that ashiire-kon represents an archaic marriage form reflecting an intermediate stage in the change from a matrilocal to a patrilocal marital system.

APPENDIX I. *Instances of Nedo-gaeri*

In fifty-eight original households which I studied, nine young wives are carrying on nedo-gaeri. Seven of these wives each have one child, and the remaining two wives each have four children. In the latter two cases, six persons—husband and wife and four children—spend every night in the wife's parents' house. The following table shows the relation of these households.

a) No. 75 (3) → No. 1
b) No. 30 (3) → No. 21 (3) → No. 72
c) No. 49 (3) → No. 52 (3) → No. 61
d) No. 36 (3) → No. 48 (6) → No. 28 (6) →
       No. 68 (3) → No. 66

These numbers refer to the households as listed in the register at the village office. The numerals in parentheses indicate the number of persons who sleep in the wife's natal house.

The simplest case is (*a*), in which household No. 75 has three members who go to household No. 1 every night. Household No. 75, which consists of six members, has only three persons who remain at night, while household No. 1 also with six members receives three additional people every night. The most complicated case is (*d*) in which five households are connected and eighteen persons move every morning and evening. It is purely by chance that of the nine cases in my investigation three is the predominant number of persons involved in the moving, followed by six, and that no other number occurs. This is merely the accidental data as of 1949 when I visited the island.

The ages of these wives and husbands are given in the following table.

Household number	75	30	21	49	52	36	48	28	68
Husband's age	22	25	28	30	30	26	33	34	25
Wife's age	18	25	24	23	21	22	30	31	21

Among these wives, the ones aged thirty and thirty-one each have four children; and the ages of their children are respectively nine, six, three, one; and six, five, two, one. As far as these data are concerned, the oldest of the wives who do nedo-gaeri is thirty-one, and the oldest child involved in this practice is nine. The common situation of these nine wives is that they are living by day with their husbands' parents who have not yet retired to separate houses. The ages of the parents are as follows.

Household number	75	30	21	49	52	36	48	28	68
Father	53	66	51	58	62	55	61	59	69
Mother	57	64	52	51	60	53	56	56	72

These figures show that the age of succession to the position of household head and the retirement age are rather high on this island, among the areas where the retirement system is observed. If the wife's parents are already retired, the wife sleeps not in the main building of her natal house but in the retirement house. This is the case in household No. 61.

Let us look at household No. 68. This household consists of five members: the husband U. G. (age 69), the wife M. (72), an adopted daughter F. (21), her husband Y. (25), and a grandchild (3). The adopted daughter and her husband were married in this household, where they live in the daytime; but they return at night to her own natal house, household No. 66. This unusual case might result from the particular circumstance that she was adopted rather late, at the age of seventeen.

Only three households in the village offer exceptions to the system of nedo-gaeri. In these cases the brides have ceased to practice nedo-gaeri before the retirement of the husbands' parents.

a) Household No. 37 consists of seven members: the husband N. K. (65), the wife H. (65), a son M. (39), his wife K. (34), and three grandchildren (13, 8, 4). The old couple still hold the leadership of the household, yet the young couple live with them day and night. One possible reason that they halted nedo-gaeri might be the death of the bride's mother at her natal home. She has already carried her clothes to the husband's house and given birth to the children at the same house, despite her situation under the authority of the husband's parents.

b) Household No. 69 consists of nine members: the husband

U. S. (57), the wife M. (50), her mother K. (88), an adopted daughter T. (29), her husband T. (36), three grandchildren (8, 5, 1), and one more person. The wife M. is the real daughter of K., and the husband U. S. came from another house. The adopted daughter T. was brought to this household when very young, and her own family has left this island.

c) Household No. 41 consists of six members: the husband M. (29), the wife M. K. (32), two children (3 and 1), a foster father Y. (69), and foster mother F. (67). The latter, having no child of their own, had adopted two boys, one of whom married and succeeded the head of household No. 40. Foster parents Y. and F. retired and established a new household, No. 41, taking the other adopted son with them. This son married the wife M. K., but he was killed in the war, and his brother M. married M. K. They all live in the same house, so that Y. and F. who had already retired are now preparing for retirement again. The young wife M. K. did nedo-gaeri for about ten years with the former husband and for about a year with the present husband. Now her name is registered as the head of household No. 41, and the old couple are treated as retired people.

In these three exceptional arrangements, the young wife K. in case (*a*) is the only true exception to the system of nedo-gaeri. Besides these three, there are four cases in which the young wives stay at the husband's house along with their mothers-in-law. In those cases the husband's fathers are already dead, and in fact the young couples are actually the heads and mistresses of the households. It is expected that the mothers will retire, although the act of retirement is delayed for such reasons as poverty.

APPENDIX II. *Instances of Households of Retired Couples*

Among the present fifty-eight households in To-shima, eighteen are recognized as those of retired people. The ages of these household heads are as follows, according to the register of households mentioned on page 260.

Husband	—	73	77	55	60	75	—	78	77	—	68	59	62
Wife	68	67	78	43	52	73	76	71	—	67	66	62	61

Husband	82	—	—	—	69
Wife	74	71	71	72	67

The fourth couple in this table is younger than retired people usually are, for the reason that this wife is a second wife. There are only two other retired people on the island—one man and one woman—who are in their fifties. These figures do not indicate the ages of retirement, but when we compare them with the figures of the previous table showing the ages of the parents who live with their sons, we see that retirement age in this island is quite high. In general, there are complicated conditions which decide the retirement age. In To-shima, retirement is related to the bride's complete removal to her husband's house. Concerning this point, it may not be proper to lay emphasis chiefly on the conditions arising from the husband's side —e.g., the late retirement of his parents—in explaining the delay of the bride's complete removal to the husband's house. I would rather take the very opposite view, namely that the reason for the delay is originally to be found on the bride's side, in her attachment to her natal house.

APPENDIX III. *Instances of Childbirth at the Natal Home*

a) Household No. 11 consists of the husband O. M. (36), the wife N. (35), and seven children (16, 14, 12, 10, 7, 5, and 2) . The hubsand's parents have just retired. The wife did nedo-gaeri for ten years after the marriage ceremony. During those ten years she bore probably five children. After that she had too many children to perform nedo-gaeri. Yet she gave birth to all of her seven children at her natal house.

b) Household No. 33 consists of the husband U. C. (52), the wife T. (41), and seven children (22, 20, 17, 14, 12, 9 and 6). This wife, like the wife in case (a), was delivered of all her children at her natal house. The difference between these two cases is that the parents in case (b) retired before the first child was born, whereas in case (a) the parents retired after all seven children were born. The father of U. C., the husband, died very early, and the mother retired and established household No. 34, before her son U. C. married the wife T. Therefore T. came to live in the husband's house as the mistress, immediately after the marriage ceremony. She did not do nedo-gaeri at all, yet she went back to her natal home every time she bore a child.

We can find many more such instances, from which I select one special case:

c) Here is a family including household No. 50 and household No. 51. Household No. 50 consists of three members: a son M. S. (26), his wife M. (26), and a grandchild (2). Household No. 51 consists of four members: the mother M. T. (67), a daughter M. (22), her husband R. (21) who has married into this family, and a grandchild (1). The son, M. S., of the old mother, M. T., married a girl from outside the island, and they are living in the main house now. The old mother is retired and has a household with her daughter, whose husband married into the family. The mother M. T. has four more daughters who all married men on the island and left their mother's house. Each of these six women had some connection with the mother's house at the confinement period of childbirth. In the following items the details of their connection are described in detail.

1) The husband U. S. (55), after the death of his first wife, married the present wife H. (43), who is a daughter of M. T. and bore five children, one of whom died young. This wife gave birth to four children at her mother M. T.'s house.

2) The wife M. (37) in No. 3 household bore seven children,

five of whom are living (15, 13, 10, 7 and 4). All but one of the children were born at the grandmother M. T.'s house.

3) The wife C. (35) in household No. 70 has now five children (17, 10, 6, 4, and 1). Three other children died. The wife C. gave birth to all of these eight children at her mother M. T.'s house.

4) The wife K. (32) in household No. 41 has two children (3 and 1) to whom she gave birth at her mother M. T.'s house.

5) The daughter M. (22) of M. T., who lives with her husband and a child in M. T.'s household, gave birth to the child in the same house.

6) The wife M. (26) of M. T.'s son bore her first child at her natal house outside the island; she is to give birth to the second child under the care of the mother-in-law M. T.

None of these six women does nedo-gaeri now. The wife H. of case (*1*) and wife M. of case (*2*) will not come back any more to their mother's house for confinement and delivery. But wife C. of case (*3*) and wife K. of case (*4*) are still expected to come to the mother's house when they are going to have a baby. Wife M. of case (*5*) and wife M. of case (*6*), who are still young and expected to bear more children, are under the care of M. T. so long as she lives. During the past seventeen years twenty-one babies were born at the grandmother M. T.'s house. Like a hen's nest, the childbed in her house has had no time to cool off.

Thus, from the foregoing summaries of household situations, we see that unless some unforeseen circumstance prevents it, a woman of To-shima will probably return to her natal house to give birth, as long as her mother lives.

Notes

1. Tokuzō Ōmachi, "Ashiire-kon to sono Shūhen" ("*Ashiire-kon* and its Environment"), *Minzokugaku Kenkyū (Studies in Folklore)* (Annual Report of the Folklore Society of Japan) (Tokyo), I (1950), 1–64.

2. The reason for the increase, small as it is, in the number of original households is not known to me.

3. See Ōmachi, *"Mori to Oyako* ("Nursemaid and Ritual Mother"), *Minkan Denshō (Folklore Journal)* (Tokyo), Vol. XIV, No. 1, 1950, pp. 5–13.

4. See Ōmachi, *Hachijō-jima (Hachijō Island)* (Tokyo: Sōgen Sha, 1951), pp. 158–64.

The Spool of Thread: A Subtype of the Japanese Serpent-Brídegroom Tale

BY KEIGO SEKI

The animal-bridegroom type of folktale[1] is well known in Japan, where it appears in several forms. Among these forms are the demon-, monkey-, and serpent-bridegroom versions, which also have been collected in China,[2] Korea,[3] Turkey,[4] and from the Tsou people of aboriginal Formosa.[5] The serpent-bridegroom tale in Japan has six distinct subtypes;[6] the distribution and development of one of them—the *odamaki* (spool) tale—is the subject of this paper.

I. CONTENTS OF THE TALE

The odamaki tale has three basic forms (herein designated as *A*, *B*, and *C*), but the three share a common introductory episode. Whereas form *A* appears to have a relatively fixed principal episode and conclusion, two distinct versions of forms *B* and *C* occur wherever the tale is found. These versions (labeled *Ba, Bb, Ca,* and *Cb*) can be compared to each other, and to form *A,* as follows:

1. *Introduction*

A young man visits a girl every night, and eventually the girl becomes pregnant. When her parents inquire about the visitor's name and family background, she tells them that she knows nothing except that he mysteriously comes to her bed each night and then departs early the next morning through a chink or hole in the door. In order to discover the stranger's identity, the parents tell her to stick an iron needle threaded with hemp into his hair or clothes. That night, the girl obeys her parents' request.

2. PRINCIPAL EPISODE

(*A*) The next morning the girl follows the thread to a pool or to a cavern which contains a stream. When she announces that she has come to find her mysterious visitor, a wounded serpent appears. The serpent says, "I am dying because of the poison of the iron. You shall bear my son, who will become a great man. Take good care of him!"

(*Ba*) Either the girl's parents follow the thread to a pool, where they find the serpent already dead or wounded and writhing with pain; or (*Bb*) the girl herself follows the thread to the pool, enters the water, and turns into a serpent.

3. CONCLUSION

(*A*) The girl gives birth to a son (or to three of them) with scales on his back. He grows up, becomes a hero, marries, and fathers children who also bear such scales.

(*Ba*) In dread of the dead serpent, the people of the locality build a shrine to appease its spirit; or (*Bb*) they fear to go near the pool in which the girl was transformed, because if they were to do so and should drop a sickle or other iron object into the water by mistake, they would become ill immediately.

(*Ca*) The girl's mother (or father) follows the thread to a cave and overhears the following conversation between a parent and son:

Parent: "You did mischief to a human being. That is why you were injured by the poison of iron."

Son: "I am satisfied because I have left my son in the human being."

Parent: "But the human being is clever. (*Ca*) She will bathe in water with sweet flag in it at the festival of May fifth. Or she will drink *sake* with peach blossoms at the festival of March third and *sake* with chrysanthemum blossoms at the festival of September ninth."[7] Or (*Cb*) "if she puts a frog in the tub which she will use at her parturition, the child will be sure to die."

(*Ca*) The mother (or father) of the pregnant girl makes her take a sweet-flag bath, or drink special wine, at the festivals of March third, May fifth, and September ninth; the tale explains that such was the origin of these festival-day customs. Or (*Cb*) the girl gives birth to a child in the tub, which contains a frog in order to assure her safety. The child dies as its grandfather has predicted.

II. DISTRIBUTION AND VARIANTS OF THE TALE

The three forms (*A, B,* and *C*) of the odamaki tale are found all over Japan, coexisting with one another and forming a definite story area or oikotype in each of four geographical regions. These regions are (*1*) Kyūshū, (*2*) Shikoku and Chugoku, (*3*) Chubu, and (*4*) Tōhoku; they are indicated on the map on the facing page.

Form *A* is in most cases told as a legend, for it attempts to explain the origin of a number of famous Japanese feudal families. It has circulated separately in the eastern and western parts of Japan, and thus has formed a distinct legend area in each of these regions. In the western region, Oita-ken in Kyūshū is the center of distribution. There, the heroine, named Uda-hime, follows the thread along with her nurse. Both of them encounter a wounded serpent, who gives the heroine a box, but advises her not to open it until the one-hundredth day after their meeting. Weary of waiting, she opens it on the ninety-ninth day instead. Within the box are three eggs or golden balls, from which three boys are born. Named Takata Saburō, Usuki Jirō, and Ogata Saburō,[8] the boys grow up to become the feudal lords of western Japan. Their names correspond with the real names of the heroic, historical personages who held sway over Kyūshū in the Middle Ages.

Only minor variations of form *A,* as it is described above, occur elsewhere in western Japan. Recent immigrants from Ōita-ken have carried this form of the tale to Kagawa-ken in Shikoku, where the only changes are that the serpent gives the heroine three boxes instead of one, and that three boys come directly out of the boxes rather than from eggs or golden balls. In Kumamoto-ken in Kyūshū, all collected texts of form *A* end with the birth of only one child. The same is true of two variants from Nagasaki-ken on the north-

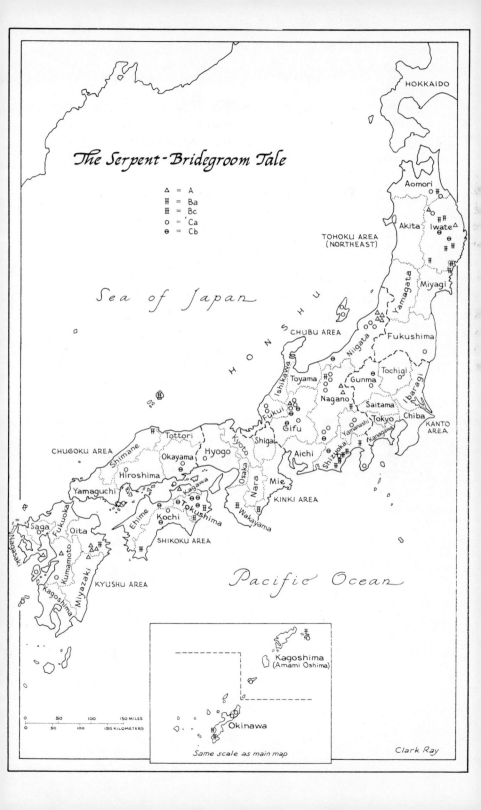

The Serpent-Bridegroom Tale

△ = A
Ⅱ = Ba
Ⅲ = Bc
○ = Ca
⊖ = Cb

HOKKAIDO

Sea of Japan

TOHOKU AREA
(NORTHEAST)

Aomori
Akita
Iwate
Yamagata
Miyagi

HONSHU

CHUBU AREA

Niigata
Fukushima

Toyama
Tochigi
Gunma
Nagano
Ibaragi
Saitama
Tokyo
Chiba
KANTO
AREA

Ishikawa
Fukui
Gifu
Yamanashi
Shizuoka
Kanagawa

CHUGOKU AREA
Tottori
Shimane
Okayama
Hyogo
Kyoto
Shiga
Aichi
Mie

Hiroshima
Yamaguchi
Kagawa
Osaka
Nara
KINKI AREA
Tokushima
Wakayama
Fukuoka
Ehime
Kochi
Saga
Oita
SHIKOKU AREA
Nagasaki
Kumamoto
Miyazaki
KYUSHU AREA
Kagoshima

Pacific Ocean

Kagoshima
(Amami Oshima)

Okinawa

Same scale as main map

50   100   150 MILES
0
50   100   150 KILOMETERS
0

Clark Ray

western coast of Kyūshū. The Kumamoto variants, however, are the most interesting, for, like the variants of form
A collected in eastern Japan, they maintain that the descendants of the serpent's child are born with sharp fangs
and with scales on their backs.

According to variants of this form told in Niigata-ken,
the distribution center in eastern Japan, only one child is
born. The child, called Igarashi Kobunji, grows up to become a man of great strength and founds a powerful local
family or shōya.[9] Every descendant of Igarashi Kobunji is
born with three scales in each of his armpits. In Iwate-ken
in the Tōhoku area and in Gifu-ken in the Chūbu area,
similar variants have been collected in which the serpent's
child also founds a shōya, all of whose members likewise
have three scales in each armpit. Though the Iwate variant
is less clearly told and less detailed than any of the texts of
form A mentioned above, it is important because it seems
to contain an element from form B. At the end of the principal episode, for example, the serpent tells the pregnant
girl: "After my death, build a shrine [see Conclusion Ba in
the chart above] and take good care of the child. He will
become a remarkable man." Finally, the variants from
Nagano-ken are similar to a unique variant from Nagasaki
in western Japan, in that the serpent visitor is a woman
rather than a man. After she gives birth to a son, she is
killed by the poison of iron. The son, named Koizumi
Kotarō, grows up to be very strong.

Both of the versions of form B likewise appear to be told
as legends. Whereas Ba is an explanatory legend which
usually tells of the origin of a shrine, Bb occurs as a local
legend about a particular pond. Ba has a heavy distribution
in the Tōhoku region and a sporadic one throughout Japan
from Nagano-ken and Shizuoka-ken to the Ryukyus. The
other version of form B (Bb)—in which either a parent fol-

lows the daughter, who goes out of the house every night, and sees her enter the pond, or the heroine herself follows the suitor and enters the pond—was collected mainly from Fukui-ken, Gifu-ken, Oita-ken, Tokushima-ken, and Wakayama-ken. Yet similar legends are connected with many ponds in other districts too.

Having a wider distribution in Japan than either A or B, form C surpasses them also in its degree of geographic variation. It is divisible into at least five versions, according to the extent of connection of its principal episode and conclusion with the traditional observances held at the March, May, and September festivals. This connection in turn is largely dependent upon the extent to which each of these festivals is observed in each of the four geographical regions of Japan where $A, B,$ and C forms of the odamaki tale occur. In this study, four versions of form C are labeled collectively as Ca, because each of them reflects some aspect of festival observance. The fifth version, which shows no festival connection whatsoever, is referred to as Cb.

The first of the Ca versions is found in the Tōhoku area, where the connection between festival and legend is not so apparent. Here, variants mention merely that the heroine takes a sweet-flag bath at the festival of May fifth. In the Chūbu and Kantō areas, however, where the second version of C is found, the May festival is more widely observed; accordingly, this version manifests a more detailed and specific connection with the festival. The third version occurs in the Chūgoku area, where all three festivals (those of March third, May fifth, and September ninth) often take place. Although the distribution of form C is light in this area, variants reveal definite connections with all three of the festivals. The fourth version, which is connected predominantly with the festival of March third, belongs to an area extending from southern Kyūshū to the Amami Islands and the Ryukyus. In this area, the connection of the tale with the festival of March third is reinforced by the widely observed custom of performing rituals at the seashore in March. These rituals form an important adjunct to the festival itself. The fifth and final version (labeled *Cb*), which lacks any connection with the March, May or September observances, has its major distribution in the Shikoku area, but also coexists with *Ca* versions in Chūbu and Tōhoku. In the *Cb* version, the heroine kills the serpent's child not by participation in the festivals but instead by placing a frog in the tub used at the time of her parturition.

III. EARLY LITERARY RECORDS OF THE SERPENT-BRIDEGROOM TALE IN JAPAN

The existence in Japan of the odamaki subtype of the serpent-bridegroom folktale can be traced back to the early years of the eighth century. The written sources which contain early texts, and the texts themselves, are given here in chronological order.

1) Kojiki (A.D. 712)[10]

The reason why Ōtataneko was known as the son of a deity is explained as follows. Once, a most fair lady named Ikutamayori-hime was visited at midnight by a young man of peerless elegance. The two were attracted to each other and planned to marry. However, in a short time the beauty became pregnant. Her parents grew suspicious about it, and asked her, "You have not a husband yet. So how have you conceived a child?" Their daughter answered, "A fine young man, his name unknown, visited me every night and stayed with me. So naturally I have conceived a child."

Upon hearing this news, the lady's parents decided to find

out who the man was. Thus they told their daughter to scatter brown clay in front of her bed and to stick a needle threaded with hemp into his clothes. The daughter obeyed their instructions and the next morning she saw the thread going out through the keyhole, leaving only three loops of thread behind. (This was the origin of the place named Miwa [Three Loops].) She followed the thread and reached Mount Miwa, where the thread entered the shrine of the deity of the mountain. She realized, then, that the young man was the deity's son. Kushimikata-no-mikoto was borne by this lady, and Ōtataneko is his third descendant.

2) *Hizen Fudoki* (ca. A.D. 713)[11]

When Otomo Sadehiko no Muraji set sail for Mimana (southern Korea), Otohimeko climbed a mountain and waved her *hiré* (a strip of cloth which ladies in ancient Japan wore on their shoulders) toward him. So the mountain peak thereafter was called Hiré-furi no Mine (the Summit of Waving-the-Hiré).

Five days after Sadehiko no Muraji's departure, a man visited Otohimeko. He came to her every night after that, slept with her, and left at daybreak. His face and figure resembled those of Sadehiko.

Being suspicious of her visitor, Otohimeko secretly attached a spool of hemp thread to the bottom of his coat. Then she and her maid followed the thread and came to a pond on the mountain top. There, they saw a creature dripping with water lying prone on the bank. Although its body was a human one, its head was that of a serpent. Transforming itself at once into a human being, the creature said: "Since I have slept this night with Otohimeko of Shinohara, I will not be separated from her."

Otohimeko's maid ran back to the house and told her

lady's parents everything that had happened. The parents sent people up to the mountain top to investigate, but they found Otohimeko and the serpent no longer there. As the searchers gazed into the pond, however, they saw at the bottom the body of a human being. Everyone said it was the corpse of Otohimeko, and so they buried it to the south of this peak where they erected a tomb.

3) *Nihon Shoki* (A.D. 720)[12]

Yamato Totohime no Mikoto became the wife of Omononushi no Kami, a deity who appeared before his wife only at night. Because she desired to see her husband in the daylight Yamato Totohime no Mikoto said to him: "Since you do not come to me when the sun is up, I cannot see your face clearly. Please stay here a little longer. Tomorrow morning I should like to see your handsome features." In response to her, the great kami said: "Your desire is reasonable. Tomorrow morning I shall be in your comb case. Do not become frightened when you see my features."

Yamato Totohime no Mikoto had a suspicion in her heart. Therefore as soon as the new day dawned, she hastened to look in her comb case, where she found a pretty little snake as long as the band on her underclothes. When she became frightened at this and cried out, the kami grew ashamed of himself and turned at once into a human being. He said to his wife: "Because you could not keep calm, you put me to shame. So now you shall be put to shame." Having spoken, he walked away into the sky and reached the top of Mount Mimoro. Yamato Totohime no Mikoto looked up at him with regret. Then she thrust a chopstick into her private parts and died. She was buried at Oichi, where people called her tomb Hashi-baka (the Tomb of the Chopstick.)

4) *Heike Monogatari* (A.D. 1190–1219)[13]

Once a woman lived in a mountain hamlet in the province of Bungo (Ōita-ken). Her daughter was courted by a man every night and soon became pregnant. Being suspicious, the woman asked her daughter, "What kind of man is he who calls on you every night?" The daughter replied, "I see him when he comes, but I don't know when he leaves me." The suspicious mother then commanded her daughter to put a mark on him the next morning before he went away, and to follow him.

According to these instructions, the daughter thrust a needle into the collar of the man's *kariginu* (a kind of gentleman's coat worn in those days) as he prepared to depart the next morning. She had inserted through the needle a thread wound around an *odamaki* (spool), and she followed this thread until she arrived at a big rock cavern at the foot of Mount Ubagadake on the borders of Bungo and Hyūga provinces. Standing in front of the cavern's mouth, she announced that she had followed him. Then a voice from inside replied: "A boy will be born to you. On the two islands of Kyūshū, he will have no equal in taking up the bow and arrow and sword." When the woman requested that the speaker show himself to her, a serpent with a needle thrust into its windpipe appeared. The woman did give birth to a son as the serpent had predicted. The son was fostered by its mother's father and named Daita. Daita's fifth descendant was Ogata Saburō Koreyoshi. The serpent father of Daita was deified, and a shrine was built for him.

5) *Miyako Kyūki* (A.D. 1701)[14]

Once there was a powerful family on Miyako-jima to whom a girl was born in answer to their prayers to the deity.

In her fifteenth year, though, the girl was possessed by a serpent and soon conceived. When her parents, surprised at this, asked her about the matter, the daughter answered that in a dream she had seen a youth who came to her and made her pregnant.

Feeling ashamed of her strange predicament, the girl intended to throw herself into a pool. But her parents soothed her, and, giving her a needle and a thread several thousand *jō* long (one jō is equal to about ten feet), told her to thrust the needle into the young man's neck when he visited her that night. The daughter did as she was told; and after daybreak she followed the thread with her father and mother. When they arrived at a place called Harimizu, there in a rock cave, with a needle thrust into its neck, lay a big serpent.

So frightened and revolted were the mother and daughter that they planned to hang themselves. But that night in a dream the serpent appeared before the daughter and spoke to her. It said: "I am the reincarnation of the heavenly deity Kuitunu, who created this island in ancient times. With a desire to establish a protective deity, I came to this land and married you. You shall give birth to three daughters. When they are three years old, with them in your arms you shall come to the hill of Harimizu [now part of Hirara city, Miyako]." So when the children were three years old, their mother went to Harimizu with them. Then a big serpent appeared, and took the children into the hill after their mother had fled from the scene. The serpent and these children became tutelary deities of the island.

These early texts of the spool tale may be classified into two groups, according to whether they are aetiological legends about the origin of a deity or kinship group, or local legends attached to a particular pond, mountain, or tomb. Those which place emphasis upon explanatory motifs are variants of form *A,* whereas those which stress the locality in which the incident is supposed to have taken place are variants of form *B.*

Three of these early texts—the ones which appear in the *Kojiki, Heike Monogatari,* and *Miyako Kyūki*—belong to form *A,* despite the fact that, as in form *B,* the serpent is deified, and despite the further fact that, unlike most modern texts of forms *A, B,* and *C,* these variants mention that the serpent appears before the girl at night in the shape of a human being. The *Kojiki*'s episode may have been collected in the Nara district, for the *Kojiki* was compiled during the Nara period (A.D. 710–94), when present-day Nara city was the imperial capital The episode in the *Heike Monogatari* is similar to variants of the legend which are told today in Oita-ken in Kyūshū. And the *Miyako Kyūki*'s variant is the same as a legend handed down on Miyako-jima in the southern Ryukyus. The remaining texts—those in the *Hizen Fudoki* and *Nihon Shōki*—differ little from each other and correspond most closely to form *B.* Like the text of form *A* in the *Kojiki,* both of them may have been collected in Nara-ken.

IV. THE SOCIAL AND RELIGIOUS BACKGROUND

The serpent-bridegroom folktale depicts an ancient form of marriage, one that in general Japanese usage is called *tsumadoi-kon.* In this marriage form, the man first courts the woman, and then, if she does not refuse permission, they begin to sleep together in her room. Examples of tsumadoi-kon abound in literature of the Heian period (794–1185).

Although the woman's parents are to some extent aware of these nightly visits, they remain silent about them until their daughter appears to be pregnant. Then it becomes necessary for the parents to obtain full knowledge of the man. In reply to her parents' questions, the woman describes her visitor and requests permission to marry him. The parents acknowledge the marriage formally at this time, and the husband continues to make nightly visits to his wife at her home. Though matrilocal residence of this kind was generally practiced in the old Japanese society before the Middle Ages, some traces of it still survive even in mid-twentieth-century Japan. One of these traces is the serpent-bridegroom folktale.

The tale reflects another aspect of matrilineal society, namely that the mother has a stronger say than the father in the matter of their daughter's marriage. In many variants of the odamaki subtype, it is the mother, rather than the father or a third person, who tells the heroine how to discover the mysterious visitor's identity. This fact is a further indication that the serpent-bridegroom folktale contains survivals which reflect social conditions existent under the matrilineal system of ancient Japan. Of course, the spool tale also reflects folk beliefs and practices which are current in Japanese society today. These include beliefs about the alleged magical properties of iron, the beneficent and malevolent powers of the serpent, and traditional customs still observed at the festivals of March, May, and September.

The iron needle used by the heroine to poison the serpent has its basis in a primitive belief widespread among many other peoples than the Japanese, the belief that iron has the power of protecting and defending human beings against evil spirits and their influences. This idea still appears frequently in the present-day folklore of Japan. Japanese peasants believe, for example, that serpents dislike iron so strongly that if a person wearing a sword attempts to sail across a lake inhabited by a serpent, the boat surely will capsize. They claim, moreover, that if a piece of iron is dropped into a pond, a heavy rain will fall and that a farmer who drops his sickle into a pool will become ill as a result.

Along with beliefs of this kind, peasants in many locales still hand down a story about the youngest daughter who was obliged to marry a serpent, but who freed herself from the creature by throwing a thousand iron needles into its pond.[15]

The mixed attitudes toward the serpent which occur in the tale have their counterparts in Japanese folk society. Though folk beliefs usually treat the serpent with awe, many of them also characterize him as an object of abomination. Until recent times, serpents often were regarded as spirits which protected a home. Thus many families honored them as tutelary deities. White serpents in particular were honored in this manner, for they were supposed to bring prosperity to the houses in which they lived. The Igarashi and Ogata families which frequently are mentioned in the serpent-bridegroom tale certainly were connected with this belief. The tale also indicates the fact that in former times some families were proud to claim descent from these serpents. On the other hand, families which did not venerate such creatures looked upon those who did so with foreboding. These families believed that many little snakes lived in the homes of people who worshiped serpents as their tutelary deities, and that such snakes could possess and cause evil to members of other families in the neighborhood. For these reasons, *hebi-gami-tsuki* (a family line or kin group possessed by a serpent deity) was commonly used as a term of abomination, and intermarriage with members of a serpent-worshiping household was rigorously shunned. Yet the existence of rituals and charms to drive off evils caused by serpents seems to indicate that, as in the serpent-bridegroom folktale, women sometimes were thought to be possessed by a serpent, even when they were unaware of it, and even when they had refrained from contact with men who worshiped the serpent as a tutelary deity.

Like the heroine in the spool tale, Japanese villagers follow traditional customs at the festivals of March, May, and September, in order to rid themselves of pollutions caused by serpents or other evil spirits. Of these festivals, the one held in May is probably the oldest, for its performance is recorded in a Japanese document written in A.D. 747. It was introduced from China earlier than that and mingled quickly with native Japanese customs. Over the centuries, it spread throughout Japan, even though its actual functions varied from one year to another and from locality to locality. The warrior dolls and paper carp displayed during the May festival indicate that in recent years it has come to be regarded as a celebration especially for boys; the March festival, when female dolls are displayed, is its counterpart for girls. In some districts, however, a traditional phrase meaning "women's house" is used in connection with the May festival. This phrase is applied to the annual occasion when the male members of a household leave the women— who are in greater danger of being possessed by serpents or other evil spirits—at home alone to purify themselves.

In the districts south of Kyūshū people go to the seashore at the time of the March festival to eat together or to bathe in the sea. Called *hama-ori* (going down to the beach), this custom is based upon a notion similar to that of the "women's house." This notion is that the purificatory qualities of the sea water will wash away pollutions caused by evil spirits. It is similar to an idea embodied in form *C* of the odamaki tale, namely that the heroine will take a sweet-flag bath at the festival of May fifth to rid herself of the serpent's child.

The heroine's participation in the festival of May fifth also reflects the importance of May in Japanese agricultural society. Because this is the month of transplanting the rice seedlings, it is also the month of religous rituals designed to ensure a good harvest. Because they are especially dependent upon rice-cultivation, Japanese farmers at this time do everything possible to honor the serpent, who is looked upon as the deity controlling water. During this month the water deity is supposed to demonstrate power over the rainfall and over the irrigation water in rice fields. Accordingly, agricultural communities formerly held a festival in his honor, at which everyone prayed for sufficient water. Maidens played a prominent part in these observances, preparing food and weaving clothes for the deity.

Throughout Japan many pools are known as Hataori-buchi (literally, Weaving in River Depths). Various explanations of this term exist, but the most prominent ones are either that a weaving sound at the bottom of each pool is heard in May, or that if a woman carrying a loom should pass by one of them, she would surely fall into the water. We have noted already that maidens once wove clothes for the water deity, who was conceived of as a serpent. When we further observe that today prayers for rain are offered beside the pond or pool in which serpents are thought to dwell, the two explanations of Hataori-buchi seem to suggest that it once was taboo to weave clothes for human beings in May. These explanations would reflect the believed fate of women who ignored this prohibition. If such a taboo did exist, then the version of the odamaki tale in which the heroine enters the pond (form *Bb*) might have had its origin in this taboo.

V. CONCLUSION

The three forms of the odamaki subtype of the serpent-bridegroom folktale correspond to actual forms of belief in the serpent. In the first form (*A*), the hero is said to be a divine serpent, and his son, born to the heroine, is said to be of divine character. Comparable to an origin legend

rather than to a märchen, this form was evolved and transmitted by families which proudly claimed descent from the
serpent's child. In the second form (B), the serpent-hero
after his death is honored as the water deity and treated
with awe. Although one possible explanation of the origin
of form Bb has been put forth already, another one is that
it might have developed under the influence of a tradition
existing even today in some parts of Japan. This tradition
is that maidens once were offered to the pond spirit in request for abundant rice crops. The Ba version of this form,
in which human characters reject the serpent as a suitor but
deify it for fear of its curse, might be derived from the same
tradition. In the third form of the tale (C), the serpent's
child is not cared for by its mother and grandparents as it
is in form A. Instead, either it is eliminated before birth
(Ca), or (Cb) an attempt to kill it, by placing a frog in the
bedside tub used by the mother during parturition, is described. (The frog is regarded as a helpful servant of the
rice-field deity.) This form may have developed among people who lived near families which worshiped the serpent as
their tutelary deity. Certainly it reflects the dread these
people had of unknown serpent suitors, the abomination
they felt towards members of serpent-worshiping families,
and the rituals they practiced to rid themselves of evils
which possession by a serpent could cause.

The odamaki subtype of the serpent-bridegroom tale,
then, is a folktale which emphasizes the attempts of human
beings to decide whether the serpent is an honorable deity
or an evil spirit. The many variants in which the heroine's
parents, or other persons, follow the thread in order to
guard her from harm while they discover her suitor's true
identity further support this supposition.

The history of the development and diffusion of the spool
tale in Japan can be divided into at least three periods. The

first of these began with the introduction of the tale from China and Korea,[16] some time before the start of the seventh century. Although the form of the tale when brought to Japan is unknown, and will remain so until a comparative study is made with corresponding materials in China and Korea, we do know that the story spread throughout the country and that, having undergone historical and local changes, it developed into two forms by the start of the eighth century: form *A* which was recorded in the *Kojiki*, and form *B* which was included in the *Fudoki* and *Nihon Shoki*.

The second period of change began after the eighth century.[17] By this time the central origin legend of form *A* had gradually lost its divine significance and was in wide circulation throughout the country, becoming connected in various localities with semi-historical figures of the Middle Ages. No longer a deity's son, the offspring of the mysterious suitor now, on the one hand, became the heroic ancestor of the powerful Ogata family of Oita-ken and, on the other hand, a local hero of Niigata-ken and Nagano-ken. Form *B* also underwent basic changes during this period. Wherever it came in contact with the origin legend of form *A*, it may have developed into an explanatory legend about the origin of a particular shrine (form *Ba*). Wherever it was attached to ponds, pools, or other bodies of water, it may have become a popular legend (form *Bb*).

The third period of change in the history of this folktale began after the Japanese Middle Ages, when the origin legend of form *A* became connected so firmly with special kinship groups (such as the Ogata family) that it lost the support of the general folk community. Even though in the meantime more and more local and explanatory legends developed from form *B*, these legends were increasingly influenced by a transition in folk psychology from animistic belief in the serpent as deity to abomination of it as a dangerous reptile. Many of these legends, therefore, were combined with religious rites performed at the March, May, and September festivals to rid people of the pollution which possession by the serpent was believed to cause. Various degrees of combination between these rites and legends, due to each variant's reflection of actual customs in a particular locality, account for the development of the numerous versions of form C. Our observation of the manner in which these versions developed should make us realize that even though we divide the development of the odamaki subtype of the serpent-bridegroom folktale into three stages, these stages did not occur everywhere in strictly chronological order, but according to the social conditions of each locality.

Notes

1. Cf. Types 425, "The Search for the Lost Husband," and 431, "The Ass," in Antti Aarne and Stith Thompson, *The Types of the Folk-Tale* (Folklore Fellows Communications, No. 184 [Helsinki, 1961]).

2. See Type 31 in Wolfram Eberhard, *Typen chinesischer Volksmärchen* (Folklore Fellows Communications, No. 120 [Helsinki, 1937]).

3. Chin-tae Son, *Chōsen Mintan Shū (Korean Folktales)* (Tokyo: Kyōdo Kenkyu Sha, 1930), pp. 132, 142.

4. See Type 98 in W. Eberhard and P. N. Boratav, *Typen türkischer Volksmärchen* (Wiesbaden: Steiner, 1953).

5. Yūkichi Sayama and Yoshitoshi Ōnishi, *Seiban Densetsu Shū (Legends of the Formosan Aborigines)* (Taipei: Sugita Shoten, 1923), p. 727.

6. The six subtypes of the serpent-bridegroom folktale are (*1*) the odamaki (spool) tale, (*2*) the prayer-for-water tale, (*3*) the kappa-bridegroom tale, (*4*) the grateful-frog tale, (*5*) the grateful-crab tale, and (*6*) the tale of the *konotori's* (Japanese stork's) eggs. See my *Nihon*

Mukashibanashi Shūsei (Compilation and Classification of Japanese Folktales) (Part II, Tokyo: Kadokawa Shoten, 1953–55), I, 13–108.

7. According to popular belief, each of these practices would reveal whether an unborn child with a serpent for one of its parents would enter the world as a serpent or as a human being. The festivals at which these practices occurred include those that took place in January and July, in addition to the festivals mentioned in the text. Collectively these festivals are known as Go-sekku (Five Festivals). The celebration of Go-sekku, introduced to Japan from China in olden times, takes place during periods of the year when various flowers and plants are in season. For example, *sake* with peach blossoms is used at the March third festival, because March is the season for peach blossoms; *sake* with chrysanthemum blossoms is used at the festival of September ninth, because in September the chrysanthemums are in bloom; and baths with sweet-flag or iris leaves floating in the tub are taken at the May fifth festival, when these flowers are at their peak. The names for these festivals up until the past generation have been Momo-no-sekku (March), Tango-no-sekku (May), and Kiku-no-sekku (September). In the March festival the toko-no-ma (alcove) is decorated with girls' dolls and peach (*momo*) blossoms. Today the common term for the March festival is Hina-matsuri (*hina* refers to a pair of king and queen dolls); the September festival has generally disappeared except in parts of Okinawa.

8. Alternate sets of names which likewise correspond closely with the real names of heroic feudal lords are (*1*) Saegi Tarō, Hokase Jirō, and Ogata Saburō; and (*2*) Tackachiho Tarō, Ogata Jirō, and Saegi Saburō.

9. During the Tokugawa period, the village head man was called a *shōya*. His family held an hereditary claim to this position of authority.

10. The *Kojiki* is one of the earliest books of ancient Japanese history, compiled in A.D. 712 for the government. Its three volumes contain myths, legends, imperial genealogies, and stories of many kinds.

11. The *Fudoki* contains the earliest extant records of local products, geography, and traditions of the Japanese provinces. It was compiled in A.D. 713 by command of the central government. A part of it, the *Hizen Fudoki,* is a description of Hizen province, including both Nagasaki-ken and Saga-ken.

12. The *Nihon Shoki* (or *Nihongi*) consists of thirty volumes. With the exception of the *Kojiki,* it is the oldest extant work of history which describes the origins of the Japanese nation and its imperial household. The work was completed in A.D. 720 by a number of compilers appointed by the government.

13. A work of epic literature, the *Heike Monogatari* describes the life of the historical Heike family from the time of its rise to political power until its complete destruction by the Genji family. Although scholars differ as to the year of its completion, the leading opinion is that the *Heike Monogatari* was completed sometime between 1190 and 1219.

14. The *Miyako Kyūki* is a collection of legends from Miyako-jima in the southern Ryukyus, made in 1701. The legend in the text is quoted from a reprinting in Moritoshi Shimabukuro (ed.), *Irō Setsuden (Traditional Stories Told by the Aged)* (Tokyo: Gakugei Sha, 1935) (pp. 45–47), in which the records of the *Miyako Kyūki* are reproduced.

15. Archaeological studies trace the use of iron in Japan back to the time of the Yayoi pottery culture, which began in the second century B.C. The use of hemp, which also plays a role in the odamaki tale, is mentioned for the first time in a document which appeared 800 years later (ca. A.D. 750). Although hemp thread rarely is used to sew clothing with today, Japanese peasants who sustain the belief that it has magic powers of purification utilize it frequently in their rituals.

16. Stories of this kind appear in Chang Wei's *Hsuan-Shih-piao,* which was written ca. A.D. 850 during the T'ang Dynasty, and in *Sangoku Iji (Memoir on Three Kingdoms),* an old Korean document of the thirteenth century. The Chinese and Korean variants indicate that the serpent was regarded as a sacred being which symbolized divinity, and that Chinese and Korean villagers often enshrined it as one of their local gods. When brought to Japan, some of these stories became attached to the shrine of Mount Miwa in the Nara district, which was the cultural center of that time. A variant from the *Kojiki* appears on pp. 274–75 above.

17. During this period, unified belief in the divine character of the serpent weakened; but the popular belief that the serpent was an embodiment of the water spirit spread throughout the country, and many lakes and ponds became associated with stories of snakes.

若者

PART SEVEN | YOUTHS

Initiation Rites and Young Men's Organizations

BY TARO WAKAMORI

Japanese young people, defined as single youths and girls eligible for marriage, are of interest to folklorists because their arrival at physical maturity or at the prescribed age of formal maturity was, and often still is, accompanied with traditional ceremonies and with membership in traditional youth organizations.[1] In Japan, it is a long-established custom to allow young men and women to seek marriage partners as soon as they have grown up physiologically, but in some districts it is equally customary to permit young men to do so when they have reached an age agreed upon by their fellow villagers. Physical maturity appears to be the older of the two prerequisites for wedlock, at least on the basis of analogies drawn by this writer between initiation ceremonies in Japan and in primitive societies. Whether marriage eligibility has been based upon either of these criteria or upon parental decision in each locale, it has usually been recognized between the ages of thirteen and fifteen with appropriate rites of passage.

Traditionally, when a Japanese young man reached the threshold of physical or socially accepted maturity, he received a white cotton loincloth as a symbol of his new position in life. The loincloth was given to him during a *heko* (dialect for "loincloth") ceremony, an initiation rite found in southern Japan with minor variations from place to place. The father or mother of the youth presented the heko, or, if neither were alive, an important man of the village did so, at the request of a relative of the young man. On the island of Taka-shima, Kita-Matsuura-gun, in Nagasaki-ken, a *heko-oya* (an appointed "loincloth father," who acts in place of the initiate's real father) presented the garment to him when he attained physical manhood, regardless of his socially recognized age. In contrast, on the islands of Goto and O-shima, respectively in Nagasaki-ken and Yamaguchi-ken, each boy usually had his heko ceremony at the age of thirteen. On these islands, and throughout the Kyūshū and Chūgoku areas as well, the ceremony was always held in January of the lunar calendar, and was conducted by the initiate's *natsuke-oya* (name-giving parent),[2] who presented him with a plain piece of white cotton cloth (rather than with a finished garment as in heko ceremonies elsewhere). On Mikura-jima in Izu province even more variation is found by the field investigator. Here, each youth took part in a loincloth ceremony at the age of thirteen. A six-foot length of new, white, cotton cloth[3] was tied around his waist by his natsuke-oya. These loincloth ceremonies generally were attended not only by the youth's immediate family but also by his kinsmen.[4]

In general, it can be said that within any given community the same standard of adulthood—physical maturity or a socially recognized age—applied to both men and women. Young women celebrated the attainment of maturity with special rites of their own. In some districts, for example, a womanhood ceremony was held at the time of a girl's first menstruation, as in the Izu Islands, where it occasioned a *hatsude-iwai* or "life start ceremony"[5] and a subsequent feast of sekihan (ceremonial rice boiled with red beans) at which her condition was announced by her parents to the invited male guests. This stage in the female life cycle was celebrated with the presentation of a *koshimaki* (a type of petticoat).[6] On some islands in the Kyūshū area a celebration was held for girls as well as boys, at the age of thirteen or fifteen, regardless of their physical maturity. The girls were given new koshimaki on this occasion, although the ceremony itself was called *heko-iwai*. In the Goto-retto in northern Kyūshū, girls were often presented at the heko-iwai with new ceremonial dresses intended for their future weddings, whereas the boys were given only loincloths. The girls put on these ceremonial dresses at home and then visited the village shrine.

The social recognition that a young man received during his heko ceremony traditionally carried a further implication: Not only had he become eligible for marriage but also he had become old enough to contribute to his community as an important part of the labor force. From another point of view, then, we can define youth as the period from the age at which a young man first attains the physical strength of an adult to the time when he can bear all the public obligations as a full-fledged villager. Accordingly the Japanese young man often joined a young people's association[7] at the time of his loincloth ceremony; the association served the purpose of integrating him into the village labor system.

Membership in a village young people's association was

often determined by feats of endurance or strength. For example, to become eligible for membership, a young man may have had to demonstrate to the village elders his ability to plow or hoe a *tan*[8] of the rice field in one day, or to shoulder unassisted a bale of rice or a stone of the same weight.[9] Once the prescribed feat was accomplished, his labor capacity was immediately recognized, and he was free to join the young people's association, to receive a full share of its production of goods, and openly to select his future wife. At this point his new social status became recognized by the entire village, with a special name-changing ceremony that replaced his childhood name with an adult one.[10]

In some areas the manhood rite itself simultaneously implied the initiation into a young people's association. Such a dual-purpose ceremony was called *genpuku* rather than *heko-iwai,* although the genpuku rite originally signified only the attainment of manhood and hence the right to marry.[11] In former times, when youths joined a young people's association in this manner, they were thus given full freedom by the village adults to visit a girl's bedchamber and solicit her charms; for *hada-awase,*[12] or premarital sexual experimentation, was deemed very advisable. Their right to indulge in sexual affairs, however, was often contingent upon their performance of a feat of strength or endurance upon the very day of their genpuku. The feat was often one of those already mentioned, such as lifting a heavy stone or plowing a rice field, but sometimes it was much more extreme. At Nichi-Sonoki-gun in Nagasaki-ken, for example, it was a strangling ordeal called *shime-korosu* in which youths were choked and made to faint for a moment. On the Izu Peninsula, it consisted of ordering the initiates to sit on firewood cut into triangular shapes, to listen in this position to the village ordinances, and to submit to beatings with thick pieces of firewood if they lapsed

from good manners and respectful posture.[13] And in Mio-
mote village in Niigata-ken, the test was an extraordinary
one: A half-burned end of firewood or charcoal was hung
from the penis as a simultaneous examination of the initiate's manly endurance and sexual virility.

In various segments of Japanese society in which no need
has existed for young men to join a village labor system,
initiation ceremonies have sometimes been shifted back to
the period of life between infancy and boyhood. That is
why, among court nobles or the aristocratic military class
of the Heian period (794–1185), a formal maturity ceremony called a *genpuku* or *kakan* was often held for boys
before they were ten years old. On the night of this ceremony, there was practiced a custom called *soi-bushi* (to lie
with) of which the central feature was the placement of an
older woman in the child's bed. This custom was probably
a survival from the pre-Heian period when the genpuku
or kakan was held upon the arrival of each youth at mar-
riageable age, and when the attainment of manhood was
climaxed with hada-awase or actual premarital relations, as
mentioned above.[14] In the medieval period (thirteenth to
sixteenth centuries) even seven-year-old boys became subject to genpuku, kakan, or heko ceremonies, on the assumption of the aristocratic samurai families that the age of
seven is the first critical and climactic age to signify a transitional period in the life cycle. At some places in Okayama-
ken and Fukuoka-ken these ceremonies were also performed
for girls, who at the age of seven were presented with a
kind of woman's petticoat during a formal *imoji* (petticoat)
ceremony.[15] The holding of maturity rites at so early an
age among various segments of Japanese society, and at
different periods in history, is the outcome of the differen-
tiation between marriage eligibility and full-fledged participation in a village labor force, which are the two essential

aspects of social recognition of puberty. Yet as we have already seen, many other segments of Japanese society manifest traditional customs in which both of these aspects of coming-of-age are closely intertwined.

Young people's associations seem to have come into being primarily as a labor organization on the one hand, and as an institution to prepare one for marriage on the other. In historical documents, however, the labor aspect of the association is far more manifest than the matrimonial, presumably because the former is more public and the latter more private in character.[16] The forerunners of these associations appeared after the end of the Kamakura period (1185–1333) when the system of *waka-tō* or *waka-shū* (group for young men of the warrior class) came into existence. Later on, when the village community assumed the character of a self-governing cooperative body at the end of the Muromachi period (1338–1573), members of these groups who had hitherto been subordinate to political authority on a higher level—namely powerful local families possessing large domains and military forces—seceded and formed new organizations of their own. These organizations, which became responsible for protecting village self-government, were the original versions of the Japanese young people's associations still in existence today.

Since their origin in the sixteenth century, the young people's associations have undergone a number of significant changes. All of these associations gradually assumed an important role in the annual shrine festivals. These previously humble religious celebrations became more and more showy as the members of the associations began to display the mikoshi (portable shrine) more colorfully than ever when they carried it about. In time, their important role in the festivals came to signify that they had attained eligibility as full-grown men. Consequently the young people's associations lost their character as purely labor organizations ruled by a leader, and in many places the conditions for joining them also underwent a change. All young men, not merely those who could qualify on the basis of their physical maturity alone, joined these revamped associations when they reached a certain age. Thus the custom of testing their degree of physical and sexual maturity became less emphasized, and only sons-in-law or adopted sons from other villages had to undergo severe trials if they wished to join.

There are indeed traditional organizations in mid-twentieth-century Japan which remind us of the precursors of the young people's associations. For example, vestiges of the medieval waka-shu system still remain on the Chita Peninsula of Aichi-ken, where many of the associations continue the tradition of investing immediate authority over the members in an older leader. This leader generally is nominated by the young men from among their own ranks, and he is in turn under a much older senior leader who is called the *kashira* (head) or the *oya* (parent), and who is the head man of a big house but not a member of the association. The senior leader does not directly intervene in the internal life of the association, but he tacitly or indirectly supervises the actions of its members. His origin may perhaps be traced to the old warrior society of Japan and, more specifically, to one of its customs according to which a fictitious male parent, *kari-oya*, was appointed at the time of a genpuku to take charge of the then-related ceremony of kakan, or putting on of the ceremonial headgear, eboshi. That a connection exists between this fictitious parent and the senior leader of the young people's association in the village community is at any rate plausible on the basis of evidence that the former was called a *genpuku-oya* or an *eboshi-oya,* and the latter is also called *oya* (or *kashira*).

Wherever these vestiges of the waka-shu system remain,

a new member of a young people's association does not need the village's public approval. Instead, all that is necessary is to pay a courtesy visit to the senior leader; this is deemed more important than visits of courtesy to other members. In contrast, wherever the master-servant relationship has not been in effect, and where a classless system for regimenting all the village young men exists in its place, it is most important for the initiate to visit his peers with the idea of establishing a horizontal relationship with them. In villages on the Izu Peninsula, however, an older person reminiscent of the kashira (boss) is appointed to introduce the initiate to the members of the association. In the historical development of young people's associations, such senior leaders may represent a transitional stage halfway between the stratified organizations of the medieval period, some of which still survive today, and the more egalitarian ones in which all the members are on an equal level with one another. Whether this is the case or not, however, the fact remains that young people in classless associations enjoy greater freedom from restraint.

Even though an initiate was led by his fictitious father or his boss into the association, he usually took a sho (1.588 quarts) of *sake* with him as his initiation gift to the members. Presenting a sho of *sake* at one's initiation was a prevalent custom throughout the country; the initiate exchanged cups with the old members to consolidate their relationship.

In any type of association, it is traditional for the members to live in special houses away from their family homes. These houses, generally called *neyado* (sleeping lodges), still remain in mid-twentieth-century Japan wherever villages continue to employ local young men's associations as collective labor forces; the more each village's economy requires communal labor, the more manifest the system of neyado. In the fishing villages, unlike farming villages where each family works its own field, cooperative labor remains important; and thus the associations still maintain many active lodges. In these lodges, the members, who have eaten and worked with their families during the day, work together at night. Gathering in the neyado after supper, they spend the evening chatting, mending fish nets, making straw goods such as *waraji* (sandals), tatami (mats), and rope. On special occasions they engage in public work: repairing village roads or shrines, thatching a house, building a bridge, or planting trees in the communal forest. Even when the lodges have lost these labor functions, the association members sometimes continue to dwell within them. Thus they may remain as work forces to be summoned in case of village emergencies, such as shipwreck or fire.[17] This is the origin of the recent conversion of many local young men's associations into permanent fire brigades.

The daily life of a typical young men's association was once as much taken up with matters concerning women as it was with providing the village with effective communal labor. Younger members of the association who lived in a sleeping lodge received a great deal of information on sex from the older ones, and so were sometimes inclined to visit women under the cover of night. These visitations were the natural consequences of the association's traditional role as a sex-information bureau, a sexual proving ground, and a matrimonial agency. This role met with full village approval, for the senior leaders[18] of the young men's lodges really acted as go-betweens in the arrangement of marriage contracts between one family and another.

Since young men joined the association with matrimony in mind, the instructions given them about relations with women comprised the strictest terms of the membership code. These orally transmitted regulations, called *okite* (rules) or *jomoku* (articles), sternly forbade the initiates to have sexual relations with married women, and instructed them instead to greet such women with constant politeness and respect. The young men were also enjoined not to violate the women of other villages, but nothing at all was said about the unmarried girls of their own community. Indeed the members of the young men's association regarded the village girls as being roped off by them from outsiders, and old men still alive today remember this fact from their personal experience.

On the other hand, the girls in most cases had no comparable organization of their own. Such organizations, if there ever were any, seem to have ceased to exist early in Japanese history, after their failure to attain sufficient autonomy. In former days, the girls' coming-of-age was celebrated by women's maturity rites, on the completion of which the girls dyed their teeth black.[19] In more recent times, their attainment of physical maturity has merely qualified them for sexual relations with the members of the young men's lodge.[20]

The young men's association has been so firmly established as a kind of marriage bureau that the preferences of association members in marriage affairs have often enjoyed priority over the preferences of the girls' families; young men have usually seceded from membership as soon as their marriages have been arranged. Some men, it is true, have been known to remain affiliated with the association until thirty or forty years of age, perhaps as the leaders of young men, particularly under the waka-shu system of the pre-Meiji feudalistic periods, in which a greater elasticity in the age qualification seems to have prevailed. As the *waka* (which implies vitality) in *waka-shu* suggests, even though the oldest member of a young men's group existent during that period was over forty, no one doubted that he was still a "young man." After all, he could still do his share in the association's public function—that of providing the village with an effective, cooperative labor force.

Changes have occurred in young men's associations whenever variations arose in the kind or quality of labor needed or in the manner in which the villagers conducted their marriage affairs. Thus, in villages where population was scant and cooperative labor was greatly in demand, some men may have remained in the associations even after marriage. In general, this practice became the exception rather than the rule, especially in those areas where such an association became an organization on the village level. Such a village organization did away with vestiges of the medieval waka-shu system, characterized by the hierarchical relationship between the regular members and their senior leaders. On the other hand, in later times when the association's authority over marriage arrangements weakened, and the influence of family leaders consequently became stronger as inter-village alliances increased, marriage no longer necessarily involved secession from the association. Young men now joined with the realization that family elders would arrange their marriage through private go-betweens hired outside of the association. Thus they became members for other than marital purposes. Nevertheless, the attitude of married men toward the lodges gradually became negative. Where this happened, the lodges themselves were often abandoned or used only as houses for night watchmen. In farming villages they were no longer used even for sleeping, but only as informal meeting places.

Although some young people's associations continue to fulfill their traditional village functions, their role in modern Japan has become increasingly unpredictable. The rapid growth of modern industries since the Meiji Restoration in 1867, and the interest of the national government in moral education, have disrupted village folk institutions such as the youth associations discussed in the present article.

Notes

1. The traditional customs described in this article have almost died out in the past fifty years. The *wakamono-yado* (sleeping lodge for young men), however, still remains in some fishing villages.

2. The natsuke-oya or godparent gives a baby its name on the seventh day after birth in a celebration still widely observed.

3. In the Ina district this loincloth is called *oba-kure* (given by the aunt), and the custom is locally known in that district as *oba-kure-fundoshi* (loincloth given by the aunt). Women present young men with loincloths elsewhere in Japan too. For example, in some villages of the Ina district in Nagano-ken, fifteen-year-old boys receive them from their mothers' sisters when they call at their homes for New Year's greetings.

4. The range of kinship, patrilineally inclined, varied from one locality to another.

5. Variant names for this rite are *hatsu-kado* and *hatsu-tabi*. Both *kado* and *tabi* signify the menstruation hut. *Hatsu* means "first," and *hatsude* implies going to the menstruation hut for the first time. The ending -*iwai* means "celebration."

6. *Koshimaki* (waist-wrapper) is an ordinary Japanese petticoat, i.e., a plain wide cloth with strings on both sides which are tied around the waist.

7. The term *wakamono-gumi* is used broadly for both young men's and young women's associations; *wakaishu-gumi* is a common village term for the young men's association, and *musume-gumi* or *musume-nakama* for the young women's.

8. A *tan* is equivalent to 992.7 square meters (or about 0.245 acres).

9. A bale of rice weighs sixty kilograms (or 132.276 pounds). Stones to test lifting power usually were used in place of actual bales of rice. These stones are often seen within the precinct of a village shrine.

10. The name-changing ceremony called *nakae-shiki* was held on

the festival day of a village shrine. A Shinto priest announced the boy's new name to the villagers. The childhood name usually ended in ——*maru*, as Goromaru; this became Gorobei, Goroemon, or something similar.

11. *Genpuku* is literally "to be invested with headgear," and was the term originally applied to the boy's maturity rite as practiced among the nobility. The oldest extant record of the word is in the *Shoku Nihongi* (797). The custom was subsequently adopted by the samurai, and after the seventeenth century genpuku was generally practiced by the common people. Today this is a standard, generic term, whereas *heko-iwai* is used only locally by villagers. *Kakan* means to place a *kanmuri*, headgear worn by a court official, on another person's head. *Kakan* was used in almost the same sense as *genpuku*.

12. *Hada* means "skin" or "body." *Awase* conveys the idea "to join together," "put together," or "unite."

13. This custom seems to have been an anomalous transformation of the various tests of bodily strength.

14. The custom of soi-bushi is widely mentioned in the eleventh-century Heian literature. In many cases the woman chosen to share the ceremonial bed with the youth was his prospective wife, and after the ritual night they indulged regularly in sexual relations.

15. The term *imoji* (or *yumoji*) is synonymous with *koshimaki*; the latter is standard usage and the former is a local and archaic word. Here *imoji-iwai* was held to celebrate the girl's seventh year, the transitional period from infancy to older childhood, whereas the womanhood ceremony in the Izu Islands, mentioned earlier, celebrated the actual coming-of-age. Imoji-iwai, however, was originally a maturity rite.

16. The historical documents referred to are unpublished medieval records belonging to old houses, temples, and shrines. One such document is the *To-ji-Monjo*, which belongs to the temple of To-ji in Kyoto. This is now being published by Todai Shiryo Hensan-jo (the editorial office for historical materials in Tokyo University), five volumes having been issued to date.

17. This work was not paid for by the village. Daily necessaries for members of the lodge were provided by their own families. Sometimes the association owned an area of field or forest, and the profit accruing from it was applied to the common expenses.

18. These older men outside the association were known as *yado-oya* (sleeping-lodge fathers).

19. The Japanese custom of *kane-tsuke* (teeth-dyeing) has changed its significance through the centuries. Blackened teeth originally were a formal sign of female maturation; next they came to identify women about to be married; and finally, up to the Meiji era, they became the badge of women already wedded.

20. One reason for the failure of the young women's association (musume-gumi) to attain autonomy is that its function, to supervise the sexual and marriage affairs of the young women, did not involve the communal labor of the village. The main work of young women lay in spinning, weaving, sewing, and helping to prepare feasts for the village-shrine festivals.

NOTES ON CONTRIBUTORS

(Listed alphabetically by surname)

TATSUO HAGIWARA, born in 1916, was a councilor of the Folklore Institute of Japan from 1953 to 1957, and a director of the Folklore Society of Japan in 1954. A graduate of Tokyo Bunrika Daigaku (University of Science and Literature), he has published extensively, in Japanese folklore periodicals, on the subjects of festivals, rituals and the Shinto priesthood.

TOSHIAKI HARADA, born in 1893, has held the position of professor of religion at Tōkai University, Tokyo, since 1959. From 1949 to 1959 he was on the faculty of Kumamoto University in Kyūshū. His most recent work is *Jinja* (*The Shrine*), published in 1961. Other major studies include *Nihon Kodai Shūkyō* (*Ancient Religion of Japan* [1948]) and *Kodai Nihon no Shinkō to Shakai* (*Beliefs and Society of the Ancient Japanese* [1949]). An article in English, "Social Organizations for the Village-Deity Cult of Japan," appeared in *Cultural Nippon*, IX (December, 1941), 1-13.

TOSHIJIRO HIRAYAMA, born in 1913, is presently an assistant professor of history at Osaka Municipal University and a lecturer in anthropology at Nanzan University. In collaboration with Kozo Nishiki, he published *Oku-Harima Minzoku Saiho-Roku* (*Record of Folklore Collected from the Remote Region of Harima Province*) (Osaka: Kinki Minzoku Gakkai, 1953).

ICHIRŌ HORI, born in 1910, presently holds the position of professor of history of religions at Tōhoku University. He has been awarded the Honored Prize of the Mainichi Press for his book *Minkan-Shinkō* (*Folk-Beliefs*) (Tokyo: Iwanami Shoten, 1951) and the Honored Prize of the Japan Academy for his book *Waga-kuni Minkan-shinkō-shi no Kenkyū* (*A Study in the History of Japanese Folk Religion*) (Tokyo: Sōgen Sha, 1953–55). In the years 1956 through 1958 he was a research fellow of the Rockefeller Foundation at Harvard University and in Europe. In 1957–58 he served as a visiting professor of history of religions at the University of Chicago. Besides having published extensively in Japanese, Professor Hori has also published articles in English on Japanese folk beliefs.

TOICHI MABUCHI, born in 1909, has been professor of social anthropology at Tokyo Metropolitan University since 1953. He graduated in 1931 from the Taipei Imperial University of Formosa, and from 1929 to 1940 conducted a series of field researches among Formosan native peoples. In subsequent years he extended his fieldwork to Indonesia, the Philippines, and most recently (1960), under a grant from the Wenner-Gren Foundation, to the southern Ryukyus. In the spring quarter, 1961, he served as visiting professor of anthropology at the University of Chicago; in 1961–62 he was a fellow of the Center for Advanced Study in the Behavioral Sciences at Stanford University; and in the summer of 1962 he was visiting professor at the Folklore Institute of Indiana University. Professor Mabuchi has published widely in both Japanese and English on the ethnology and folklore of southeast Asia. He was a councilor of the Japanese Folklore Institute until it closed in 1957.

NARIMITSU MATSUDAIRA, born in 1897, has held the position of professor of politics at Meiji University in Tokyo since 1960. A graduate of the department of law of Tokyo Imperial University, he was the director of the Society of Politics in Japan in 1954. His main publications have concerned Japanese festivals and have been written both in Japanese and in French.

NOBUHIRO MATSUMOTO was born in 1897. A 1920 graduate of Keiō University, he went to France to study at the Sorbonne in 1924. Since 1924 he has held the position of professor of history at Keiō University and has specialized in Oriental history. His major writings on ancient Japanese mythology and culture include *Nihon Shinwa no Kenkyū (Study of Japanese Mythology)* (Tokyo: Kamakura Shobō, 1946), and *Indo-Shina no Minzoku to Bunka (The Races and Culture of Indo-China)* (Tokyo: Iwanami Shoten, 1942).

TAKAYOSHI MOGAMI, born in 1899, is a professor at Nihon Daigaku (University of Japan, Tokyo). Between 1948 and 1957 he served as secretary of the Folklore Institute of Japan, and in 1957 he was a director of the Folklore Society of Japan. Although he is a graduate of Tokyo Imperial University's department of economics, Professor Mogami has published widely on Japanese folklore. His books include a field report on the folklore of Kurogochi and a study of the memorial-grave system in Japan.

HIROJI NAOE, born in 1917, has been an assistant professor of Japanese history at Tokyo Kyoiku University since 1952. From 1942 to 1945 he lectured at Catholic University in Peiking, China. In 1948 he was made a director of the Folklore Institute of Japan, a position he held until 1957. In 1953 he was a director of the Folklore Society of Japan. Professor Naoe has published on various aspects of Japanese folklore, with special emphasis on household religion.

MANABU OGURA, born in 1912, presently teaches at Sakuragaoka Senior High School in Kanazawa-shi. Mr. Ogura, a member of the Folklore Society of Japan, has published studies on the folklore of Noto and Kaga provinces. In 1961 he was granted the degree of Doctor of Literature.

TOKUZŌ ŌMACHI, born in 1900, has been a lecturer at Chūō University since 1955 and at Tokyo Joshi Daigaku (Women's Christian College of Japan) since 1956. From 1939 to 1945 he was a professor at the National University of Manchuria, and in 1946 became a director of the Folklore Society of Japan. He is also a former chairman of the Folklore Institute of Japan. In 1937 he collaborated with Kunio Yanagita in writing a book on Japanese marriage customs. His more recent publications include studies of the folklore of Hachijo-jima and of Takaoka-mura in Hitachi province.

TOKIHIKO ŌTŌ, born in 1902, presently occupies the position of professor of folklore at Seijo University. Professor Ōtō, who graduated with a degree in social philosophy from Waseda University, was the director of the Folklore Institute of Japan from 1947 to 1957. He is also a member of the Japanese Folklore Society. His major publication is a book on the cultural history of contemporary Japan.

KATSUNORI SAKURADA, born in 1903, graduated with a degree in literature from Keiō University in 1929. He joined the Research Staff of the Attic Museum in Tokyo in 1935, and in 1940 became a part-time official of the Fisheries Bureau in the Ministry of Agriculture and Forestry. He was made president in 1950 of Nippon Jomin Bunka Kenkyūsho (The Institute of Folk Culture in Japan, formerly the Attic Museum), and was also appointed a councilor of the Folklore Society of Japan. His extensive writings have centered on the folk culture of fishing villages. Among them may be mentioned *Gyoson Minsoku Shi (The Folklore of Fishing Villages)* (Tokyo: Issei Sha, 1934), *Tosa Shimanto-gawa no Gyogo to Kawafune (Fishing and Boats in the Shimanto River)* (Tokyo: Attic Museum, 1936), and *Gyojin* (Fishermen) (Tokyo: Rokunin Sha, 1942).

KIYOKO SEGAWA, born in 1895, presently is a lecturer at Ozuma Joshi Daigaku (Ozuma Women's College). Since 1934 she has studied Japanese folklore under the guidance of Kunio Yanagita. She joined the research group which surveyed the mountain and fishing villages. From 1947 to 1957 she was a representative to the Folklore Institute of Japan; she has also been a councilor of the Folklore Society of Japan. Mrs. Segawa has published numerous books and articles concerning marriage, clothing, and food customs in Japan, especially as found on the islands of Mi-shima and Himaka.

KEIGO SEKI, born in 1899, has been a professor of sociology at Tokyo Gakugei University since 1956. A graduate of Toyo University in Tokyo, Professor Seki joined Kunio Yanagita's folklore group in 1933. His major interest centers in the folktale, and he has published several major studies, classifications, and collections of Japanese folktales. An English translation by Robert J. Adams, selected from his collection, has just appeared (*Folktales of Japan* [Chicago: University of Chicago Press, 1963]).

TARO WAKAMORI, born in 1915, is a history graduate of Tokyo University of Literature and Science, and has been a professor at that institution since 1950. Also in 1950 he became a director of the Folklore Society of Japan. Professor Wakamori's impressive list of publications includes studies on folk tradition, on history and folklore and on the Miho Shrine.

KUNIO YANAGITA was born in 1875 in Tahara-mura, Hyōgo-ken. At the age of fifteen he went to Tokyo to live with his brother and there received a degree in political science from Tokyo University in 1900. In 1910 he initiated his folklore publications with *Tōno Monogatari* ([*Tales from Tōno*] Tokyo: Kyōdo Kenkyū Sha), and in 1913 he founded the journal of local-life studies, *Kyodo Kenkyū*. In 1914 he was appointed chief secretary of the Upper House of the Diet, and in 1921 and 1922 he served as a delegate to the League of Nations at Geneva. In 1923 he took a position as editorial writer for the Asahi Press, and that year he began lecturing on folklore at Keio University. In 1941 he was awarded the Asahi Prize for his achievements in folklore. He was appointed an adviser to the Privy Council in 1947 and was elected to membership in the Japan Art Academy the same year and to the Japan Academy in 1948. He received an award of the Order of Cultural Merit in 1951. His published writings on all aspects of Japanese folk culture number close to a hundred volumes and more than a thousand articles. Further information on his work and leadership in folklore studies is given in the introduction. Professor Yanagita lived in Seijō-machi on the outskirts of Tokyo and maintained active contact with professional folklorists and serious-minded amateurs until the end of his life. He celebrated his eighty-eighth birthday on July 30, 1962, just before his death on August 8.

GLOSSARY OF NAMES AND TERMS

ABA. Lit., hem of a fishing net; a float in the fishing net, rectangular and usually made up of paulownia wood.

AE-NO-KOTO. A harvest festival held in the Noto Peninsula on November ninth of the lunar calendar. Also called *ta-no-kamimatsuri*. The purpose of this festival is to greet the visiting deities of the wet rice field.

AGARI-USHI. *See* DAIKOKU-AGE.

AI-BI. Lit., sharing the fire; in some areas of Japan, a rite observed by women immediately after leaving their menstrual seclusion. It is essentially a purification rite.

AKA-BI. Lit., red fire; a word associated with childbirth taboos.

AKA-FUJŌ. Lit., red pollution; in the Kyūshū area it implied the menstrual pollution.

AKIBA. The name of a deity first enshrined on Mt. Akiba, worshiped as a YASHIKI-GAMI (q.v.).

AMA-GOI. Lit., prayer for rain; a ritual observed by rice farmers.

AMA-ZAKE. Lit., sweet *sake*; generally used in ritual or ceremony.

AME-NO-HIHOKO. A culture hero of ancient Japan (or Silla, southern Korea) who traveled to Silla (or Japan) and brought back many treasures.

310

AME-NO-KOYANE-NO-MIKOTO. A semimythological being who is believed to be the ancestral head of the Fujiwara clan.

AME-NO-MEHITOTSU. The One-eyed Deity of Heaven who is believed to be in charge of the metal industry.

ANEI. Dial., sister (-in-law).

ARA-MI. Lit., rough abstinence; the avoidance of the uncleanness connected with childbirth, practiced by the members of a family in which a birth has recently occurred.

ASHIIRE-KON. Lit., putting-one's-feet-in marriage; a specific form of matri-patrilocal marriage.

ATAGO. Name of a mountain in Kyoto, where a shrine for the chief fire deity (Kagutsuchi) is located; hill shrines dedicated to Kagutsuchi are found in all the chief cities in Japan.

BETSU-YA. Lit., separate house. *See* KARI-YA.

BOCHI. A graveyard. *See also* HAKA.

BON. The best-known Japanese festival, roughly analogous to All Souls' Day, celebrated in mid-July, and combining old pre-Shinto beliefs with Buddhistic rites. *See also* URABON.

BONTEN. Also called *bonden*; the literal meaning is unknown. It is a sort of large *hei* or *go-hei*, a tall bamboo rod adorned with paper strips, found in the Tōhoku area. *See also* GO-HEI.

BOSAN. Lit., visiting the grave; now refers to all practices commemorating the dead at the grave.

BOTA-MOCHI. Rice-cake dumpling covered with sweet bean paste.

BUN-YA. Lit., secluded hut; the separate corner of the house in which menstruating women lived on Sado Island. *See also* KARI-YA.

CHI. Blood; but since the word is tabooed in mountain speech (*yamakotoba*), *hedari* is substituted.

CHI-JIN. Lit., the deity of the earth. *See also* JI-GAMI.

CHINJU or CHINJU-SAMA. Lit., a deity who makes peace prevail and protects; a tutelary deity. The presiding deity or guardian of a place.

CHINJU-NO-KAMI. The deity of the village shrine; a recent synonym for UJI-GAMI (q.v.).

CHIN-KON. Lit., to put a soul at peace; a ritual for the renewal and repose of the emperor's soul.

CHŪIN. The mourning period of forty-nine days which is observed after a death.

CHŪRŌ-IRI. Lit., joining the elders; the rite performed when one formally joins the company of the elderly, around the age of forty.

DAIKOKU or DAIKOKU-GAMI. The deity of general good fortune; also the deity to whom the people in rural areas pray for a good crop.

DAIKOKOKU-AGE. A harvest festival held in northern Kyūshū on the day of the ox in November of the lunar calendar. Also called Agari-ushi.

DAIKOKU-MAI. Lit., the dance of the deity Daikoku; a ritual performed by outcast people during the New Year celebrations to dispense the grace of the deity Daikoku to the villagers; both the performers and their performance are called Daikoku-mai.

DAIKOKU-NO-TOSHITORI. Lit., the New Year Celebration for Daikoku. This harvest festival is held on December ninth of the lunar calendar in the Tohoku area; also called Daikoku-no-yome-mukae (literally, Daikoku's receiving a bride).

DAIKOKU-NO-YOME-MUKAE. See DAIKOKU-NO-TOSHITORI.

DAIKON. A long radish, sometimes having green leaves. The two-forked *daikon* is used as a sacred offering.

DAIKON-NO-TOSHITORI. Lit., New Year celebration for *daikon*.

DAISHI-KŌ. Lit., a cult association (*kō*) which worships Kōbō Daishi, a Buddhist saint (*daishi* originally meant "son of deity"); actually, a sort of harvest ritual held in the Tōhoku and Kantō areas on November twenty-third of the lunar calendar.

DENGAKU. Orig., rice-transplantation music or chant; the ancient agricultural music and dances.

DŌROKU-JIN. The guardian deity of roads and travelers; sometimes the guardian deity at the village boundary.

DŌZOKU. A patrilineal group, often including nonrelatives affiliated because of economic or ritual dependence. The hierarchical character of this kinship group is reflected in the emphasis laid on the head-family descent through primogeniture, in the conduct of ritual affairs, and in landholding relationships. This term (which can be translated as "the same kinship group") has been newly coined by Japanese rural sociologists and is not found among folk names for kinship groups.

EBESU. See EBISU.

EBESU-ABA. See EBISU-ABA.

EBISU or EBISU-GAMI. Ebisu is thought to be one of the Seven Deities of Good Luck (Hichi Fuku-jin); he protects occupations and brings wealth to his worshipers. Sometimes he is worshiped as the deity of the wet rice field by the farmers of eastern Japan. Fairly frequently he is the deity protecting fishery activities and is often personified as Ebisu Saburo carrying a red snapper under his arm; a shark, a whale, or even a floating corpse may be honored by fishermen as an embodiment of Ebisu. Among fishermen the term *ebisu* is a substitute for both *kujira* (whale) and *iruka* (dolphin), the latter two words being tabooed in open-sea speech. *See also* EBISU-ABA, EBISU-KŌ, OKI-KOTOBA, and TA-NO-KAMI.

EBISU-ABA. A fishing-net float; *see also* EBISU.

EBISU-ISHI. A stone believed to embody EBISU (q.v.), and worshiped as such.

EBISU-KŌ. The day on which Ebisu-gami is worshiped. There are two great Ebisu-kō days each year: January twentieth and October twentieth. In Niigata-ken fishing activities are proscribed on October twentieth when the ŌSUKE-KOSUKE (q.v.) is believed to come upstream. *See also* EBISU.

EBISU-MAWASHI. A ritual performed by outcast people during the New Year celebrations. Its purpose is to dispense the grace of the deity Ebisu to the villagers; both the performers and their performance are called Ebisu-mawashi.

EBOSHI. Formal headgear formerly worn by nobles at the imperial court.

EBOSHI-OYA. Lit., *eboshi*-parent, i.e., the person who puts the *eboshi* on the young man's head during the *genpuku*. *See also* EBOSHI and GENPUKU.

ENGAWA. A Japanese verandah; a woman in menses retires to it during the tabooed period.

ETE or ETE-KŌ. A special term substituted for "monkey" in both the open-sea speech and the mountain speech, in which the ordinary word *saru* (monkey) is tabooed; *see* OKI-KOTOBA and YAMA-KOTOBA.

FUJUKU-NICHI. Lit., the unripe days; on these days sowing and transplanting are tabooed. Among them are the day of the rat (*ne*), the day of the horse (*uma*), and the day of the chicken (*tori*).

FUNADAMA-SAMA. The guardian deity of a ship.

FURUMAI. Lit., giving a feast; the banquet in honor of a deceased person, which continues for a week following the death. *See also* KUYŌ.

FŪSŌ. Lit., wind funeral; a method of burial practiced in Japan in ancient times. The villagers covered a body with straw, clothes, or a box, and left it exposed to the air.

GEN. Lit., luck; a term used by fishermen. *Man* is a synonym.

GENPUKU. Coming-of-age ceremony; the initiation rite prerequisite to joining a young people's association, held when the youth is fifteen. Dictionary spelling: *gembuku;* also called *wakashū-iri.*

GENPUKU-OYA. The person who acts as godparent in the GENPUKU (q.v.)

GION. The name of a nationally known festival held in Kyoto, but used in this volume to refer to a local festival for fishermen held on the island of Tsushima on June fifteenth.

GO-HEI. A short stick to which are attached paper or cloth strips. Originally it was used in Shinto rituals as an offering to a deity. Later it came to symbolize the presence of the deity itself. The *go-hei* is also called *hei*—the prefix *go-* being honorary. See also HEI-GUSHI and TAKAMA.

GOKUIZAKE. A ceremony observed in fishing villages when the drag-net fishing is completed.

GORIN-NO-TŌ. A five-layer stone monument for graves. The five layers represent sky, wind, fire, water, and earth.

GORŌJI. Dial. form of GORYŌ-SHIN (q.v.).

GORYŌ-SHIN or GORYŌ-JIN. Lit., deified soul; that of a drowned man. *See also* GORŌJI.

GOSAI. Lit., honorable festival; the festival held in Ise province at Izogu Shrine on June twenty-fifth and twenty-sixth. See also KAERI-GOSAI.

GO-SEKKU. The five festival days of the year, January seventh, March third, May fifth, July seventh, and September ninth.

GŪJI. The Shinto priest's role as the chief of a shrine.

HACHIMAN. Lit., Eight Banners; Emperor Ojin deified; originally a deity of the forge, later a deity of war. He has now become an agricultural and fishing deity and patron of such primitive products as spears and agricultural instruments.

HADA-AWASE. Premarital sexual experimentation; *hada* means "skin" or "body"; *awase* means "to join together," "to put together," or "to unite."

HAFURI. Lit., one who purifies; this term describes the essential function of a Shinto priest, but in recent times it has been applied mostly to the local priests of lower grades or to some assistants in religious performances. *Hōri* is a synonym.

HAFURU. Lit., to throw; a local term for the burial grave.

HAKA. A grave (*baka* is a combining form of *haka*). *See also* BOCHI.

HAKUSAN. The name of a deity, used as another name for the YASHIKI-GAMI (q.v.).

HAMA-ORI. Lit., going down to the beach; the rite of going down to the sea to bathe or to eat by the water. *Hama-ori* is observed by those who believe the sea water will purify them of pollutions caused by evil spirits or other evil influences.

HANA-KAGURA. A series of popular Shinto dances with accompanying music, presented in the Aichi area in December of the lunar calendar.

HANA-MATSURI. Lit., a flower festival.

HANAMI-SHOGATSU. Lit., New Year for flower-viewing; at this time, ground-rice cakes in the form of flowers are hung on the branches of small willow trees, and rooms are decorated with these trees. Actually it is a winter festival intended to secure a good harvest for the coming year.

HARAI. A Shinto purification rite.

HARAMIDO. Dial., a pregnant woman.

HARU-KOMA. Lit., spring horse. When the ritual performers of outcast descent go from house to house on New Year's Day, reciting incantations which dispense the grace of the deity for the coming year, they usually carry with them a wooden horse's head. Both the performers and their performance are called Haru-koma.

HARU-TA-UCHI. Lit., to cultivate the wet rice field in the spring; a ritual mimicry, performed by outcast actors during the New Year celebrations, of the wet-rice-field cultivation.

HATAORI-BUCHI. Lit., the weaving-depths of a river; a legend is told in a number of localities that the sounds of weaving come from the river bottoms in the month of May.

HATSU-BATSUHO. Dial. for *hatsuho* (the first fruit). The term refers to the meal taken by women at the end of the menstrual abstinence period during the New Year celebrations. In Chikura, this word also denotes the rice given to a new baby at his first meal.

HATSUDE-IWAI. Lit., life-starting ceremony; synonymous with HATSU-KADO (q.v.).

HATSUHO. *See* HATSU-BATSUHO.

HATSU-KADO. The rite of passage which marks the beginning of womanhood, held at the time of a girl's first menstruation. Synonymous terms are *hatsu-tabi* and *hatsude-iwai*.

HATSU-TABI. *See* HATSU-KADO.

HEBI. Snake. *See also* MI, NAGA-MONO, and OKA-NO-ANAGO.

HEBI-GAMI-TSUKI. A family line or kin group possessed by a serpent deity.

HEDARI. One of the words in YAMA-KOTOBA, the mountain speech used by hunters. *Hedari* is substituted for the tabooed word *chi* (blood).

HEI. *See* GO-HEI.

HEI-GUSHI. Equivalent to GO-HEI (q.v.) and *hei,* but often used to denote a smaller type of *go-hei. See also* TAKAMA.

HEKO. "Sash" in standard Japanese, but here used as a dialect term for a man's loincloth.

HEKO-IWAI. A ceremony in which a young man is presented with a loincloth, signifying that he is physically and socially mature.

HEKO-OYA. Lit., loincloth parent; the person who presents the loin- cloth in the *heko* ritual.

HI. Fire. *See also* HI-GAKARI and HI O KUU.

HI-GAKARI. Lit., infected by fire. *See also* HI and HI O KUU.

HIGAN. Lit., the Other Side (of the river); a seven-day period com- prising the vernal or autumnal equinox, together with the three preceding and the three following days. It is often the occasion of visits to the family graves.

HIKAN. A class of tenant farmers; *nago* is a synonym.

HIMACHI. Orig., the activities of a group of people in the same com- munity who spent the night together keeping abstinence in worship of a certain deity. The religious meaning is now lost, and the term signifies being off from work or having a party or entertainment.

HIMA-YA. *See* HIYA.

HI O KUU. Lit., to eat fire; to receive the influence of fire. *See also* HI and HI-GAKARI.

HIRE. A strip of cloth which ladies in early times used to wear about their shoulders.

HIREFURI NO MINE. Lit., the Summit of Hirefuri. This legendary name was given to a mountain peak where a young woman stood to bid farewell to her lover by waving (*furi*) her HIRE (q.v.).

HITO-DAMA. Lit., man's spirit; a phosphorescent ball, supposed to be the spirit of a dead person, which rises from the ground and moves from place to place.

HITOTSU-ME-TATARA. A mythological one-eyed and one-legged monster.

HIYA. The secluded hut for menstruating and parturient women in Nagano-ken; also called *hima-ya*. *See also* KARI-YA.

HŌIN. Buddhist ascetics. This word is used only in the Tōhoku district; the term used elsewhere is YAMA-BUSHI (q.v.).

HŌIN-KAGURA. Music and plays performed by the Shinto priests who were formerly Buddhist ascetics, *yama-bushi* or *hōin*. These plays are popular in northeastern Japan.

HO-KAKE. The ritual, held at the beginning of the harvest, in which newly reaped "rice ears" (*ho*) and parched rice are offered to the deity of the rice field.

HONDAWARA. A seaweed, used as an ornament during the New Year celebration. In ancient times *hondawara* was a symbol of happiness.

HONE-ARAI and KAISŌ. The washing (*arai*) of the bones (*hone*) and their reburial (*kaisō*), which occurs three years after death.

HŌRI. *See* HAFURI.

HŌYŌ. A memorial service in which a Buddhist priest recites sutras and a feast is held for the invited relatives of the deceased. This is held seven times during the forty-nine days after death.

HYŌCHAKU-GAMI. Drifted deity; a deity believed to have come to this world from the world of the gods by floating on the sea. Such deities are often believed to be embodied in objects, such as small stones, which drift ashore. *Hyochaku-jin* is a synonym. *See also* YORI-GAMI.

I. The wild boar, the twelfth of the twelve horary signs.

ICHINEN-KANNUSHI. A Shinto elder serving for a year in the capacity of village priest.

IHAI. A wooden memorial tablet for the dead.

IKAKE. A scooping implement made of bamboo.

IRI-RYŌ. The spirit (soul) of a living person.

IMI. Taboo; there are two general types of taboo found in Japan: prohibitions against touching or approaching sacred objects and against contact with persons or objects polluted by death or childbirth.

IMOJI. Sometimes *yumoji*; orig., Japanese court ladies' term meaning "petticoat"; a type of petticoat which is given to young women during a rite of passage and which signifies that they have become adults.

INARI. A Shinto deity (often identified with the rice-field deity) of food and fertility, closely associated with, and sometimes designated as, a fox deity.

INKYO-YA. The house of retirement.

I-NO-KAMI. *See* TA-NO-KAMI.

I-NO-KO. Lit., Child (*ko*) of the Wild Boar (*i*); the day of the wild boar in October when the rice-harvest festival is held.

ISHI. Stone.

ITABI. Lit., board monument; a grave marker made of a flat stone resembling a board.

IWAI-GAMI or IWAI-JIN. Terms used in some areas to refer to the YASHIKI-GAMI (q.v.).

IWASHI. Sardine; *see also* KOMA-MONO.

JI-GAMI. The deity of the earth, also called *chi-jin, ji-no-kami, ji-nushi,* or *ji-shin-sama. See also* TA-NO-KAMI.

JIKA-NO-HI. "The day of fire on earth," on which sowing is tabooed. There are a total of twelve *jika-no-hi* each year. Among them are *mi,* the day of the snake in January; *uma,* the day of the horse in February; and *tatsu,* the day of the dragon in December.

JINJA. A Shinto shrine.

JI-NO-KAMI. *See* JI-GAMI.

JI-NUSHI. Lit., a landlord; *see also* JI-GAMI.

JI-SHIN-SAMA. *See* JI-GAMI.

JI-ZAMURAI. Land-owning farmers who were armed as samurai until 1588 when they were forbidden to bear arms. This ban was issued to draw a clear line between true samurai and non-samurai (such as farmers and priests) and thus to deprive the latter of fighting power against the government.

JIZŌ-DŌ. The name of a number of shrines consecrated to Jizō, a Buddhist deity of mercy who is especially concerned with rescuing souls of the dead from damnation.

JŌ. A unit of linear measurement, approximately equal to ten feet.

JŌMOKU. The articles or regulations which govern an organization.

JŌNOMI. A scupper. *See also* JŌNOMI-ISHI.

JŌNOMI-ISHI. A stone (*ishi*) which has been picked up by a pregnant woman and which is used to seal the JŌNOMI (q.v.). It also plays a part in a fishing ritual.

JŪ-YA. Lit., the night of the tenth; the name used in the Kanto and Chubu areas for the *kariage matsuri,* the festival at the end of the harvest. *See also* I-NO-KO, SAN-KU-NICHI, SHIMO-TSUKI MATSURI, and TŌKAN-YA.

JŪYA-NEMBUTSU. The rite of supplication to the Buddha or Buddhas on behalf of the spirits of the dead.

KAERI-GOSAI. Lit., returning Gosai; the second day of the festival of Gosai, held at the Izogu Shrine in Ise province. *See also* GOSAI.

KAGASHI. A scarecrow, sometimes regarded as a symbol of the rice-field deity.

KAGI-AZUKARI. *See* KAGI-TORI.

KAGI-TORI. Lit., key-taker (or key-holder); a village elder who plays a prominent role in village festivals along with the KANNUSHI (q.v.), the TOYA (q.v.), and the UJI-KO (q.v.) representative. Also called *kagi-azukari* (key-keeper).

KAGOYA. Palanquin bearer.

KAGURA. Sacred Shinto music and dances with flute and drum; music often accompanied by a dance. *See also* HANA-KAGURA.

KAISŌ. *See* HONE-ARAI.

KAKAA. Dial. or slang for wife or mother; used as a mode of address.

KAKAN. Lit., putting on the headgear; the ceremony of investing a youth with a man's headgear on his attainment of maturity.

KAMADO-GAMI. The deity of the hearth; *see also* KŌJIN.

KAMA-HARAI. Lit., purification of the hearth; an end-of-the-year ritual for the hearth deity, performed by the lower class of female shamans.

KAMI. This especially significant term is sometimes translated as "god," although "deity" is preferred in the present volume. *Kami* can mean either a discrete spiritual being or a spiritual force which may manifest itself in natural phenomena, in animals, and in ancestors, heroes, rulers, and the divinities of old.

KAMI-DANA. Lit., the shelf for deities; an altar.

KAMI-KATA-ISHI. A sacred stone on which a deity is thought to have floated to shore.

KAMI-SAMA NO OSATO. Lit., the home of the deity; a temporal home (a shrine) in which a deity is believed to dwell.

KAMI UTA. Sacred Shinto songs.

KANE-TSUKE-IWAI. The rite of passage in which girls' teeth are dyed black. This is an elaborate group ceremony held on the second of January for girls who have reached the age of fifteen.

KANEYAKO-GAMI. The ancestral god of the foot-bellows workers.

KANNON-DŌ. The name of a number of shrines consecrated to Kannon, a Buddhist deity of mercy.

KANNUSHI. A Shinto priest; orig., a presiding elder at Shinto functions.

KANZEON-BOSATSU. A Buddha of mercy; also called Kannon.

KAPPA. A goblinlike water demon, usually, but not invariably, malevolent.

KARA-SAKE. Lit., salty salmon. The fish is gutted and dried in the winter.

KARIAGE MATSURI. The festival at the conclusion of the harvest. It is also called *san-ku-nichi* in the Tōhoku area, I-no-ko in the Kinki area, Shimo-tsuki matsuri in Kyūshū, and *jū-ya* or *tōkan-ya* in the areas of Kanto and Chubu.

KARIGINU. Lit., hunting clothes; a type of gentleman's coat worn in ancient times.

KARI-YA. Lit., temporary house; a special and secluded hut for the use of women in menses. This term is not universal; in other areas the words *koya, bun-ya, betsu-ya,* or *taya* are used.

KASHIMA-ODORI. Lit., Kashima dance; a dance, popular in the Kanto area, introduced by the KOTOBURE (q.v.).

KASHIRA. A headman or leader.

KATSURA. Japanese Judas tree.

KAYU. Rice gruel.

KENGU. Lit., offering; the ritual of offering up food to the dead, which continues for forty-nine days following a death.

KEZURI-BANA. Lit., flower made of shaven wood; a stick, half of which is shaved into thin strips curled to give the appearance of a flower.

KIRI-BI. Lit., separating fire; a fire struck with flint and steel; a term referring to the isolated meals taken by a woman in menses.

KIYO-BAKA. Lit., clean (or pure) grave. *See also* MAIRI-BAKA.

KOBUSHI. A kind of magnolia.

KODOMO-IRI. Lit., joining the children; the ritual of joining the company of children, held when a child reaches the age of seven.

KO-IE. Lit., little house; the secluded hut used during the tabooed menstrual period.

KŌJIN or KŌJIN-SAMA. The deity of the hearth; sometimes, the deity of the rice field, the grounds, or other places around the home and the farm. The *kōjin* is often regarded as a rude, ill-mannered deity.

KŌJIN-MORI. Any grove consecrated to *kōjin*.

KŌJIN-MOTO. The person who organizes and manages the *kōjin* cult group.

KOMA-MONO. Lit., small thing; used in *oki-kotoba* (open-sea speech) in place of the tabooed word *iwashi* (sardine).

KOME. Rice; a word tabooed in *yama-kotoba* (mountain speech); hence *kusa-no-mi* (grass seed) is substituted.

KŌ-MOTO. Lit., center (*moto*) of a cult group (*kō*). *See also* MIYA-MOTO.

KONKON-SAMA. A name for the *ji-no-kami* in Shizuoka-ken, where the fox is believed to be the servant of the deity and is sometimes identified with the deity himself. "Kon, kon" is a cry imitating the sound of the fox's voice.

KŌNOTORI. Japanese stork.

KOSHIMAKI. Lit., loincloth (for women); a type of petticoat presented during a rite of passage at the time of a girl's first menstruation.

KO-SHŌGATSU. Lit., little New Year; a rite to ensure a good harvest, held on January fifteenth of the lunar calendar.

KOTOBURE. Lit., to spread things abroad. The lower class of priests received this name from their proclamations concerning auspicious times.

KOYA. The name for the secluded hut used by women in menses in Mie-ken. *Taya* is a synonym. *See also* KARI-YA.

KUJIRA. Whale, a word tabooed in *oki-kotoba* (open-sea speech); hence the word EBISU (q.v.) is substituted.

KUMANO. The name of a deity enshrined at Kumano; another name for the YASHIKI-GAMI (q.v.).

KURO-FUJŌ. Lit., a black pollution; in the Kyūshū area it means "death pollution."

KUSA-NO-MI. Grass seed; *see* KOME.

KUSHI. A skewer. *See* HEI-GUSHI; (*-gushi* is the combining form of *kushi*).

KUYŌ. A ritual to comfort the soul of a recently deceased person. *See also* FURAMAI.

MAGARI. Bend; used in place of the word *neko* (cat) which is tabooed in mountain speech (*yama-kotoba*).

MAI-DAYU. Male dancers in Shinto rituals.

MAIRI-BAKA. One of the two graves used in the double-grave system. The *mairi-baka* (also called *kiyo-baka*) is a symbolic, memorial grave at which rites for the soul of the dead are held after the prescribed period of mourning at the burial grave has passed. *See also* HAKA, MATSURI-BAKA, and UME-BAKA.

MAN. *See* GEN.

MANAITA-ISHI. Lit., a chopping-board rock; a big, flat rock, usually one which has been found in the river or ocean, which looks like a chopping board and is utilized as part of a ritual.

MAN-NAOSHI. Lit., mending (bad) luck. One ritual expression of *man-naoshi* is the fisherman's practice of drinking *sake* in a sort of salute or supplication when there has been a scarcity of fish. Another is a ceremony performed by the women of a fishing village, who gather at a shrine and implore the deity to grant the men a rich catch. During this ceremony the women recite chants and take their meals together.

MANZAI. Lit., to live long; a New Year's rite of blessing, performed by a special minority group; the performers are also called *manzai*. *See also* SAIZŌ and TAYŪ.

MARE-BITO. Mysterious visitors of eminence, e.g., *kami*.

MATSURI. Ritual or ceremonial performances in general.

MATSURI-BAKA. Lit., ritual grave. *See also* MAIRI-BAKA.

MATSURI-GOTO. Lit., ritual or ceremonial affairs; in archaic Japanese it implied political administration on both the village and national level.

MI. (The day of) the snake. *See also* JIKA-NO-HI and HEBI.

MI-KAWARI. A harvest ritual held in Chiba-ken at the time of the winter solstice. This rite may be a survival of the ancient *niiname* festival.

MIKO. A female dancer who takes part in Shinto rites. Originally signifying a female shaman or a nun, the term is now applied to maidens participating in ritual performances (including dancing) at Shinto shrines.

MIKO-MAI. A dance done by the MIKO (q.v.); a type of sacred Shinto dancing.

MIKOSHI. A portable shrine carried on the shoulders of many people, often the young men of the village. At the festival they carry it around the area protected by the deity.

MINAKUCHI MATSURI. Lit., irrigation-inlet ritual; the ritual or festival which takes place at the time of the sowing of seed in the rice nursery.

MISAKI. The forerunner or messenger of a principal deity. It may lead people to death and is venerated as a vengeful spirit.

MISO. Bean paste, a common food.

MI-TAMA-SHIRO. Lit., the thing on which the spirit rests. Used to refer to the object into which a *kami* has entered.

MI-TAMA ÙTSUSHI. Lit., transferring of a spirit. The act of transferring a *kami* to a sacred tree or other object.

MITEGURA. Silk or paper cuttings used as a symbol of the deity.

MIYA-MAIRI. A ritual in which a new baby is taken to the shrine of the family tutelary deity by a grandmother or other female relative; this is sometimes done when the child is a week old but usually takes place on the thirty-second or thirty-third day after birth.

MIYA-MORI. Lit., the keeper of the shrine; an elder charged with the performance of religious services at a shrine. See also MIYAZA and TŌYA.

MIYA-MOTO. Refers to the Shinto priest in his capacity as center (*moto*) of a cult group connected with a Shinto shrine (*miya*). Also called *kō-moto.*

MIYAZA. A special cult group, organized by the heads of families in a village, for the purpose of worshiping the village tutelary deity. *See also* TŌNIN, TOSHIYORI, TŌYA and UJI-GAMI.

MIZU. Water, a word tabooed in mountain speech (*yama-kotoba*); hence *wakka* is substituted.

MOCHI. Glutinous rice cake; a staple article of diet.

MOGARI. A custom of the ancient noble classes, requiring relatives of a dead person to stay in seclusion for a certain time at a designated place near the grave in order to watch the body.

MONOYOSHI. Lit., all things are going to be good; incantatory blessings bestowed at the end of the year by the visiting magician-beggars, who are also called *monoyoshi. See also* SEKIZORO.

MURAGE. A chief of blacksmiths, an archaic term.

NAE. A rice seedling.

NAE-IMI. A taboo against touching the rice seedling.

NAE-JIRUSHI. The wooden signs used in the Tōhoku area to mark the rice-seedling bed; originally set up as *yorishiro* (resting places for the deity). *See also* NAE-MI-DAKE and TANANBŌ.

NAE-MI-DAKE. A bamboo stick set up in the rice-seedling bed. It is a type of YORISHIRO (q.v.) used in Fukushima-ken. *See also* TANANBŌ and NAE-JIRUSHI.

NAGA-MONO. Lit., long thing; used as a substitute for *hebi* (snake), the latter word being tabooed in the open-sea language of the fishermen and the mountain speech of the hunters. *See also* OKA-NO-ANAGO.

NAGARE-BOTOKE. A floating Buddha; the term is used by fishermen to denote a floating corpse, the discovery of which is regarded as a good omen.

NAGERU. Lit., to throw away; a dialect term for burial.

NAGESHO. Lit., a place where things are thrown out; a dialect term for a burial grave.

NAGO. *See* HIKAN.

NAMAHAGE. The ogre who is said to punish idle children; one of the "mysterious visitors" of the New Year.

NARIKI-ZEME. Lit., torturing the fruit tree; a ritual observed at the time of the New Year.

NATSUKE-OYA. A godparent.

NE. An abbreviated form of *nezumi* (rat); it is one of the twelve horary symbols or signs. *See also* FUJUKU-NICHI.

NEDO. Lit., the place to sleep in. *See also* NEYADO.

NEDO-GAERI. A custom involved in the practice of *ashiire-kon* marriage whereby the bride works for her husband's family in the daytime and returns to her parents' house after supper.

NEKO. Cat; a word tabooed in *oki-kotoba* (open-sea speech) and *yama-kotoba* (mountain speech). *See also* MAGARI and YOKOZA.

NEYADO. A night dormitory for young people. *See also* NEDO.

NIGI-MI-TAMA. Peaceful spirit or soul.

NII-BOTOKE. Lit., a new Buddha; but used to refer to the soul of a recently deceased person.

NIINAME or NIINAME-NO-MATSURI. A harvest festival annually held at the imperial court and observed by the emperor himself. It includes a ritual in which the first fruit of the season's rice crop is tasted.

NIO. A heap made of reaped rice plants.

NIRAI-KANAI. Eternal land beyond the seas, in Okinawan dialects.

NISO-NO-MORI. The Grove of Niso; in the villages of Fukui-ken, sacred groves owned by the head families of kinship groups, who hold there an annual rite for their ancestral spirits. The meaning of the word Niso is not certain.

NIWA-SHIGOTO. Work (*shigoto*) done in the yard (*niwa*), such as threshing and husking rice.

NO-GAMI. *See* TA-NO-KAMI.

NORITO. A sacred written address to Shinto deities.

NUSHI. Lord or master.

OBA-KURE. Lit., something given by the aunt; refers to the loincloth given to a young man by his aunt during a rite of passage. This custom is found in parts of Nagano-ken.

ODAIKO. A type of drum.

ODAMAKI. A spool (of thread).

O-FUDA. An amulet made of wood or paper, distributed by a shrine to the worshiper for the purpose of purification or as an aid in praying for the assistance of a deity.

O-HAKE. A holy rod, sometimes used in the worship of the *uji-gami*; the etymological meaning of this word is unknown today.

O-HAKE-TSUKI. Tsuki means "to build up." This is a specific type of O-HAKE (q.v.) which is raised or erected to a great height.

OKAMI. Wolf. The word is tabooed in *yama-kotoba* (mountain speech); hence *yase* (lean) is substituted.

OKA-NO-ANAGO. Lit., a long thing on land; in Kagawa-ken, used in *oki-kotoba* (open-sea speech) to avoid the tabooed word *hebi* (snake).

OKI-KOTOBA. Lit., open-sea speech. The term refers to the set of word substitutes used by fishermen in place of tabooed words.

OKITE. The rules which govern an organization.

OKINA. Old man.

OKYAKU. Lit., guest; used in open-sea speech in place of the tabooed word *ushi,* meaning "cow" or "ox."

ONARI. Beautifully dressed virgins who serve the consecrated diet during the *ta-ue* ritual.

ONMYŌ-DŌ. A Japanized branch sect of Taoism.

O NO MAI. The term for each of two sets of dances performed at the beginning of the YŌKA MATSURI (q.v.). *See also* TSURUGI NO MAI.

OREGAE. Lit., my own house; the dialect term used by a bride to refer to her natal house.

ŌSUKE-KOSUKE. A special name for the salmon which in the Tōhoku area is said to appear on the day of a certain ritual.

O-TA-NO-KAMI. *See* TA-NO-KAMI.

OTARIYA. A festival held at certain shrines in Tochigi-ken at the end of November and in mid-December of the lunar calendar. During these rites the MIKOSHI (q.v.) are carried from hamlet to hamlet. The festival is also called Yūgyō.

O-TA-UE. Honorific form of TA-UE (q.v.).

O-TOJIME-NO-MATSURI. The rite of closing the shrine's door in the festival of Haushiwake Shrine, in Akita prefecture, on November 8 of the lunar calendar.

OTOME. Maiden, virgin, or girl; a semiclassical word.

OTONA. Lit., an elder; the Shinto priest in his capacity as an elder. *Tone* is a synonym.

OTONA-IRI. The ritual which installs a man, at the age of sixty, as one of the village headmen or leaders.

OTONA-SHŪ. Lit., group of elders; those controlling the cult-group called MIYAZA (q.v.).

O-USHI-SAMA. A deity of agriculture, worshiped on the day of *ushi*, the ox.

OYA. The parent or leader.

ŌYA. Lit., a big house; refers to a family's main house, as distinct from the house of retirement (*inkyo-ya*).

OYAJI. In ordinary speech, this word means "father"; it is also a substitute for *saru* (monkey) or *kuma* (bear), words which are tabooed in the mountain speech of the hunters. *See also* YAMA-KOTOBA.

OZAKAE-MATSURI. A harvest ritual held at several Shinto shrines in Shimane-ken.

PURI. A harvest festival in the southern Ryukyus.

RYO-ZUKE. A form of ritual magic practiced by fishermen: Men who have pregnant women in their families are sometimes invited aboard the fishing boats in order to ensure a large catch.

SA-BIRAKI. *See* SA-ORI.

SABURŌ. A common male name in Japan.

SAGE. The leader of those who join the work of transplanting rice seedlings; he holds a *sage* stick in his hand and leads the *ta-ue* songs. The literal meaning of *sage* is not clear. *See also* TA-UE.

SAIMON. A written invocation, directed to KAMI (q.v.) and inviting them to join the worshipers.

SAITŌ-GOMA. The Shugen-dō rite of burning specially prepared firewood, while praying for peace and a good crop. *See also* SHUGEN-DŌ.

SAIZŌ. A buffoon in the *manzai* performance, who may represent a spirit of the earth. *See also* MANZAI.

SAKA-DARU. Barrel of *sake*.

SAKAKI. A tree (*eurya ochnacea*) which is considered sacred.

SAKE. Rice wine, the most popular Japanese drink, originally used in rituals.

SAKI-TAMA. Happiness-bringing spirit; *saki* implies happiness or good luck.

SAKU-GAMI. *See* TA-NO-KAMI.

-SAMA. A title of respect added as a suffix to the names of persons, deities, and sometimes to objects.

SAMISEN. A common, three-stringed Japanese musical instrument resembling a banjo; also called *shamisen*.

SANABURI. *See* SANOBORI.

SANBAI-SAMA. The deity of the wet rice field; *see also* TA-NO-KAMI.

SAN-KU-NICHI. *See* KARIAGE MATSURI.

SANOBORI. A ritual performed when the transplanting of the rice seedlings is completed; also called *sanaburi*.

SA-ORI. A ritual performed at the beginning of the rice-seedling transplantation; also called *sa-biraki* and *wasa-ue*.

SA-OTOME. The village girls who work together in transplanting the rice seedlings. They wear, as a uniform for the planting, white towels on their heads and red cords around their shoulders.

SARU. Monkey, a tabooed word in *oki-kotoba* (open-sea speech); hence *etekō* is substituted.

SARU-HIKI. The outcast people who perform the SARU-MAWASHI (q.v.).

SARU-MAWASHI. Lit., the monkey show; a New Year's rite for the purpose of purifying the stable (the monkey is considered the guardian of the stable and of horses). Also called *saru-ya*. *See also* SARU-HIKI.

SARU-YA. *See* SARU-MAWASHI.

SA-TSUKI. An old name for the month of May in the lunar calendar, when the rice seedlings are usually transplanted. *See also* TA-UE.

SEDO. Backyard.

SEDO-UJIGAMI. *See* YASHIKI-GAMI.

SEKIHAN. Lit., red rice (rice cooked with red beans); cooked only on ceremonial days and at certain festivals.

SEKIZORO. Lit., this is the end of the year; incantatory blessings bestowed at the end of the year by outcast beggars. *See also* MONO-YOSHI.

SENGEN-KŌ. A special cult association for the worship of Mount Fuji.

SETSUBUN. A purifying ceremony during which beans are thrown into each room of a house to drive out the evil spirits, usually performed on the evening before the first day of spring. Setsubun literally means "The Parting of the Seasons."

SHAMISEN. *See* SAMISEN.

SHANICHI. The day for serving the deity of the earth.

SHICHI-FUKUJIN. The Seven Deities of Good Fortune.

SHICHIHON-ZAME. A sacred, seven-tailed shark associated with the festival of GOSAI (q.v.).

SHIME-KOROSU. Lit., to throttle one to death; the present use refers to an initiation ceremony in which youths are choked and made to faint momentarily.

SHIMO-TSUKI. Lit., the month (*tsuki*) of frost (*shimo*); the old name for November in the lunar calendar.

SHIMO-TSUKI MATSURI. *See* KARIAGE MATSURI.

SHINMEI. Another name for the goddess Amaterasu-Okami, enshrined by some families as a YASHIKI-GAMI (q.v.).

SHINMEI-CHO. A list of KAMI (q.v.) in use by A.D. 743, containing 3,132 names. Only those *kami* were listed to whom official GO-HEI (q.v.) were offered at the beginning of the year.

SHINMEI-GŪ. A shrine for SHINMEI (q.v.).

SHIRA-FUJŌ. Lit., white pollution; in the Kyūshū area it implies the childbirth pollution.

SHIRITAKA-GAI. A type of shellfish.

SHI-RYŌ or SHI-REI. The spirit (soul) of one recently deceased.

SHŌ. A measurement equivalent to 1.588 quarts.

SHŌEN. A tract of land controlled by the imperial family, noblemen, or shrine priests of the high class. The *shōen* system was comparable to the manorial system in medieval England. The institution was abandoned in the early sixteenth century, but parcels of land continued to be called *shōen* until modern times.

SHŌYA. In the Tokugawa period the village headman was called a *shōya*. His family held hereditary rights, and he had power to control the villagers.

SHŪGEN. A new and relatively elaborate kind of marriage ceremony.

SHUGENDŌ. A religious sect led by ascetics called *yama-bushi* and representing an amalgamation of Shintoism and Buddhism, with emphasis laid on the mountain worship traditional to folk Shintoism.

SOI-BUSHI. Lit., to lie with someone.

SŌJI-NO-MONO. One who cleans or purifies.

SO-REI. Ancestral spirits.

SŌSŌ. A funeral rite.

SUTEBA. Lit., a place where things are abandoned; a dialect term for a burial grave.

SUTERU. Lit., to abandon; a dialect term for burial.

SUZU. A bell carried by the MIKO (q.v.) during certain Shinto dances; it is also used in folk festivals and in Nō and Kabuki performances.

TAIHŌ. Lit., great treasure; the holy rod consecrated to the village tutelary deity in Ibaragi-ken.

TAKAMA. Lit., high heaven. A rather uncommon name for a *hei*, a holy rod consecrated to the village tutelary deity. The *hei* is erected high in the air and the deity is supposed to use it to descend from heaven, hence the term *takama*. *See also* GO-HEI.

TAKASE. *See* UMA.

TAKO-NO-MAMMA. Lit., food for the octopus.

TAMACHI. Meaning is now obscure, but the word once meant "soul" or "soul power."

TAMASHII. The human spirit or soul.

TAMA-YORI. One possessed by a spirit or deity, an archaic term.

TAN. A roll of cloth about twelve yards long, or about .245 acres of land.

TANANBO. A large branch erected in a rice field and regarded as a bench for the deity of the rice field. *See also* NAE-JIRUSHI and YORISHIRO.

TANEMAKI-ZAKURA. Lit., the cherry blossoms that bloom at the time of sowing; a kind of magnolia. *See also* KOBUSHI.

TA-NO-KAMI. The deity (*kami*) of the wet rice field (*ta*). This deity is also called *no-gami* in the Tōhoku area; *saku-gami* in Yamanashi and Nagano-ken, *tsukuri-gami* in the Kinki area, *i-no-kami* in the San'in region, Ebisu-gami in western Japan, Sanbai-sama in the Chugoku area, and *ji-gami* along the Inland Sea; sometimes also called *o-ta-no-kami, o* being simply an honorific prefix.

TA-NO-KAMI-MATSURI. *See* AE-NO-KOTO.

TA-NO-KAMI-NO-TOSHITORI. Lit., the ceremony of adding a year to the rice deity's age. This harvest festival is usually held in October of the lunar calendar. It is also called *daikon-no-toshiya*.

TATAMI. Mats made of a condensed layer of straw covered on both sides with woven rushes.

TATARA. Foot bellows; Also a place name in Japan and Korea.

TATSU. *See* JIKA-NO-HI.

TATSU-GASHIRA. A dragon head.

TA-UCHI SHŌGATSU. A ritual, held on January eleventh, in which the head of the family plows—actually or in pantomime—for the first time in the year; *ta-uchi* implies "to cultivate the wet rice field," and *shōgatsu* means "the New Year."

TAUDO. The villagers who join in the transplantation of rice seedlings.

TA-UE. The transplantation of the rice seedlings from the seedling bed to the wet rice field (*ta*); *ue* implies "to plant."

TAYA. *See* KARI-YA and KOYA.

TAYA-BEYA. A term popular in Tottori-ken; the separate corner and hearth which a woman in menses occupies during the tabooed period.

TAYŪ. A protagonist in the *manzai* performance who might represent a greater spirit of the eternal land; *see also* MANZAI.

TAYŪ-SAN. Specifically, a male dancer in Shinto rituals, but the local Shinto priests are sometimes called by this term; *see also* MAI-DAYŪ.

TENGU. A long-nosed, red-complexioned goblin who is supposed to live in mountains; sometimes associated with the *yama-no-kami* (mountain deity).

TENJIN-SAMA. The deified spirit of a famous statesman who was exiled from Kyoto, the capital, in the early Middle Ages.

TENKA-NO-HI. Lit., the day of fire in the heaven; it corresponds to both the day of the chicken (*tori*) in January and the day of the monkey (*saru*) in December, when thatching is tabooed.

TŌBA. A long, thin, wooden stave, bearing inscriptions from the sutras, which is erected behind the grave stone on the thirty-third anniversary of death to mark the end of Buddhist services for the soul of the dead; also called *sotōba*.

TŌKAN-YA. Lit., the night of the tenth; a harvest ritual held on October tenth of the lunar calendar in the Kanto and Chubu areas. *Jū-ya* is a synonym.

TOKO-NO-MA. An alcove used as an ornamental recess for flowers and hanging scrolls.

TOKOYO. Land of Eternal Life.

TOKOYO-NO-KUNI. The eternal land of the ancestral spirits or the land of the deities.

TONE. *See* OTONA.

TŌNIN. Lit., the person in charge or the person concerned; equivalent to TŌYA (q.v.).

TORI. *See* FUJUKU-NICHI.

TORII. An arch before a shrine.

TORI-OI. Lit., to drive away injurious birds; a rite performed from door to door by outcast female magicians who were also called *tori-oi*. In the Tōhoku district today children carry on the ritual.

TOSHIGOI-NO-MATSURI. The February ritual to pray for a good crop.

TOSHIYORI. Lit., the aged; those who take a central position in a MIYAZA (q.v.).

TŌYA. A person charged with the service for the tutelary deity of the village. The position of the *tōya* rotates among the heads of village families under the *miyaza,* a cult group organization; *see also* MIYAZA and UJI-GAMI.

TSUKURI-GAMI. *See* TA-NO-KAMI.

TSUMADOI-KON. An ancient form of marriage in which a man pays nightly visits to a woman who, if she accepts his advances, is then considered his wife. The girl's parents are not told of the union until she becomes pregnant. The elements of the word are "wife" (*tsuma*), "visiting" (*-doi*), and "marriage" (*kon*).

TSURUGI-NO-MAI. Lit., sword dance; the second of two dances performed at the YŌKA-MATSURI (q.v.).

UBUSUNA. Lit., native soil.

UBUSUNA-GAMI. Equivalent to UBUSUNA-NO-KAMI (q.v.).

UBUSUNA-NO-KAMI. Lit., the deity of native soil; today nearly synonymous with UJI-GAMI (q.v.), although the two words originally differed in meaning.

UBU-YA. A special, isolated hut used by women after giving birth; confinement to this hut is still required in some areas as part of the parturition taboo.

UBU-YU. The baby's first bath, a ritual performed shortly after birth.

UCHI-GAMI. See YASHIKI-GAMI.

UCHIGAN-DŌ. The shrine of *uchi-gami*. See also YASHIKI-GAMI.

UCHIKATARI. In ASHIIRE-KON (q.v.) a celebration held on the fourteenth day after the birth of a baby, when the wife and the baby visit the husband's family for the first time.

UIDE-IWAI. The celebration held when a girl returns from the secluded hut after her first menstruation. *Uide* means "going out for the first time"; *iwai* means "celebration" or "ceremony."

UJI-GAMI. Lit., the deity (*kami*) of an *uji* (lineage or clan); the word is usually, however, used to refer to the tutelary deity of a village; in urban areas it is the tutelary deity of a ward of the city; and in some localities it refers to the deity of the house and grounds. See also YASHIKI-GAMI.

UJI-KO. Parishioners who worship the same UJI-GAMI (q.v.).

UMA. Horse. This word is tabooed in *yama-kotoba* (mountain speech); hence *takase* (high back) is substituted. See also FUJUKI-NICHI and JIKA-NO-HI.

UMARE-GO. A ritual for the newborn child held at the first winter festival following the birth.

UME-BAKA. One of the two graves used in the double-grave system. The *ume-baka* is the actual burial grave. See also HAKA and MAIRI-BAKA.

URABON. The same as the Bon, derived from the Sanskrit. See also BON.

USAGI. Hare. This word is tabooed in *yama-kotoba* (mountain speech); hence YAMA-NO-NEGI (q.v.) is used.

USHI. Ox (or cow), the second of the twelve horary signs. *Ushi* is also one of the words tabooed in open-sea speech. *See also* OKYAKU.

UTAI. Recitation of verses from the Nō drama.

UTSUGAN. *See* YASHIKI-GAMI.

WAKA. A combining word element meaning "young"; when used as part of a word, it often implies especially the vitality of youth.

WAKAME. A kind of seaweed.

WAKA-MIYA. Lit., young deity; a harsh and malevolent deity or spirit enshrined as a son of a stronger deity so that the former will be consoled and soothed.

WAKA-MIZU. Lit., young water. At the beginning of the spring planting rituals, the rice seeds are soaked in *waka-mizu,* the first water drawn on New Year's morning, which has been kept for this occasion.

WAKA-SHU. Youths of about sixteen years of age.

WAKASHU-IRI. *See* GENPUKU.

WAKA-TŌ. The persons who attend a noble when he travels abroad.

WAKKA. An Ainu word meaning "water," used in mountain speech to replace the tabooed word *mizu* (water).

WARAJI. Sandals made of rice straw.

WASA-UE. *See* SA-ORI.

WATARI-BARAMI. Wandering pregnant woman.

YAKUSHI-NYORAI. A Buddha in charge of medicine.

YAMA-BUSHI. *See* SHUGENDŌ.

YAMA-IRI. Lit., going into the mountain; a rite performed by the *yama-bushi. See also* SHUGENDŌ.

YAMA-KOTOBA. Lit., mountain speech. The term refers to a set of word substitutes used by mountain hunters in place of certain tabooed words.

YAMA-NO-KAMI. The deity (*kami*) of the mountain (*yama*).

YAMA-NO-NEGI. Lit., priest of the mountain; this word is a substitute for USAGI (q.v.).

YASE. Lit., lean; used in place of the tabooed word *ookami* (wolf) in YAMA-KOTOBA (q.v.).

YASHIKI-GAMI. A deity of the house and grounds who is enshrined at the corner of the yard or in a distant site owned by the family. In northern and eastern Japan, he is called *uji-gami* or *uchi-gami*, and in the southern half of Kyūshū he is called *utsu-gan*. Other appellations are *yashiki-ujigami, sedo-ujigami,* and *iwai gami.*

YŌKA-MATSURI. The festival of the eighth day; usually celebrated on the eighth day after New Year's as a prayer for an abundant harvest.

YOKOZA. Orig., master's seat; used in *oki-kotoba* (open-sea speech) for *neko* (cat). *See also* MAGARI.

YOME-KATAGI-KON. Stealing the bride; a marriage practice popular in the western part of Japan, particularly in Kyūshū. The elements of the word are *katagi* (dial., to carry up), *yome* (bride), and *kon* (marriage).

YOME-NIGIRI. Lit., bride's rice balls; rice balls served at the marriage ceremony.

YORI-GAMI. A deity who comes floating ashore; that is, a deity who arrives from the world of the deities by floating ashore—or visiting deities who make regular appearances at festivals. *See also* HYŌ-CHAKU-GAMI.

YORISHIRO. Any object upon which the deity rests after descending.

YŪGYŌ. *See* OTARIYA.

Index

335